Ceramic Design

CERAMIC

JOHN B. KENNY

DRAWINGS BY CARLA KENNY

CHILTON BOOK COMPANY

RADNOR, PENNSYLVANIA

Other Books by the Author
THE COMPLETE BOOK OF POTTERY MAKING
CERAMIC SCULPTURE
THE ART OF PAPIER MÂCHÉ

DESIGN

To all of the ceramic artists
who gave so generously
of their time and their talent,
this book
is affectionately dedicated.

Second Printing, May 1964
Third Printing, November 1965
Fourth Printing, March 1967
Fifth Printing, August 1968
Sixth Printing, August 1970
Seventh Printing, October 1971
Eighth Printing, October 1973
Ninth Printing, September 1974

Foreword

Wнат is good design? How does one recognize it?

Those are tough questions. There are principles of design, of course —rhythm, balance, proportion, harmony, contrast, and so on. But they don't help us much in finding an answer. The trouble with principles is that soon they become accepted as rules. And there are no rules in art. There can't be. Whenever you come across something masquerading as a rule of design, it is a good idea to break it.

Perhaps we should start with a simpler question: What is design? Even that one is difficult to answer. Webster himself has trouble. At one time he calls it ". . . a plan; a scheme; a purpose; an intention." And then he tries again: ". . . a secret; a sketch; an arrangement of details which make up a work of art."

Yes, design is all of those things. Certainly it is the arrangement of details, and it does involve sketching and planning. But to the ceramist, design means more than that—much more. It means order out of chaos; form out of shapeless mass. It is something that comes to life in his material as he works with it, something mysterious that he creates through combinations of shape and color and texture. It is something for which he must search, and when he finds it, his work is satisfying and good. His quest is never ended—he must go on searching as long as he lives and works.

Ceramic materials lend themselves well to modern design, and designing with clay is a rewarding experience. Anyone who has held clay in his hands and felt its responsiveness to his slightest touch has known the urge to go farther—to explore—to try out all the possibilities of this fascinating material. It is through such exploration that design comes into being.

In this book we shall explore together. There are many paths; we shall try as many as we can. First of all, we'll study ways of shaping clay, then explore the possibilities of other ceramic materials. We'll work with color as well as shape, decorating ceramic forms and making pictures in clay.

In our quest for form, we'll take a look at the past—yet not be bound by tradition. And we'll look, too, at what is being done today—to appreciate, not to imitate.

We'll study nature and natural forms to find inspiration for patterns and shapes, but not to copy. We'll try untrodden paths. We'll make some things unlike anything ever made before—yet be not satisfied with mere novelty. We'll make some things for use, some things for decoration, some things just for the joy of making them.

We'll have fun with clay!

Contents

The search for form. Types of forms. Exploration. A small armature. Abstract creations. A word about clay. Geological formation of clay. Buying clay. Freeform. A few rules. Wedging. Joining clay. Keeping work moist. Drying. The leather-hard state. Shrinkage. Water of plasticity. Chemically combined water. Hollowing out. Grog. A working surface. Tools.

Ⓥⓘ

The search for form continues. Bringing shapes to life. Symbolism. Heads. People. Animals. Making a clown. A ballerina. Birds. Clay caricatures. Crèche figures. Ceramic chessmen.

Making a coil-built form. Surface texture. Applied design. A bowl for a fountain. A multiple spouted vase. Enlarging a figure by the coil method. Coil building as an approach to design.

Designing with layers of clay. A hanging form. Work in a cloth sling. Draping over a clay mound. Designing a pattern. Making a rectangular platter. A boxlike shape. Making a planter. Applied decorations. A teapot made of layers of clay. Figurines as candle holders. Shaping clay over a balloon. A piggy-bank. Other forms.

Centering. Throwing a bowl. Opening. Throwing a tall cylinder. Throwing the pieces of a tea set. Handles. Spouts. Lids. Using a pair of calipers. Turning a foot. A piece thrown in two sections. A piece thrown in three sections. A wheel at floor level. Design on the potter's wheel.

A new direction in ceramic design. Throwing a sculptural flower holder. Cutting and joining pieces. Creating a figurine on the potter's wheel. A humorous flower holder. Abstract sculpture made on the potter's wheel. Design through the combination of wheel-thrown shapes and slabs.

Design by cutting clay while in the leather-hard state. Carving a draped shape. Hollowing out sculpture. Making a hanging planter. A combination of modeling and carving in ceramic sculpture. Carving an architectural ornament. Carving a factory-made plate. A head carved from a piece cast in a mold. Changing the character of cast pieces by carving. Pieces thrown and carved. Incising. Design principles in carving clay shapes.

The qualities of ceramic sculpture. Texture. Making pieces hollow. Building hollow forms. Making a figure for a fountain. Armatures. Waste molds. Shims. Making a plaster of Paris replica of a clay figure. Combinations of materials in ceramic sculpture. Designing a form to fit on a metal rod. Grog in sculpture. Organic material. Color in sculpture. Waxing. Milk. Glazing sculpture. Tools. Sculptural ceramic design.

Color in clay. Color of natural clays affected by the fire. Oxides added to clay to produce color. White bodies. Body stains. Engobe. Engobe recipes. Colors for engobe. Grog, a source of color. Exploring color effects. A line blend. Design with color.

Main ingredients of glaze. Alumina. Silica. Flux. Coloring oxides. Lead glazes. Recipes. Color additions to glazes. Alkaline glazes. Egyptian paste. Frit. Frit glaze recipes. Opaque and semi-opaque glazes. Mat glaze.

Colemanite or boro-silicate glaze. Rutile. Bristol glazes. Stoneware glazes. Porcelain glaze. Salt glazing. Special effects. Specks. Glaze over glaze. Flowing glazes. Glazing textured ware. Crackle. Jewel glaze. Lustre. Chromium red. Selenium red. Purple glaze. Black. Brown. Mixing glazes. Gums. Settling. Applying glazes. Dipping. Brushing. Sponging. Spraying. Pouring. Glazing unfired ware. Glaze defects. Crazing. Crawling. Blistering. Pinholes. Running. Dryness. Roughness. Shine. Shivering. Planned crawling. Foam glaze. Commercial glazes. Compounding glazes. Experimentation. Glaze tests. Keeping records.

Glass a ceramic material. Its role in ceramic design. Experimentation. Fusing glass to clay. A tile with raised ridges and pools of glass. Bottle glass. Melting temperatures. Firing. Filling openings with glass. Filling openings in vertical pieces. Melting broken glass. A separator, whiting. Glass bending. A mold for bending glass. Decalcomania on glass. Cutting glass. Making a glass bowl. Cutting curves. A glass relief. Glass colors. A glass picture. Gemmail. A glass pictorial panel. Glass design. Laminating. Using organic materials with glass. Possibilities of glass for the ceramist.

Effect of fire on clay. Fuels. Wood. Gas. Oil. Electricity. Wood-burning kilns. Down-draft kilns. Electric kilns. Elements—nichrome, Kanthal, Globar. Top loading kilns and front loading kilns. Stacking. Precautions. Stacking glazed pieces. Kiln wash. Dry-footing. Stilts. Temperature measurement. Cones. Pyrometers. Cut-off devices. The firing cycle. Water smoking. Dehydration. Maturing. Cooling. Reduction. Effect of reduction on clay and on glaze. Bucchero ware. Celadon. Copper-red. Controlling reduction. Salt glazing. Tunnel kilns. The fire an element of design.

Drawing for the ceramist. The language of drawing. Exercises. Drawing on a blackboard. Pencil drawing. Brush drawing. Tones. Problems of form. Geometric patterns. Designing within a circle. Designing for tall cylindrical shapes. Designing within a square. Rectangles within rectangles. Combinations of geometric shapes. Cut out shapes. Stencils. Overlapping shapes. The bird in design. Natural forms. Weeds. Sea shells. Flowers. People. Landscape in design. Dots. A wandering line.

Intersection. Radiation. Symmetry. Four-point symmetry. Symbols. Design in the world about us. Creativity. The sketchbook, its importance in ceramic design.

Pictures on pots. Ancient examples. Techniques. Engobe decoration. Slip painting. Sponging. Stencils. Masks. Sgraffito. Spatter. Thread decoration. Wax resist. Combinations of methods. Decorating a plate. Mishima. Slip trailing. Making a cooky jar with an inlaid design. Slip trailing used with molds. Combing. Feathering. The decorating wheel. Underglaze painting. Overglaze painting. Majolica. Making a series of coasters. Glazing and painting figurines. The special quality of majolica. Commercial decoration of ware. Decalcomania. Meeting a challenge through design.

Ceramic design in two dimensions. Ceramic murals, an ancient art. A single tile. Murals made of numbers of tiles. A mural in a subway passage. Ceramic murals on store fronts. Tiles for murals. A paddle for making tiles. Using glazed commercial tiles. Ceramic tiles in wooden frames. Making a large clay layer. Cutting a layer into shapes. A panel made of pieces cut from a layer. Treatment of tile plaques. Cementing tiles. A panel set in plaster of Paris. A pictorial panel. Panels made in a single piece. Making a sculptural panel. Pressing a plaque in a mold. Making a panel by cutting and modeling. The place of two-dimensional ceramic design in modern living. Mosaic. Ceramic tesserae. Glass tesserae. Preparing a mosaic design. Cement and mastic. Grout. Edge treatment. Wooden edging. Making a mosaic panel by the direct method. Mosaic design in cement. Edge tiles. The indirect method of making mosaics. Application. A table top made by the indirect method. Cement mortar. Mosaics for outdoor use. Coloring cement. Exploring the possibilities of mosaic design.

The place of ceramics in modern architecture. Planning architectural ceramics. Ceramic murals set in large walls. Ceramic plaques designed by artists, manufactured in factories. Ceramic murals on building exteriors. Cooperation between the artist and the manufacturer. Staff artists in terra-cotta plants. Making a large architectural terra-cotta statue. Designing with unfired terra-cotta shapes. Opportunities for the ceramist.

List of Illustrations

Photo Series

Plates

Color Plates

1
Shape

Oᴜʀ Qᴜᴇsᴛ for design begins as a search for form.

Form is something we all know. Our acquaintance with it began in the cradle the first time we reached out to grasp something. We know form by touch as well as by sight. We know it not only as shape but as weight, balance, movement. We know it as a contrast between rough surfaces and smooth. Our whole life is a series of experiences with forms.

The world is filled with forms. There are forms of growth and life, the patterns we find in living seashells, in fruits and flowers. There are forms of death and decay, empty seashells broken by waves on the shore, pieces of driftwood, rotting tree stumps. There are shapes of movement, volutes and spirals; shapes of movement arrested, icicles, candle drippings.

There are geometric shapes, spheres, prisms, cylinders; functional shapes, bottles, chemical retorts, teapots. There are structural shapes, buildings, factories, pipes and pipe fittings, machines. There are shapes that are purely accidental.

We begin our search in our material, *clay*.

PHOTO SERIES 1

Exploring form

Take a lump of clay and roll it into a ball. *The process of design has begun.* Roll the ball into an elliptical shape, then flatten it slightly. Stand it on a clay prop and study the form.

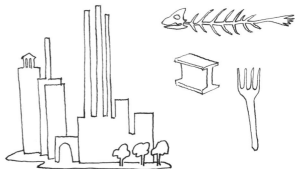

Roll another ball and flatten it into a disk, then twist it.

An armature will prove helpful here. A block of wood with a hole bored in it to hold a piece of wire (coat hanger wire is good) makes it an easy matter to put one clay shape on top of another. Take note, however, that clay shrinks as it dries and, if we want to save the pieces we make, when they are put on the wire they must be rotated and moved up and down so that the hole is quite a bit larger than the wire; as the clay shrinks it will be able to move along the wire without damage.

Make another ball, this time hollow. Start with a lump of clay and open it by pressing the thumb into the center. Model the walls between the thumb and the fingers until you have something that looks like a deep cup without a handle. Prepare another piece of clay to put over the opening.

Put the two pieces of clay together and seal the joints with the fingertips. What you have now is a hollow clay sphere. This can be paddled with a wooden tool; the air trapped inside will keep the form from collapsing. If the clay is quite soft and plastic (as it should be for this work) you can push a drinking straw through the side and inflate the sphere by blowing into it gently.

Paddle the sphere into a slightly different shape and stand it on a clay pedestal. Model a cup shape and paddle it into a rectangular form; this time, don't try for a smooth surface, but strike it roughly with the edge of the paddle so that texture is created. Stand this on a different kind of pedestal.

Make a different shape and rest it on two supports. (The photographs shown here are not to be copied, of course—they are merely illustrations of how it *could* be done. The shapes you make will be original.)

Make some more shapes. Paddle a hollow sphere into a cube. Make a cylinder and cut it into slices. Form narrow strips of clay and bend them. Make combinations of these shapes.

Make a form by combining shapes. Cut an opening. See what effect this opening has on the form.

Make some more shapes by cutting, twisting and combining.

Roll a form somewhat like a cigar. Cut it in half diagonally, reverse one part and join the two halves again.

Put the shape just made in a different position; combine it with another form.

Try more combinations and textures.

Now make something fantastic—something *way out!*

Continue to explore the realm of the fantastic. See what can be done by combining many different shapes. Make another armature by drilling a number of holes in a wooden block and inserting pieces of wire on which forms can be threaded.

Explore the possibilities of cutting a flat layer. Pound the clay on a piece of oilcloth (shiny side down) until the layer is about ½″ thick, then cut a variety of forms, bend them and combine them in different ways.

Try still more combinations. Be completely free. Enjoy the thrill of making something that is different from anything ever seen before.

The series of exercises we have just completed taught us something about clay—how it feels, how to manipulate it, how it responds, when it can stand on its own feet and when it needs help. Most important, however, it taught us something about form.

The things we have made are experiments, but don't destroy them right away. Put them aside while you work on other projects. After a few months have passed, get them out and study them again. You will find that some of them are not exciting—back to the clay bin with them. But the others—ah, some of them are good! They have originality and interest. Keep them, you may fire them.

A few words about clay: What is it? Where does it come from? How does one obtain it?

Briefly, clay is decomposed rock, a product of weathering that has been going on for thousands of centuries and is going on right now. Clay is one of the most abundant substances on the face of the earth and it is being made at a rate faster than all the ceramists in the world can use it up. The geologist knows clay as a chemical combination of elements, alumina, silica, and water, plus impurities. The ceramist knows clay as a plastic material which obeys his lightest touch and which, once it has been dried and fired, holds the imprint of his fingers forever.

We get clay by digging it from the ground, or by purchasing it from a ceramic supply house. In the section on materials in the Appendix, we'll say more about clay and how to prepare for use clay which you dig yourself. For the moment we will rely on the dealer.

Buying clay

There are many different kinds of clay, suitable for many different purposes. Some are good for working on the potter's wheel, others are better for sculpture. Some are coarse and rough, others are smooth. Some become hard in the kiln at a comparatively low temperature (about 1900°F.). Others require much higher temperatures before they mature (2300°F. or more). Some can be used just as they come from the ground, others must have things added to them (when minerals are added to clay or when different clays are combined, the product is called a *clay body*). Clays vary in color, too. Some are red after they have been fired. Others are buff or brown, or white, or black.

At the start, when you buy clay, get it in plastic form. Ask for a good modeling clay, preferably one which has been pugged and de-aired. (We will be using technical terms occasionally, but these are all defined in the section on materials or in the Glossary.) One thing is important—things made of clay must be fired. Buy clay that will mature within the temperature range of your kiln.

Now for a different approach, starting with a lump of clay and an idea —a bowl, not round, not square; something nonsymmetrical, unplanned at the beginning, completely free in form.

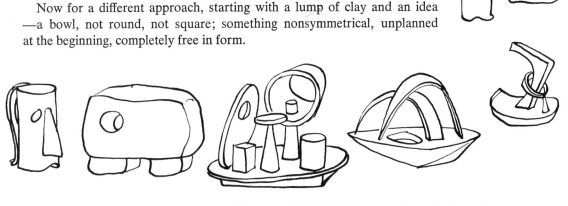

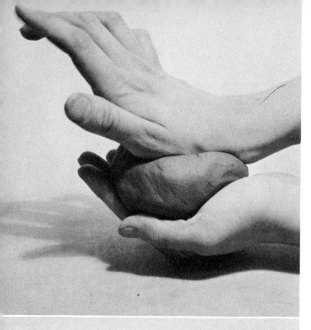

A free-form bowl

Hold a ball of clay in the left hand and press into it with the heel of the right hand.

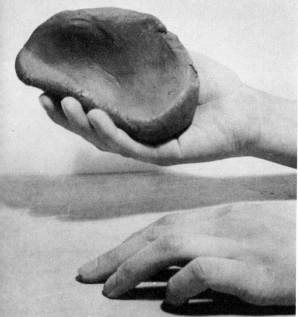

This makes the beginning of a rough bowl shape. Work on this with the fingers of both hands, pinching the wall, making surfaces smoother. Try to achieve rhythmic, sweeping lines. A wooden modeling tool will help on the outside; a spoon is good for working on the inside surface.

⑧

Study the form. Be critical. How does it look? How does it feel? How does it balance? If the shape is not pleasing, alter it. If walls seem too heavy, squeeze them thinner, or use a scraper to cut off some of the clay. Put it on a temporary three-legged stand to judge the profile. Would this stand make a good base? Doubtful—seems a bit awkward.

How would it look with three legs? Not bad.

Or a simple cylinder base? The proportions here could be better. This cylinder seems too tall for a base; too short for a pedestal.

How does it look on something really tall? This base seems too big—overpowering.

A smaller base. This has possibilities. But there is no single right answer to the question of which base to use. It's a matter of judgment. You may prefer no base at all. If you decide to have a base, weld it firmly in place, then set the piece aside to dry. After that a bit of sponging and it is ready for the kiln.

We have completed another exercise in design. Make a number of shapes this way, no two alike. You will find that your appreciation of form will increase and you will find, too, that you will begin to "see" shape with your fingers.

A FEW RULES

In the Foreword we said that rules were meant to be broken, but we were speaking then about rules of design. In working with clay, there are some rules which *must* be obeyed.

• Wedge your clay before you use it. Wedging is a process of making a lump of clay smooth and homogeneous by cutting it in half and slamming the two halves together on a board or on a plaster slab. Do this at least 20 times. A wedging board with a plaster slab and a wire for cutting the clay is shown in the sketch.

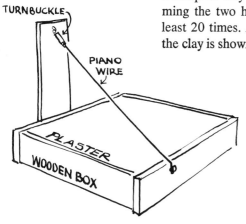

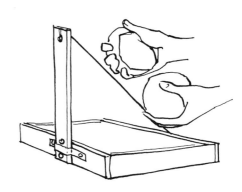

• When you join two pieces of clay, to make sure the joint will hold roughen the two surfaces, moisten them with water or slurry, press firmly together and then weld the joint with a small wooden tool. (Slurry is a thick clay slip.)

• Keep your work moist. Plastic clay starts to dry as soon as it is exposed to the air. If a piece of work takes longer than one or two hours it will need to be moistened with a sponge or sprayed. A knife drawn across the bristles of a stiff brush that has been dipped in water makes a good moistening spray, or you can use a Flit gun.

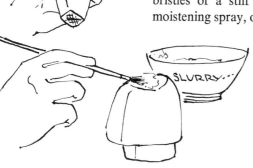

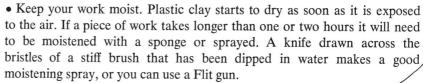

• Clay that is not being used must be kept in a covered container so that it does not dry out. If work must be interrupted, a plastic bag will keep it in good working condition for several days.

• As clay dries, it passes through a stage called "leather hard." It still contains moisture at this point but it is no longer plastic. It can be carved easily, but any attempt to change the form would break it. This is the time when clay can be shaped with a knife or smoothed with a metal scraper.

• Clay shrinks as it dries. It shrinks again when it is fired. The potter must plan to make an original clay shape slightly larger than he wants the finished piece to be. The rate of shrinkage is different in different clays. More about this and ways to measure shrinkage in the section on materials.

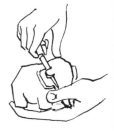

• Uneven shrinkage during drying will cause trouble. If some parts of a piece dry more rapidly than others there will be warping or breaking. Two pieces joined together must have the same moisture content or they will separate during drying no matter how carefully the joint was welded.

• Drying should be as slow and even as possible. It is best to leave work in a damp closet or covered in some way to slow the drying process. Tall pieces should dry with a slightly dampened cloth over the top so that this portion does not become bone dry while the bottom is still leather hard.

• A piece should stand on two strips of wood while it is drying so that air can reach the underside. If the shape permits, a piece may do part of its drying upside down.

• Drying in the air is only half the potter's problem. The other is drying in the kiln. Clay contains two kinds of moisture—water of plasticity, which makes it workable, and water that is chemically combined. Leave a piece of clay in strong sunlight for several hours until it becomes dry as dust— chemically combined water will still be there. Soak that bone-dry lump of clay in water and it will become plastic once more. But once clay has been put into the kiln and heated to red heat, it becomes permanently hard; no amount of soaking will make it plastic again. The chemically combined water has been driven off.

• Water in clay must be able to escape. If you were to put a solid lump of clay the size of a baseball into your kiln and fire it, the moisture in the center would be trapped and turned to steam. The result—an explosion ruining everything in the kiln. To guard against this, any portion of a piece of work more than 1″ thick should be hollowed out. With larger pieces where walls must be heavier, the potter adds things to the clay to make it more porous. Best for this purpose is grog, clay which has been fired, then ground and screened. Dealers sell grog in grades of coarse, medium, or fine.

● Work on a surface that is easy to pick up—a plaster bat or a piece of wooden board. A board with two wooden strips fastened to the underside is easy to handle.

● What about tools? Aren't we going to talk about these? Later perhaps, not right now. Tools are not so important. The craftsman uses them merely as extenders for his fingers—to add extra strength or reach. Tools are usually available when they are needed. Often a block of wood or a kitchen knife is all the potter requires.

Tools alone do not make design. They help, of course, and so does the material, but it is the mind of the craftsman, his imagination, his drive, his continued prodding, his restless search for something new and exciting, his critical judging, his relentless appraisal; it is all of these that, working through his hands and his material, create the mysterious thing we call design.

2
Sketch

OUR SEARCH for form continues. In the last chapter we experimented with shapes and then we made a bowl. This seemed a logical way to start; after all, pottery began with making containers, things to hold food, cups to drink from.

We could have begun with a different approach. Let's take another look at the shapes we made in the first photo series. Even though we made these with no thought of copying anything in the world around us, some of the shapes, as we re-examine them, will suggest natural objects to us, people, for example, or birds, or groups of buildings. If we stick two pellets of clay on the shape shown in Picture 1 of the series, the shape will turn into a face staring at us.

Roll a long thin rope of clay and put two clay pellets at one end—the rope of clay becomes a snake. What was at first just a clay shape, now represents a living thing. It calls to mind all those qualities we think of when we hear the word "snake." This is *symbolism*.

Symbolism has been an important part of art since the beginning of time; in fact we might say that art started as symbolism. When primitive man made shapes of stone or wood or clay, those shapes stood for things, sometimes men, or animals, more often supernatural forces of good or of evil—spirits that could do him harm or protect him from his enemies, make his crops grow, or bring rain. To him, art was a form of magic.

Let us see if we can work some magic and bring clay shapes to life.

13

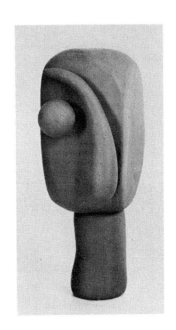

Plate 1—Heads.

• Make a number of heads. Look at those shown in Plate 1 but don't copy them; don't copy any real heads either, create original shapes.

Three wise men of Gotham.   Jeannot and Pierre.

Plate 2—People.

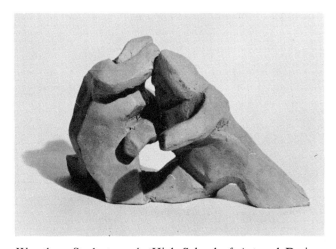

(15) • Make some people. Study
the ones in Plate 2, then design your own.

Wrestlers. Student work, High School of Art and Design.

Mother and child. Student
work, High School of Art
and Design.

Family group, garden sculpture by Maria Wishner.

Figure.

The objects shown in the illustrations and the things you have made are close to abstractions, but they have meaning. Make more. Strive for simplicity and originality. Try to capture the spirit of life without any attempt at realism. See how deliberate distortion of a natural form can give a stronger suggestion of its true nature than could be obtained from a careful copy.

Now for another approach, this time a bit more realistic but still not a copy. We'll make a clown. A clown is a figure of fantasy; in modeling him we can give full rein to our imagination and not feel bound by any obligation to get proportions right or details accurate.

A clown

We will use a block of wood with a hole in it and some lengths of coat hanger wire as temporary supports.

Clay has been rolled into two cigar shapes and a ball. One cigar shape has been threaded over a piece of wire. The other has been cut in half.

Ⓖ

The pieces are assembled to form the beginning of a little clown. A section of wire holds the second leg in place while another supports the head. We shall not let these wires hamper our design.

Some modeling of forms. We are making a suggestion of anatomy on the arms and legs, but we are thinking also of interesting arrangements of shapes.

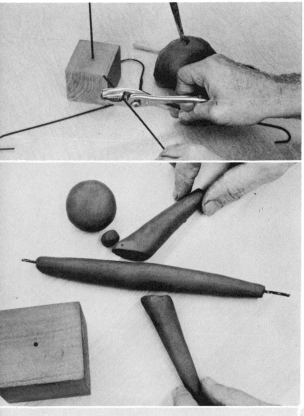

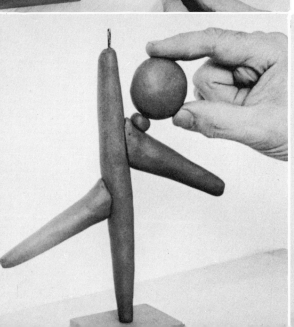

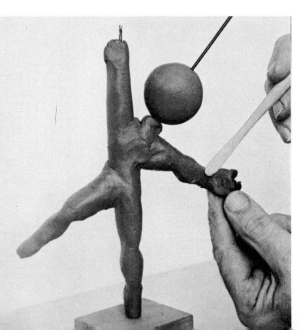

Our little clown is finished. Bits of clay have been pressed into place to give him fancy cuffs and a ruffled collar. Pellets of clay the size of a pea were pressed through a sieve to form the pompoms on his hat. In the background is a ballerina made in the same manner. Let's fire them. We must enlarge the holes so that after the clay has come out of the kiln the wires will still fit.

The fired pieces can balance each other. The ballerina is in two parts separated at the middle so that her body can be twisted. An extra bead of clay has been added at the middle to give her a long waist.

A horse has joined the troupe.

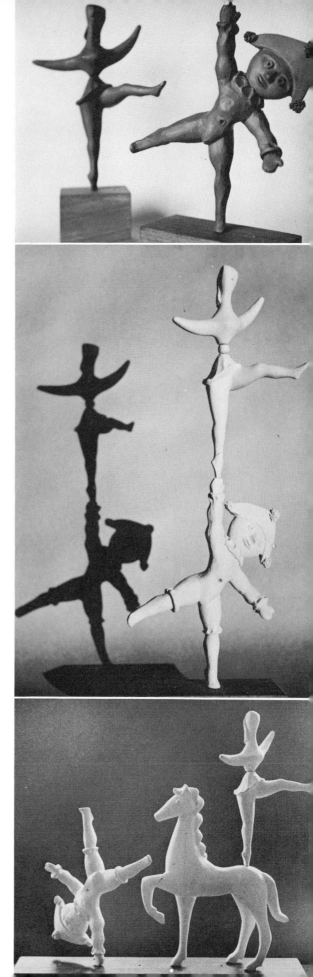

Now let us try another approach to the problem of creating designs based on natural forms. We'll make a pair of birds.

Birds

Roll a cigar shape. Bend it slightly and support it on a clay base. What we have suggests a simplified bird form.

(18)

Make another shape just like the first one. Add details—crest, wings, tail feathers. Here we have quite a different bird. This one is interesting and has rococo charm, but the one we made before was interesting too, in a different way. Let's keep both of these birds. We shall use them later.

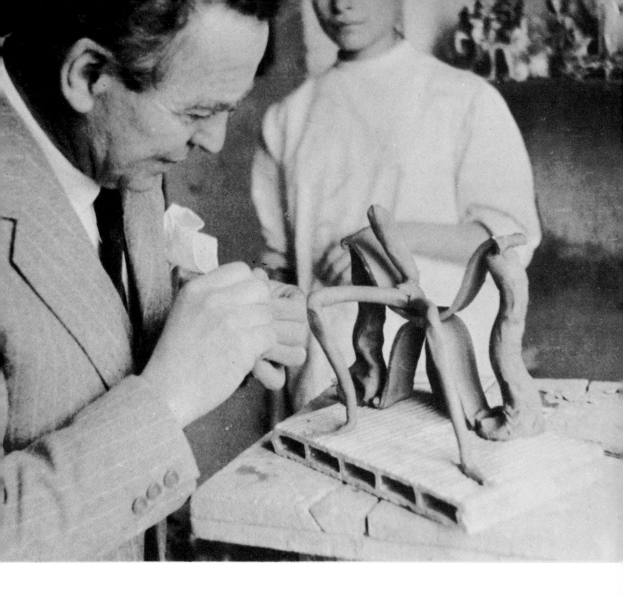

Plate 3—Fusco Martini at work on a figure of Hamlet. Thin strips of clay are rolled for him by an assistant.

Sketches in clay are often made as preliminary studies for works that will be made larger and more carefully. Clay sketches, however, have value in themselves. Note the work of Fusco Martini, shown on Plate 3. This Florentine artist has achieved a reputation with his clay sketches, most of them caricatures of people. Martini builds his figures with coils and layers of clay that are prepared for him by an assistant. Here we see him at work on a figure of Hamlet. The studio of this artist is a fascinating place. The walls are lined with shelves and every inch is crowded with tiny figures in action. There are ancient automobiles, animals, birds, lawyers, artists, musicians, etc., etc.—all of them wildly exaggerated, yet all possessing the essential truth of good caricature. A portion of these shelves is shown in Figs. 1, 2, and 4 in the color section.

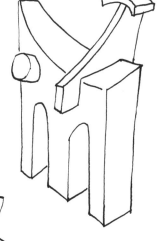

Plate 4—Crèche figures by Jean Derval.

On Plate 4 is another kind of sketching shown in the group of crèche figures by Jean Derval. These owe their charm to their delicate simplicity. More crèche figures by the same artist are shown in Fig. 6 in the color section.

In still another vein are the figures by the French artist Antoine Prinner shown on Plate 5. These highly original and imaginative creations are portions of a chess set. The white pieces are the people of the sun and the black pieces are those of the moon.

Plate 5—Chessmen by Antoine Prinner.

Sketching in clay is a rewarding activity. It is fun and it leads to good design. Often a small sketch has more gayety and life than a larger piece which is made from it. Watch for the carefree, sometimes accidental effects which occur in your sketches. These are what make your work good—preserve them.

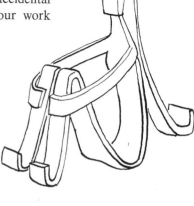

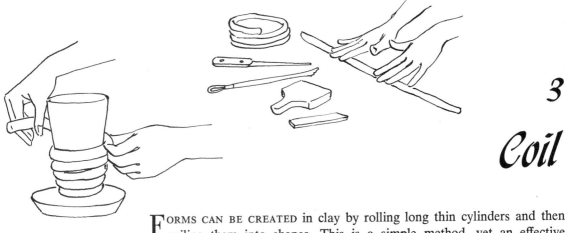

3
Coil

FORMS CAN BE CREATED in clay by rolling long thin cylinders and then coiling them into shapes. This is a simple method, yet an effective one for achieving quick solutions to some design problems. We'll go through the steps of making an oval-shaped dish with a high foot.

Coil building

We start with a ball of clay about the size of a golf ball. This is flattened into an oval shape. A long thin cylinder of clay is rolled and coiled on the base to start the outline of the dish we have in mind. The edge of the base was roughened and moistened before the coil was put in place.

The coil has been wrapped around. The inside surface is being smoothed with the fingers. As successive coils are added, the top of each coil is roughened and moistened before another coil is placed on it.

The finished height has been reached, the dish is turned upside down. Here we see the fingermarks that were made when the coils were welded together. A base has been formed. This will be put in place

on the bottom of the dish. The clay is very soft at this stage. It is supported on the inside by a cushion made of crumpled newspaper.

Attaching the foot. The fingermarks make an interesting pattern. Some potters like to retain this in the finished work, and on large pieces it makes an effective type of design. For a small piece like the one we are making, however, leaving this rough texture would make the piece unduly heavy.

The foot in place. The outside surface has been smoothed with a steel scraper.

Using a spoon to press in a surface pattern. The pattern selected here suggests the actual pattern that was made by the fingers when the shape was formed.

Completing the surface decoration.

The finished piece.

Here is another application of the coil method, used this time to make a large bowl for a fountain.

PHOTO SERIES 6

Coil building upside down

A small clay sketch has been made for the bowl of a fountain. An outline has been drawn for the top edge of the finished bowl and a coil of clay is placed on it.

More coils have been added and welded into place.

The bowl nears completion. Note the cushion of newspaper on the inside.

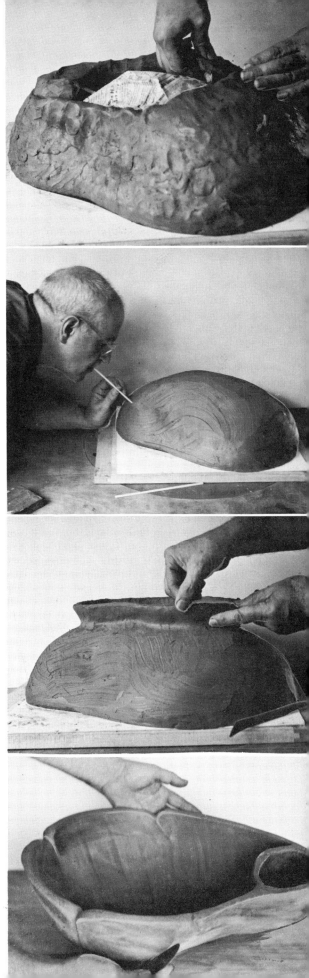

The upside-down bowl shape has been finished by paddling. A straw has been pushed through the clay shell. By blowing gently, the ceramist is able to inflate the form.

Adding a foot.

The bowl turned right side up. A partition has been added at one end to form a chamber that will hold a small electric pump. The outside of the bowl has been carved slightly to suggest a large shell form. A mermaid holding a fish will complete this fountain. She is shown on page 170.

Plate 6—Multispouted vase by Sheldon Carey of the University of Kansas.

㉖

Plate 6 shows a multiple-spouted vase by Sheldon Carey of the University of Kansas. This interesting ceramic creation was made by the coil method. Coils were used to form a kind of hollow football which the artist paddled into shape while it was still plastic. This plastic football was supported in a mortar while three legs that had been thrown on a wheel were attached. (The method of making legs like this is shown in Chapter 11.) After the legs were attached, the form was turned over and supported in a cloth hammock that had three holes cut in it. The legs projected through the holes in the cloth. The cloth was tied to the rim of a pail. Then various sized spouts were arranged on top of the form and moved about until the artist achieved what he considered the best design. The spouts were then attached with slurry. After the form was firm enough to stand by itself, holes were cut through the spouts, opening entrances into the body of the piece.

When the work became leather hard the entire outside surface was covered with dark engobe and a line design was scratched through. This method of decoration, called "sgraffito," is described in Chapter 19.

Coil building is not limited to bowl forms and vase forms. Sculpture can be made that way as well. Let's take another look at the little clown sketch that we made in Chapter 2. If we wish a larger edition of this sketch we can make it by the coil method. Here are the steps:

Cloth hammock
with holes
cut in

Pail

Sectional View

A coil-built figure

An armature has been made by boring a hole in a block of wood and inserting a wooden dowel. A second dowel has been tied crosswise to the first one. The block and the two dowels have been wrapped in newspaper so that it will be easy to pull them out of the clay form when it is finished. Clay is coiled around the base of the first dowel.

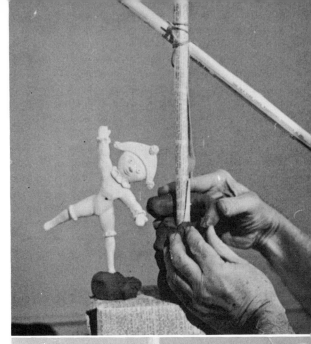

Coils have been wrapped around the upright dowel and around the transverse. This is the beginning of two legs and an arm. A third dowel, also wrapped in newspaper, is put in place as a support for the other arm. A piece of string tied to the top of the upright dowel holds the end of this third dowel in place.

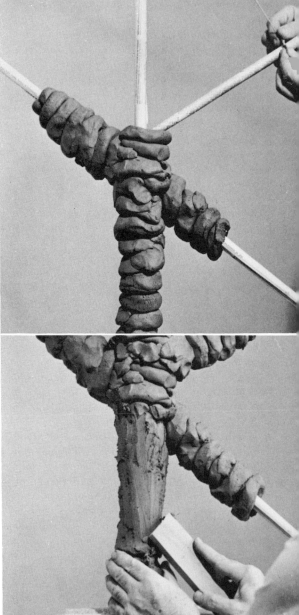

A block of wood is used to weld the coils together and begin modeling of the final shape.

Welding of the coils and modeling continues. Coils are put in place to form the head.

The modeling nears completion.

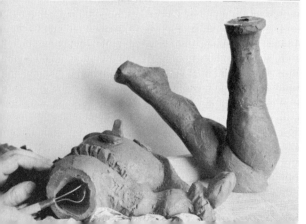

The clay is leather hard. The figure has been cut in half and the inside is being trimmed. Note that the sculpture rests on a cradle of crumpled newspaper during this operation.

The finished sculpture. The figure is in two parts so that it may be mounted on a base with a wooden dowel for support in many different positions.

Coil building is one of many approaches to ceramic design, a good one. The method can be used to make an almost infinite variety of shapes and objects—things round, and symmetrical, or of free form, large or small, heavy or light, textured or smooth. Note the unusual planter by Lyle Perkins shown in Plate 22.

Coil building is rewarding. There is a great deal of satisfaction in watching something grow under the fingers. In the process of growth, ideas develop; often they change, and the resulting piece turns out to be quite different from what was originally planned. Here is the combination of mind and material producing design.

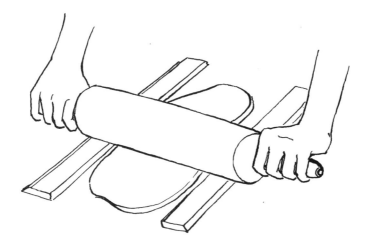

4
Roll

CERAMIC DESIGNS can be created from layers of clay rolled with a rolling pin. Use two wooden guide strips ¼″ thick (a pair of rulers will do), size of a large grapefruit. Thoroughly wedge the clay, then roll it into a ball. Put a piece of oilcloth on the table—shiny side down—and put the ball of clay on it. Pound the clay with the fist into a pancake shape. Next, put the guide strips on each side of the pancake, and roll.

Lift the layer of clay and turn it once or twice during the rolling process. If you have trouble with the clay sticking to the oilcloth or the rolling pin, dust them with a bit of flint or talcum powder. You may use a second piece of oilcloth placed on top of the layer, shiny side up so that the clay layer becomes the filling of a sandwich. This will make the rolling process easier. Newspaper can be used instead of oilcloth if you work rapidly and discard each sheet of paper when it becomes damp.

If, despite all the care you took in wedging, some bubbles appear in the clay while you are rolling, puncture them with the point of a knife. Press the clay flat and roll it smooth.

Pick up the layer of clay and let it hang. There is beauty in the curve a plastic material takes as it hangs freely this way. We'll design a piece of pottery making use of this curve.

PHOTO SERIES 8

Clay shaped in a cloth sling

A pattern has been cut from a piece of newspaper that was folded in half and in half again to make the shape symmetrical. The advantage of using newspaper is that patterns may be cut, judged, compared, and discarded until we have a shape that is right. The clay layer is cut to the shape of the paper pattern.

Rig a hammock or sling by fastening a piece of cloth (cheesecloth is good) to the sides of an empty carton. Fasten the cloth to the edges of the carton with snap-on clothespins. Place the layer in the cloth sling. If it is necessary to adjust the fastening of the cloth so that the clay hangs with a natural curve, this can be done by moving the clothespins.

Legs must be formed now so that they can dry at the same rate as the clay layer. Four legs have been rolled and placed in the sling. Now the work should be covered with a dry cloth and left for two or three hours.

Later. The layer, now leather hard, has been lifted out of the sling and rests upside down on a support while the legs are attached. The support is a metal can with a cushion made of a folded towel on top of it. Care must be taken in at-taching the legs. Both portions of the joint must be roughened, moistened, and firmly welded together. The joint will hold better if slurry (thick clay slip) is used instead of water.

The completed form.

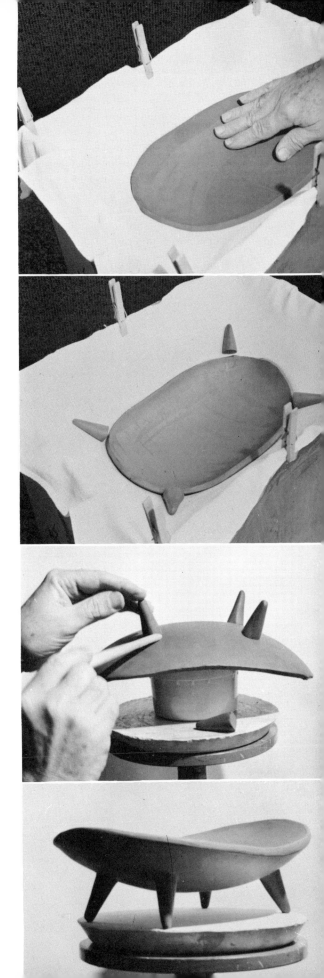

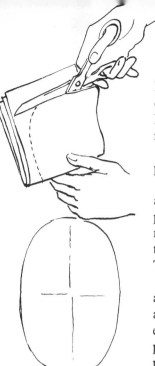

A layer of clay may be shaped over a mound, a process called "draping." Draping is usually done over a mound of plaster of Paris, but it can be done, too, over a mound of clay. A clay mound is quicker and simpler. Let's try this method, this time planning a more conventional shape, a rectangular serving platter.

The first step is to build a clay mound. This mound will shape the platter, so building the mound is actually an exercise in design.

We start by cutting a pattern out of a sheet of newspaper folded in half and in half again, as we did in the previous series. The shape of this pattern will determine the proportions of the platter we are planning to make. We have a rectangular shape in mind; our pattern must be longer than it is wide. But how much longer? One and one half times as long? Twice as long? Three times? What ratio will give the best proportions?

There is no ready answer to this question. We said earlier that there are no rules of design, and here there is no mathematical formula we can apply. Think of what the platter will be used for. A long thin shape, for example, might be just right for a celery dish, while for some other purposes it would be absurd. Try different patterns until one is found which pleases the eye. The corners of the pattern must be rounded and the sides should flare outward slightly.

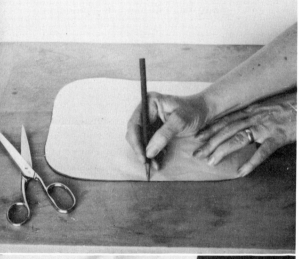

A *rectangular platter*

The pattern is traced on a board. A wooden drawing board serves well here, or a piece of plywood. We could also use a plaster slab.

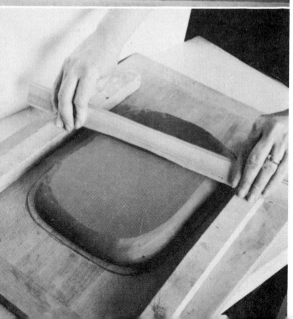

Within the outline just traced, a clay mound is constructed. This will form the inside of the platter. Remember that clay shrinks. The mound will have to be higher than we want our finished platter to be. Unless this mound is at least 1¼″ high, the finished platter will be extremely shallow. Two strips of wood of the proper thickness can be used as guides to get the height of the mound right. A third strip of wood (or a rolling pin) drawn across the two guide strips will make the mound even in thickness with a flat area on top. The edge of the clay mound should be kept ¼″ inside the outline.

The mound is covered with two layers of thin cloth. Why *two* layers? So that the piece will lift off the mound easily. One layer of cloth will stick to the mound while the other will lift off with the platter. Care must be taken in placing the layers of cloth so that wrinkles are avoided as far as possible. (*Note:* Instead of using cloth we could use dampened paper towels.)

The next step is to roll a layer of clay ¼″ thick and cut out a shape that is ¼″ wider all around than the one that was traced on the board.

The shape cut from the layer of clay is placed over the cloth-covered mound and gently pressed into place.

A rolling pin makes the bottom of the platter smooth and even.

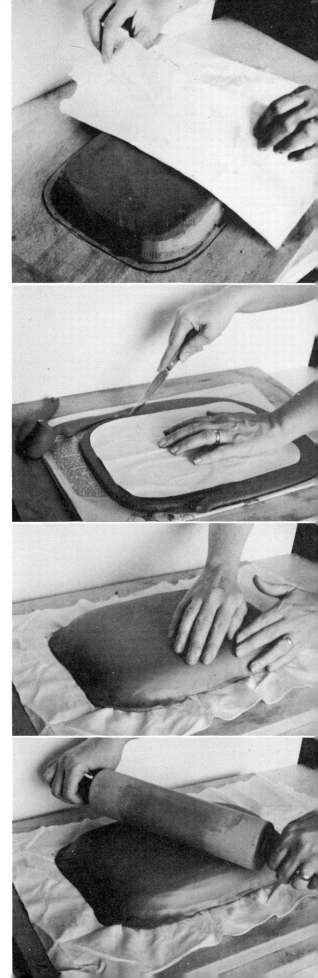

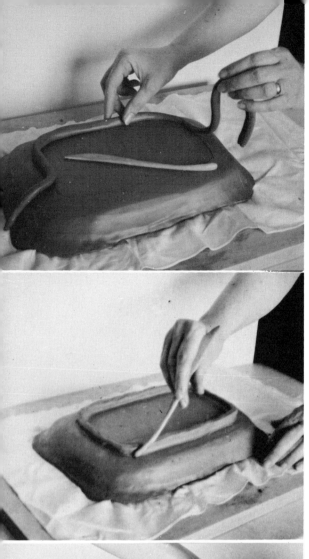

The platter will need a foot. For this, a strip of clay ¼″ wide is cut from the same layer that was used for the pattern of the platter.

The foot is pressed firmly in place.

In a few hours the layer of clay will be firm enough so that we can lift it off and study what we have made. At this point we must be critical in judging the design. If the shape does not please us for any reason, we must have the courage to discard it and start again. It is not difficult to alter the clay mound, and the satisfaction of achieving a better design will compensate us for the extra work.

The finished platter. The clay that was used fired a deep red. The beauty of this color was retained on the outer surface. The inside was sprayed with a gray-green engobe (see page 185) and then the whole piece was sprayed with a clear transparent glaze.

Rectangular shapes, decorative boxes, planters for flowers, etc., can be made from layers of clay cut into patterns, then folded and joined at the corners. Here are the steps.

A *planter*

Instead of a clay mound, a cardboard box is used as a temporary support. Again we must remember that clay shrinks as it dries. If a layer of clay were formed over a rigid box with square corners and allowed to stand until it became leather hard, the shrinkage during drying would tear the clay apart. To prevent this, the cardboard box must be wrapped in several layers of newspaper. This makes a cushion that will yield as the clay shrinks. Also, the newspaper will make it easier to lift the piece off the box.

A layer of clay has been rolled ¼″ thick and a box pattern has been cut out of the layer.

The sides folded up and joined. To make sure that the joints will hold, the pattern was cut larger than necessary so that the sides could be joined, not as two pieces of wood would be, but squeezed firmly together. Excess clay is cut off.

Two hours later. When the clay became firm enough to hold its shape, the box was removed. The clay is not yet leather hard. Thin strips of clay are worked into the corners to seal the joints on the inside.

A cross brace is fastened in place. This strengthens the planter and helps it to hold its shape.

The clay box is finished. How is the design? The proportions seem good. The box is functional; it will serve its purpose. But we must admit that the form is not very interesting. Perhaps it can be helped by some texture or ornamentation.

A high base seems to improve the design. A surface decoration has been made of lines pressed in with the tines of a fork. The piece now has more interest. It is a simple, rather severe design. Everything about it is square. The pattern made by the fork repeats the lines of the box itself, and while this makes for harmony, we are apt to feel a need for more variety.

Another treatment. A different texture has been cut with a wire loop modeling tool. Instead of a base, four cubes are used for feet. Strips of clay have been attached to the ends to serve as handles.

This design seems to have possibilities. There is a sharp contrast between the irregular, almost haphazard grooves made by the cutting tool and the straight edges of the box. This gives the variety that we missed in the first box.

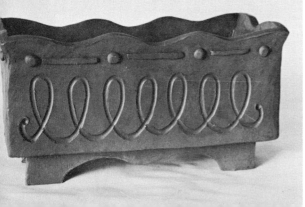

Something more elaborate. A looped design has been drawn on the side with the round end of a wooden modeling tool. A piece has been added to the top to make a slightly flared, scalloped rim. Strips and balls of clay have been pressed on the surface to make a decorative band around the top. The foot has been cut to repeat the scalloped shape of the top.

What is the effect of all this ornamentation? We have achieved something quite ornate; it was fun making it. But such a busy decoration on the side of the container would probably detract from the beauty of the plants it would hold, so let's remove the looped design and the balls and strips of clay and return to the irregular, grooved texture shown above.

Here is the finished planter, glazed with a semiopaque white glaze which gives a good surface appearance with the warm red of the body showing through.

We did not exhaust the design possibilities of this box. We could have continued trying textures, wiping them out and then trying again, changing the shape and the size of the foot, putting on and taking off handles, and so on. Experimenting this way is good exercise in design.

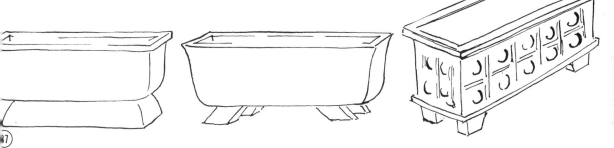

If we wish to construct a planter similar to the one we just made but wider at the top than at the base, a rectangular carton would not do for a support. It would be a simple matter, however, to construct a support for such a shape by cutting a pattern out of cardboard as shown in the sketch, folding it into shape and sealing the corners with Scotch Tape. This would then serve as a mound for forming a clay layer, just as the box did in the last series.

Now let's watch the making of a slightly more complicated shape—a teapot.

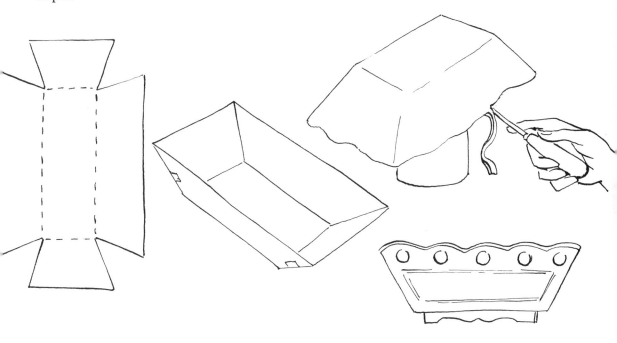

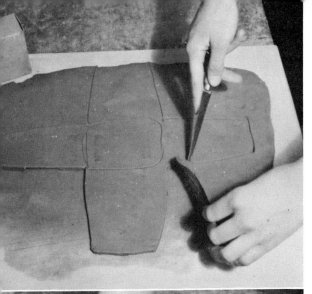

A *teapot*

A layer of clay has been rolled ¼″ thick. A pattern is cut from the layer.

The sides of the pattern are folded up and the corners squeezed together.

(38)

A thin coil of clay has been welded into the corners on the inside. Now a thin coil is welded on the top edge to provide a shoulder and to give extra strength.

Another coil is welded onto the base to serve as a foot.

Making the lid.

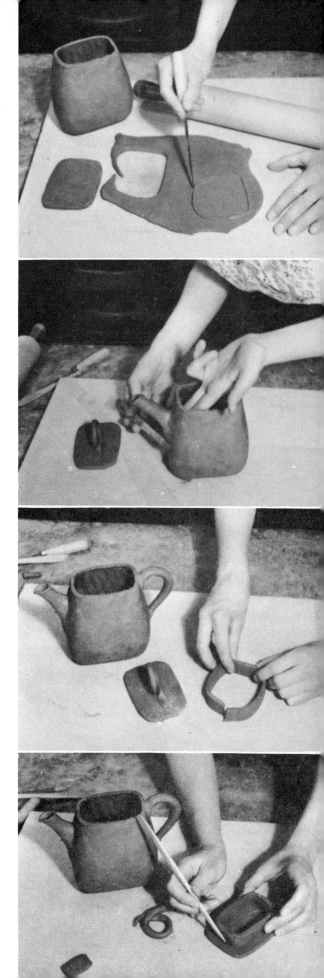

Another portion of the clay layer was rolled to make a spout. Here it is being attached. A hole was cut in the side of the pot before this operation.

Bending a strip of clay to make a flange for the lid.

Attaching the flange to the underside of the lid. The loop that served as a temporary handle has been removed.

A knob seems to make a better handle than the loop. Here a knob is attached and welded into place.

The finished glazed teapot. How is the design? Not bad. The shape is quite simple; it is functional. A high gloss, crystalline-type glaze adds interest.

Here is another way of working with layers of clay to make a pair of figurines that can serve as candleholders.

PHOTO SERIES 12

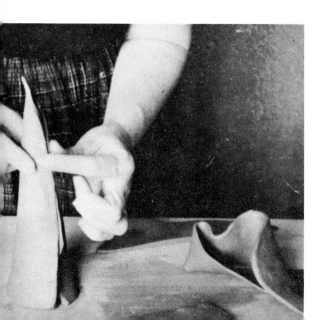

Angel candleholders

A layer of clay has been rolled and two pieces shaped like pie sections have been cut out. One of these has been rolled to make a tall narrow cone. The joint is being sealed.

Two cones have been completed. Now balls of clay are fastened on the tops to make heads.

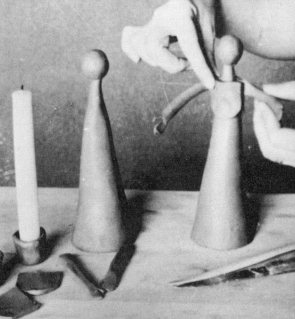

Two small pieces of clay have been cut to make the body. These are fastened in place along with thin rolled cylinders that will serve as arms. Two receptacles to hold candles have been made by wrapping strips of clay around the end of a candle.

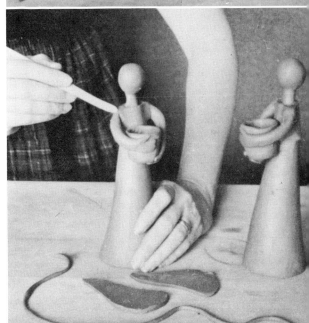

Completing the figurines, with the arms grasping the candleholders. A pair of wings have been cut from a clay layer and a long, very thin strip of clay has been rolled.

The thin strip was cut into shorter pieces and attached to the heads to make hair. Wings are now fastened in place.

Two tiny halos complete the figures. In Chapter 19 we shall see how these are glazed and painted.

These are a few of the many things that can be made of layers of clay rolled with a rolling pin. All kinds of temporary supports can be used in this work—paper cups, cracker boxes, cardboard shapes that you build yourself. Even toy balloons.

What? *Did you say balloons?*

Yes. Believe it or not, layers of clay can be shaped over balloons. The globular forms made this way can be used for many types of ceramic design. The method is amazingly easy. The clay must be quite plastic. As the layer is wrapped around the balloon, the excess folds are pinched together and squeezed off, then the whole surface is paddled and smoothed with a wooden tool.

PHOTO SERIES 13

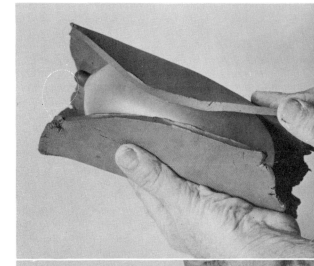

A *piggy bank*

A layer of clay is wrapped around a long sausage-shaped balloon.

Joints are sealed and smoothed.

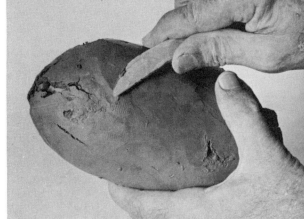

Legs and features are added. Oops! Our piggy bank looks more like a bull. Oh, well, it is too late to change it now.

The modeling completed. When the figure is leather hard, a slot will be cut in the back to receive the coins. Cutting the slot will puncture the balloon, which can then be drawn out through the slot with a bent wire.

The bank glazed and fired.

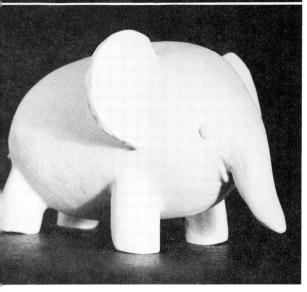

Here is another piggy bank. This one turned out to be a white elephant.

Plate 7—Flower Girl.

When a round balloon is used, the shape formed resembles a teardrop. Plate 7 shows such a shape attached to a cylinder to make a head. Features were added in the same manner as those of the bull. When this head was completed and in the leather-hard state, an opening was cut in the top so that it could serve as a flower container. Only the inside was glazed.

Work with layers of clay has many advantages for the artist seeking solutions to design problems. He can be completely free. The process is simple and it is fast. In making a free-form dish over a clay mound, one need not spend a long time shaping the mound before covering it with cloth and draping a layer of clay. As soon as the clay is hard enough to be handled it can be picked up and examined. If the design needs improvement, alter the clay mound and drape another layer, repeating the process until the result is completely satisfying. This is one of the ways to achieve ceramic design.

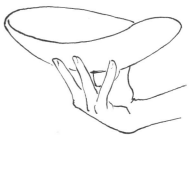

Plate 8—Gong by Pat Lopez. An amusing figure, the head (the gong) made of a thrown shape; the body a rolled slab. *Photograph by Bob Lopez.*

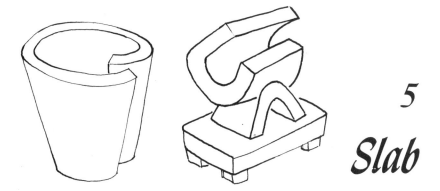

5

Slab

S HAPES CUT FROM LAYERS of clay do not have to be formed over mounds. They can be used to build free-standing constructions. In Chapter 3 we saw the coil method used to make a piece of sculpture following the outline of the sketch of the little clown. This could have been done by the slab method. We'll enlarge the little dancer, this time working with layers of clay.

PHOTO SERIES 14

A slab-built figure

An armature has been constructed by standing a wooden dowel in a block of wood. One leg of the dancer has been shaped by cutting a layer of clay, then making it into a cylinder and modeling the form. This first leg was then threaded over the dowel. Here the second leg is being formed out of a clay layer.

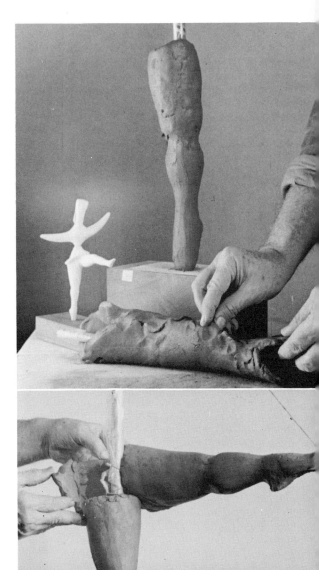

The second leg being put in place. Another dowel wrapped in newspaper serves as a support. The end of the dowel is held up by a piece of string fastened to the top of the first dowel.

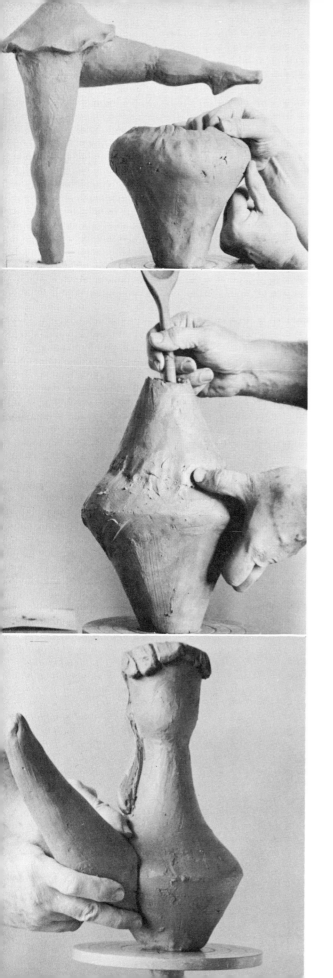

The ballerina's skirt has been put in place and another layer of clay is being formed into the waist and chest.

Another layer of clay is added to form the neck and the head. The long handle of a wooden spoon is used to weld the joints on the inside.

The head has been roughly modeled and another layer of clay has been added for the hair. Arms are being attached.

The finished ballerina. The figure is in three pieces so that, like the clown, it can be mounted on a stand in a number of different positions.

Now let's use the method of slab-building to make another fountain bowl.

PHOTO SERIES 15

Building a fountain

Layers of clay have been rolled. A round shape has been cut for the bottom of the bowl of the fountain. A rectangular piece cut from a layer is wrapped around a newspaper core. This will be the portion of the fountain housing a pump. The core is the pump itself wrapped in many thicknesses of newspaper. This is a way of making sure that the pump will fit in the space provided for it when the fountain is completed.

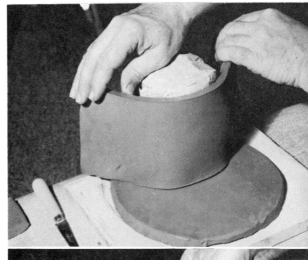

Another strip cut from a layer is put in place to form the side of the fountain bowl.

The side of the bowl is welded firmly to the base. Here we can look into the space where the pump will be concealed. An opening will be cut at the base of the inner wall so that water will be able to flow from the bowl into the pump.

A coil of clay is added to the rim of the bowl for extra height.

The bowl is turned upside down and a footing is added. A coil of clay was rolled for this. The outside surface of the bowl has been modeled into a shell shape.

3. Reclining Figure, Jacqueline Lerat.

1 and 2. *Above*. Shelves in the studio of Fusco Martini, Florence, Italy.

4. *Left*. Lawyers, Fusco Martini.

5. *Right*. The Happy Couple, Jean Lerat.

6. *Above*. Crèche figures, Jean Derval.

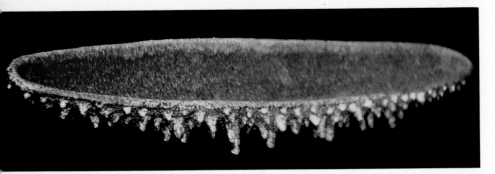

7. *Above*. Draped stoneware form, Lyle Perkins.

8. *Left*. Women on a balcony, Lucerni.

9. *Right*. Vase, product of Keremikos, Athens.

10. *Below*. Vases, Fantoni, two with raised line design.

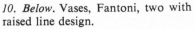

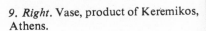

A figure of a mermaid holding a shell has been modeled separately. This will fit over the pump housing.

The mermaid in position. When this fountain is completed and operating, the pump will send water from the bowl up to the shell held in the hands of the figure. From there the water will fall into the shell at the mermaid's base, and from there it will pour back into the bowl to begin its cycle again.

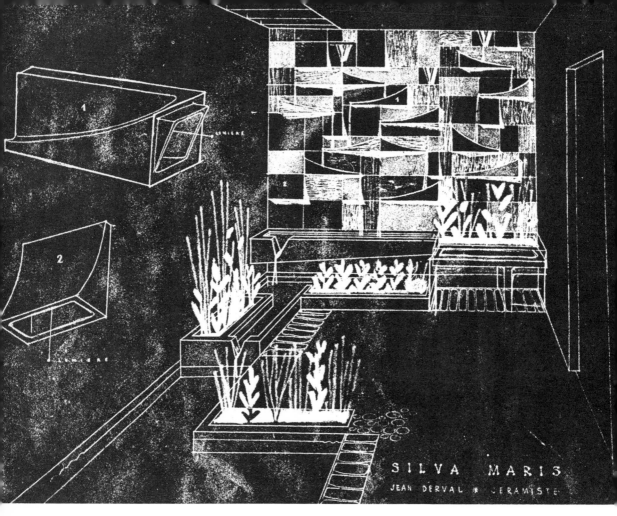

SILVA MARIS

JEAN DERVAL * CERAMISTE

Plate 9—Drawing by Jean Derval for a fountain to be built in the lobby of a residence.

A fountain of similar design is shown in operation in Fig. 21 in the color section. In this fountain the bowl is shallower and the pump is concealed in the body of the mermaid.

Fountains like this are attractive ornaments in a living room. They can act as punch-servers during parties or provide a gentle sound of running water as a background to conversation. Fountains have always had their place in the garden, among the flowers or at the edges of pools. They are beginning to be used in larger form, as arrangements covering entire walls in public rooms or in private dwellings, arrangements that have the water moving across and down the wall, cascading from level to level, making a kind of water sculpture. Designing fountains like these offers a challenge to the ceramist.

Plate 9 shows a drawing by Jean Derval for a fountain to be installed in an entrance lobby. The end wall is covered with tiles in various colors. The fountain is made of ceramic units (No. 1 in the drawing) which combine a sloping trough for the water with a box to hold a light. In the arrangement planned here, the water will come from three different sources at the top of the wall, will flow from left to right and back again as it falls

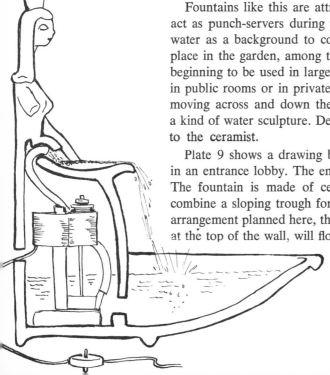

from one unit to another one lower down, until it enters a series of pools, finally reaching the pool at floor level shown in the lower left of the drawing. In its path the water will be lighted by lamps concealed in the No. 1 units which project horizontal beams, and by lights in other units (No. 2 in the drawing) which project beams downward. An exciting design, combining elements of clay, water, and light.

In Plate 10 we see Derval making a clay sketch for still another fountain. This artist's constructions are carefully thought out beforehand, often drawn with all of the detail and accuracy of a set of architect's plans. Instead of using clay slabs that are soft and plastic, that change shape as they are squeezed together, he cuts the slabs to the exact shapes called for by the pattern, bends them when necessary, then allows them to dry until they are leather hard before he joins them. The drying process often takes a full day. When he joins the pieces he sticks them together with slurry and reinforces the corners by welding thin coils of clay into the inside.

After devoting several pages to things made of clay rolled with a rolling pin it seems rather late to confess that there is a drawback to this method, namely, when we treat clay like dough and roll it flat we create tensions in the clay which are apt to make it warp as it dries. But confess we must, for it is true. This is not too serious in most cases, for the shapes that are made out of the plastic clay layers usually counteract the tendency to warp. But in the type of work Derval does, rolling clay would not work. The layers must be cut.

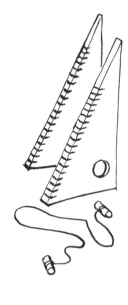

Derval cuts his layers of clay with a *taglietelle,* a tool that comes from Italy (the word means a type of noodle). It consists of a pair of wooden triangles, about 12″ high with a 6″ base. There is a series of cuts on the long side ¼″ apart. A piece of piano wire is held so that it goes through the lowest pair of cuts, then it is drawn through a mass of clay so that it cuts a layer at the bottom ¼″ thick. The wire is then shifted to the next higher pair of cuts and drawn through the clay again. This process is con-

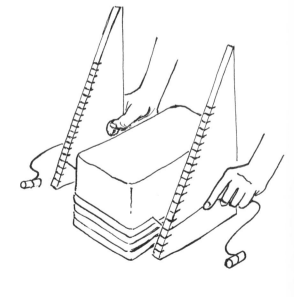

Plate 10—Jean Derval making a sketch for a fountain.

tinued until the whole mass of clay has been cut into a series of layers, all accurate, all the same thickness. Layers that are cut this way have a pleasing surface texture, especially if the clay contains grog.

Now, by way of contrast, let's watch an artist who works in a completely different manner. Here is Rudi Autio building a piece of abstract sculpture out of cut clay slabs.

Slab-built sculpture

The artist starts with a mass of clay that has been thoroughly wedged. The clay is pounded into a rough block on the table and a layer is cut from it with a handy tool made by bending a steel reinforcing rod (the kind used in concrete) into a U shape, then stretching a piece of piano wire across the ends. The wire is fastened 1″ from each end of the rod. Thus when the wire is drawn through the clay with the ends of the rod resting on the table, it cuts a layer 1″ thick.

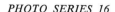

The top of the mass of clay is lifted off. The bottom layer is the one that will be used.

Starting to build.

Construction continues. A wall has been built in the form of a rough cylinder and a crosswall for bracing is built in the center.

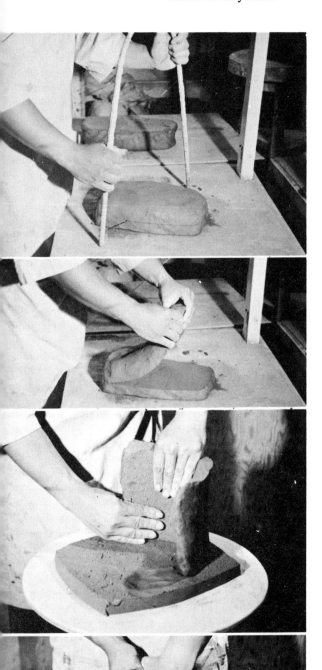

54

Making ready to place another cylindrical wall.

Completing the second wall.

Adding more slabs.

The finished construction. The artist is painting the lower portion with engobe.

What we have just watched is a method of creating form similar to that we practiced in Chapter 1. This is a new direction in ceramic design. Autio is one of the contemporary American potters who have turned their backs on tradition, who work with vigor and strength, pushing and pounding the clay into shapes that are surprising, often startling. What emerges is seldom a preconceived form, but the result of forces working on materials; sometimes it is accidental. This type of pottery is not functional. The artist here takes the role of the explorer, pushing a path into the unknown.

Interesting things can be done with slabs—especially when you work on a large scale and make forms that are bold and rugged. You don't need to do a great deal of manipulating; make things that look like slabs shaped into pottery forms, but still retaining the character of thick, cut layers of clay. For example, cut a rectangular slab about 12″ × 16″ × ¾″ thick. (Be sure to use clay with at least 30% grog added to it for this.) Cut 4 rectangular blocks of clay about 2½″ high by 1¼″ thick; attach these near the corners to serve as feet. Let the center of the slab sag so that it curves upward at each corner. You now have a serving platter, quite unlike the one that was made in Photo Series 9, in Chapter 4. That one was light, conventional in design. Its shape was determined by the mound on which it was formed. The more direct method we have just described produces a platter of a different character. Its shape comes from the natural sag of the clay. This platter is for a different kind of use—serving on a patio, for example, or on a buffet. A piece made this way, rugged though it may be, can have all the satisfying quality of good ceramic design.

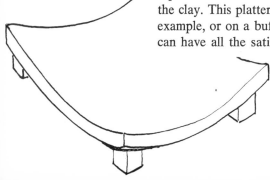

Plate 11—Slab-built lamps by the author.

The gong by Pat Lopez shown in Plate 8 was made of a layer of clay wrapped around a post to form the costume of a figure. A wheel-thrown bowl forms the head. The lamps shown in Plate 11 were built directly from slabs, and so was the vase more than 4 feet high, by F. Carlton Ball, shown in Plate 12.

There is almost no limit to the variety of shapes that can be made by slab building. Probably more than any other single method of shaping clay, it offers the ceramist a chance to experiment and to explore. Try it.

Plate 12—Flat slab-built stoneware vase, 52″ high, by F. Carlton Ball. Top glazed with satin mat gray-green glaze. Major portion of body stained with Barnard clay. Bisque surface. Fired to cone 10 in a reduction atmosphere.

6
Drape

I N CHAPTER 4 we explored ways of shaping layers of clay over clay mounds. If we take the trouble to make a mound out of plaster of Paris we shall find that the forming process is much simplified. The work is quicker, the inside surface of the piece is smoother—in fact, the job is better all around. A plaster mound used this way is called a "drape mold." We shall make a drape mold and in the process we'll learn some things about plaster of Paris.

Plaster of Paris is a valuable aid to the potter. It is made from gypsum —a rock that is hard and white. In its pure form it is called "alabaster." When this rock is heated to about 500°F., water of crystallization is driven off, the material becomes soft and crumbly, easily crushed into a fine powder. When water is added to this powder, crystals reform and the powder turns back to a hard substance much like the original rock.

This property makes it possible to use plaster to reproduce the shapes of objects—either natural forms or things made out of clay or almost any material. The shapes that are duplicated may be simple or extremely complicated. Don't make the mistake, however, of considering plaster merely a copying device; it is more than that. It is an important tool for the potter and, most important, it is another avenue toward ceramic design.

One special property of plaster makes it extremely valuable to the potter. When it is dry it acts like a sponge on clay, drawing moisture out of any clay that rests upon it. This makes it good for working bats or for bowls in which to dry clay slip. It also makes it excellent for molds.

MIXING PLASTER

Before we make a drape mold, let's learn the steps of mixing and pouring plaster of Paris by making a plaster bat.

Use a metal pie tin as a mold. Wipe the inside surface with oil or Vaseline. This will keep the plaster from sticking fast to the metal.

Put clean cold water into a clean container. This may be a regular mixing bowl or a plastic bowl. The plastic is easier to clean when you

are through. Or you can use a half gallon milk container and throw it away when the job is done.

The proper proportions are 2¾ lbs. of plaster to 1 quart of water. However, if there is no scale handy for weighing out the plaster, the quantity can be estimated.

To make a bat, a pint of water will be enough. Sprinkle the plaster into the water slowly. If you are unable to weigh out 1⅜ lbs. of plaster, the right amount for a pint of water, continue sprinkling until the plaster forms a small mound above the surface of the water.

Let the plaster slake (that is, soak up water) for two minutes. Then stir.

Stir with your hand or with a long-handled spoon. Stir from the bottom so that the whole mass is kept in movement. There will be air bubbles—stir in such a way that these are forced to the surface, then blow on them to break them. Lift the container in which you are mixing and tap it on the table from time to time—this will force bubbles to the top. If any scum forms on the surface, skim it off (scumming is a sign that the plaster is old. If there is much scumming, discard the plaster and get a fresh supply). Continue stirring for two or three minutes until the plaster starts to thicken. When it reaches the consistency of heavy cream, it is ready to pour.

Pour without splashing. Immediately after pouring stir the plaster with your finger or a stick, but don't touch the metal pie pan. Lift the pan and tap it on the table to dislodge air bubbles and to make the top surface smooth and even.

Now let the plaster set. As it hardens it goes through what is called the "cheese state" when it has the consistency of cream cheese. If we were planning to model with plaster, this is the point at which we cut it and shape it. As setting continues, crystallization begins and the plaster becomes hard. While the crystals are forming, the plaster expands slightly and gives off heat. When it becomes cool again it has set. At this point the plaster bat can be lifted out of the metal pan and the edge trimmed. Plaster bats like this are useful in a studio. Whenever you are casting with plaster have one or two pie pans handy, oiled, ready to receive any excess of plaster not needed on the job you are doing.

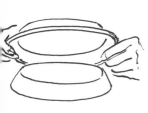

For ceramic work, the best type of plaster to use is pottery plaster. This must be stored in an airtight container, otherwise it deteriorates. Buy plaster in small quantities as you need it.

A word about disposal of waste. Plaster work can create quite a mess. Work on newspapers to protect the tabletop. Don't rinse bowls and tools under a faucet—that way you would be certain to clog the drain. Rinse off all waste plaster in a pail of water. When the plaster has settled to the bottom, pour off the water and discard the refuse. (*Note:* If you have a garden or a lawn, waste plaster of Paris is a good fertilizer.)

Now for our drape mold. Let's make a mold for a free form, somewhat triangular in shape.

Making a drape mold

We start by making a clay mound. This must have the shape of the inside surface of the piece we want to make.

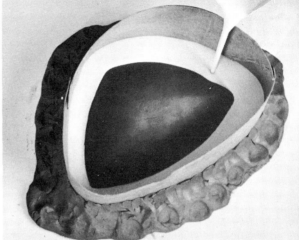

The mound has been put on a sheet of glass. A piece of cardboard that has been given a coat of size is set in place around the mound to serve as a retaining wall to hold plaster. This is called a "cottle." Clay pressed around the base on the outside of the cottle anchors it firmly to the glass. Plaster is poured. When the plaster has set, it is lifted off the glass and the clay mound is removed.

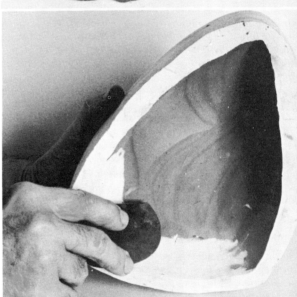

This plaster cast is a negative of the clay shape. Since we want a positive we shall have to pour plaster into the negative. Before doing this, work on the inside surface with a metal scraper to get it as smooth and true as possible. Sandpaper cannot be used here because the plaster is too wet. Emery paper would serve, however, or a special type of garnet paper made for wet work.

SIZING

Plaster can be poured over clay or glass and it will lift off easily. However, if we were to pour it into the mold we have just made, it would stick fast unless we used some substance as a separating compound. Oil or

Vaseline won't work here because they would spoil the surface of the plaster casting. Best for this purpose is *soap size*. This can be bought in prepared form from ceramic suppliers. Use it thinned to a consistency just slightly thicker than water. Apply a coating with a sponge. Wring the sponge out and wipe off all the size. Apply another coat and wipe it off again. Do this six times. Squeeze the sponge out each time but *don't* rinse it in water.

Sizing the inner surface.

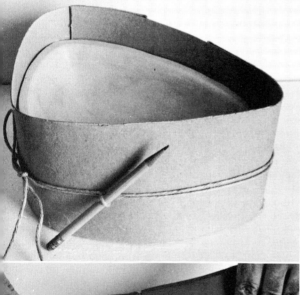

Ready to pour the final drape mold. Cardboard (again sized) is wrapped around the first portion of the mold and tied in place with twine. A pencil is used as a tourniquet to tighten the binding. This way it is possible to tie the wall firmly against the plaster and no clay is needed. Plaster will be poured now and the resulting piece will be the drape mold.

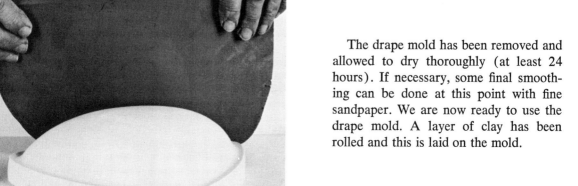

The drape mold has been removed and allowed to dry thoroughly (at least 24 hours). If necessary, some final smoothing can be done at this point with fine sandpaper. We are now ready to use the drape mold. A layer of clay has been rolled and this is laid on the mold.

The layer has been pressed into shape. Excess clay has been trimmed from the edges. Three feet are added.

When the clay has become firm, it is lifted off and smoothed and given its final surface.

Another design, using the same drape mold. Here, instead of legs we have made a high footing. The surface is given a rough texture by being struck repeatedly with a piece of wood. This variation from the more usual type of design seems to have promise. We will glaze and fire this one.

The glazed piece.

The design of a piece made over a drape mold can be varied by trimming the edge in different ways. Surface patterns or decorations can be pressed into a clay layer before it is draped. More about this in Chapters 8 and 12.

In the next series the ceramic artist Lyle Perkins, of the Rhode Island School of Design, demonstrates this method.

PHOTO SERIES 18

Draping a large form

The artist starts with a large mass of clay and pounds it flat with his hands. A piece of heavy cloth has been spread on the table. Here he is smoothing the surface of the layer by rolling a piece of pipe over it.

Instead of lifting the clay layer and putting it over the drape mold he puts the mold in place on the clay. Note that this mold has three feet or stilts, made by cutting the bottoms out of three cardboard cups, putting them in place at the bottom of the mold, and pouring additional plaster into them.

The clay is formed over the mold by lifting the cloth and turning the cloth and mold over together.

The cloth is peeled off, and the clay is pressed firmly onto the mold.

Trimming the edge. The mold stands on its three legs.

Adding shapes. The artist is interested in creating a new and original form, so instead of conventional feet he sticks on a large number of clay nodules.

Sponging the edge. The beauty of this piece will be due in part to the contrast between the smooth inner surface and the knobby exterior. The glazed piece is shown in Fig. 7 in the color section.

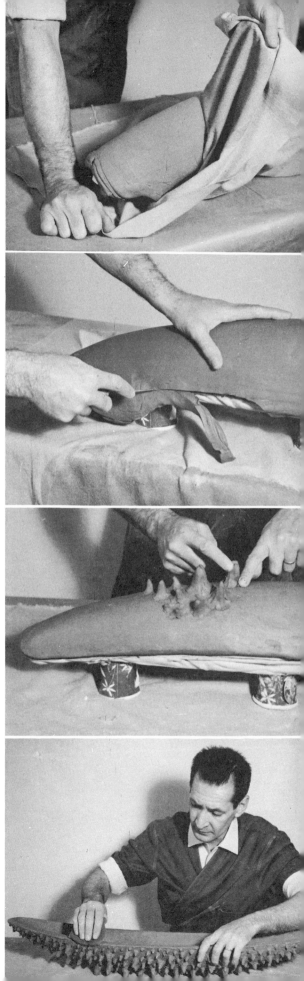

Here is another way of using plaster drape molds devised by the artist Rolf Key-Oberg.

A device for lifting a large piece off a drape mold

An opening the exact size and shape of a plaster mound was cut in a piece of plywood. The plywood has been placed over the mound like a collar.

When the artist has formed a layer of clay over the mound and attached feet, he lifts the piece off the mound by lifting the plywood. This permits him to remove the work from the drape mold at an earlier stage of the drying. The piece is left on the plywood to harden, then it is turned over onto a plaster bat to complete the drying.

66

The finished bowl. This was carved when it was leather hard, then sprayed with engobe. The line design, characteristic of this artist's work, was made by dipping a thread in gum tragacanth and laying it on the surface of the piece before spraying.

11. Platter, Jean Derval.

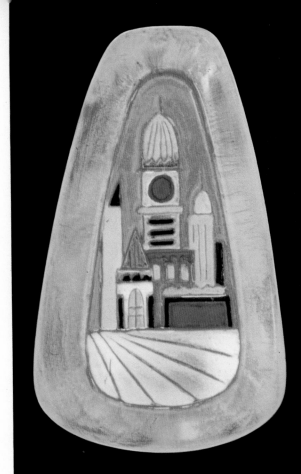

12. Decorative Dish, Harris Strong.
Design in raised lines.

13. Ash Tray, flow glaze, Harper.

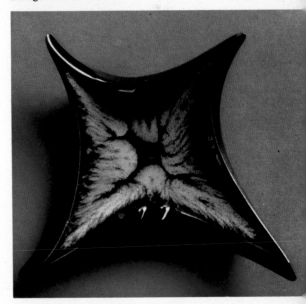

14. Ash Tray, flow glaze, Harper.

15. *Left*. Platters, Fantoni

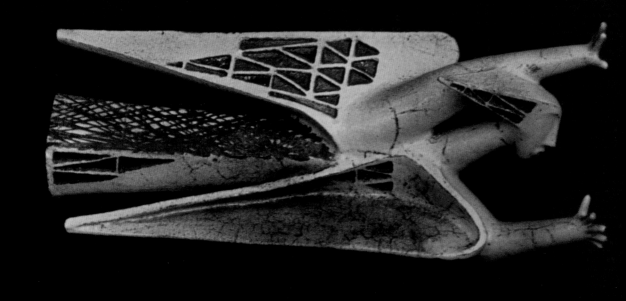

16. *Above*. Angel, wall sculpture, five feet long, Jean Derval.

17. *Above*. Owl on a Fence,
Rosemary Zwick.

18. *Left*. Girl, Rosemary Zwick.

19. *Above*. Mother and Child, garden
sculpture, Jacqueline Lerat.

20. *Left*. Cyclists, Jean Lerat.

Here is the method used by Key-Oberg to make a vase out of two draped shapes.

PHOTO SERIES 20

A vase made in two parts

A layer of clay has been pressed over a plaster mound. Note the plywood collar.

A second layer has been pressed over the mound; now the two pieces are ready to be joined. Slurry is used to fasten the joint. After the two halves are put together, the joints will be carefully welded on the outside and the inside.

The completed piece. Again we see this artist's unique line decoration.

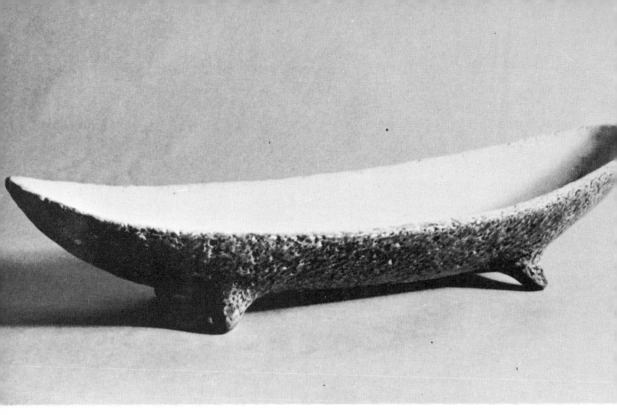

Plate 13—Long oval dish made over a drape mold. Heavily grogged clay was scraped on the outside with a toothed scraper. This gives a rough texture which contrasts with the smooth white inner surface. By the author.

Pieces made over drape molds need not reproduce the exact shapes of the molds. Forms made this way can be altered by carving when they are leather hard, or, before they reach the leather-hard state, while they are still resting on the mold, they may be altered by bending. Different types of base or foot can be tried out while the piece is on the mold also, and so can a variety of exterior surface textures. We shall see in a later chapter how drape molds can be carved to produce raised line patterns in the shapes draped over them.

A number of drape molds of different sizes and shapes are good to have in the studio; they not only help the potter to produce ware but they assist him too in his search for form.

7

Turn

So FAR the objects we have made have been of all shapes except round. And yet, the circle is the basis of most pottery forms. Why, then, have we avoided it? Because we have been working freehand, and while it is possible to make something freehand that is almost round, almost is not good enough.

The perfect circle, the wonderful shape of geometry, is never found in nature. Like the wheel, it is one of man's creations. Its full beauty is seen only when it is true. To create circular forms in clay, we need a turning device, a wheel.

The art of forming clay on a potter's wheel, or throwing, is a way of working which we shall study in detail in Chapter 10. Before we come to that, let us consider how shapes can be made on a wheel by holding tools or templates against clay as it revolves. Bowls can be made freehand then turned true in this manner, or cylindrical forms made by the coil method, or by slab building can be turned in similar fashion.

The best way to do this is with a power-driven wheel and a mechanical device to hold the shaping tool or the template. Such a device is called a "jigger"—we will speak about jiggering a little later on in this chapter. If your studio doesn't have such equipment, it is still possible to turn shapes on a banding wheel or whirler, spinning it with one hand while the other hand, firmly pressed on some supporting device, holds a tool against the clay. Here are the steps for making a piece of pottery by turning a clay mound on a whirler, then draping and shaping a bowl over the mound.

PHOTO SERIES 21

Turning a shape on a whirler

A mound of clay on the banding wheel is turned into shape with a wooden block.

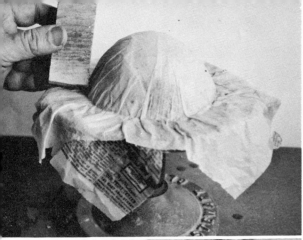

When the clay mound is completed it is covered with two layers of wet paper toweling. The wooden block presses the towel firmly into place so that there will be no big wrinkles to cause serious distortion on the inside surface of the piece we are making.

The layer of clay has been rolled. This is pressed into place over the mound.

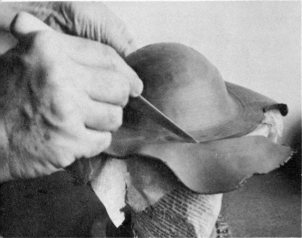

Trimming the edge.

Making a high, pedestal-type foot. A strip of clay is formed into a cylinder over a core of newspaper.

The pedestal has been trued and attached. A wooden modeling tool is held against it to make an ornamental band.

⑦1

Finishing the top and smoothing the inside surface.

The glazed piece.

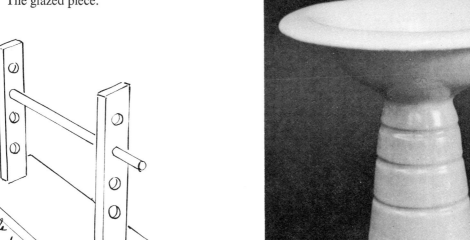

Adjustable armrest...

Note that it was necessary to brace the hand firmly during the turning operations shown in this series. An adjustable armrest like the one shown in the sketch would prove helpful.

A plaster bat that fits the top of your whirler is a handy thing to have. Here are the steps in making such a bat.

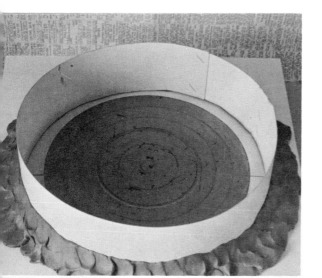

A plaster bat to fit a whirler

The head of the whirler must be oiled. Then a cottle, in this case a strip of cardboard, is fastened in place around it. Since the head of the whirler is fastened to a shaft it is necessary to rig up a device so that the shaft can go through a hole in a heavy piece of cardboard or plywood permitting the head of the whirler to rest on a flat surface.

Pouring plaster. After the plaster has been poured, it is stirred.

When the plaster reaches the cheese state, the whirler is turned and the bat is made true by holding a metal scraper against it.

When the plaster has set and cooled the bat can be lifted off the whirler. If this bat were made with a convex surface it could serve as a drape mold for plates. We shall see an illustration of this in Photo Series 27 in Chapter 8.

Another type of bat with a high beehive-shaped dome can be used to make a variety of bowl shapes.

A bowl-forming bat

A bat like the one made in the last series is placed on the head of the whirler. Notches have been cut in the bat. A small lump of clay has been placed in the center and plaster of cream consistency is being poured over it.

The plaster is beginning to thicken. More is piled on.

While the plaster is still fairly soft, the mound is turned true by holding a metal scraper against it.

As soon as the plaster sets, final scraping and smoothing is done. This process is called "running" plaster.

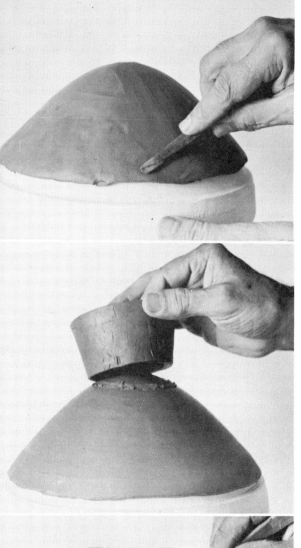

Using the mound. After the mound has dried for several days a layer of clay is draped over it. This will be turned true.

A cylinder of clay to serve as a base is put into place. The edge was roughened and coated with slurry so that the joint will hold.

The joint between bowl and base is welded with a wooden modeling tool. The lines made by this tool will be obliterated and the surface made smooth with scraper and sponge.

The finished piece.

Much variety of form and texture can be obtained by working with this same plaster mound.

Turning bowl shapes

A base for a bowl is formed out of a layer pressed over the mound and then cut into a scalloped shape.

The base attached to a bowl. A band of decoration has been made around the rim of the bowl.

The bowl completed.

(75)

The lines formed by the tool that joined the base to the bowl could have been retained as ornamental texture, as shown in this photo. The pattern of the base was repeated at the rim.

Here are three different proportions of bowl and base made over the same mound.

Plate 14 shows a ceramic lamp that was made by the coil method and then turned true on a whirler. The lamp consists of a round base that holds a bulb. The shade is a cylinder of fiberglass.

Plate 14 — Ceramic lamp, base turned on a whirler. Shade is cylinder of fiberglass. By the author.

Jiggering

Commercially, practically all plates are made by a jiggering process. The jigger is a wheel that holds plaster bats with convex surfaces similar to the one made in Photo Series 22, and a hinged arm that can be raised and lowered. A template fastened to this arm has the shape of the profile of the bottom of the plate. The convex surface of the bat forms the upper surface of a plate. When the jigger is used, a layer of clay is pressed onto the bat, the wheel is set in motion, and the template is lowered to exactly the proper distance so that when it cuts away the excess clay, what is left on the bat is a perfectly formed plate.

It used to be that jiggering machinery was heavy and extremely expensive, but recently the manufacturers of equipment for studio potters have begun producing simpler, less costly jiggers. This is good news, because jiggering is the only satisfactory way to shape clay into plate forms. The studio potter who plans to make and decorate plates would do well to consider either buying or building a jigger arm to use with his power-driven wheel.

Shapes that are turned are often made to serve as models from which molds are cast. Plate 15 shows a vase form made of solid clay, upside

Jiggering a bowl...

Jiggering a plate...
Sectional view

Plate 15—Vase shape turned out of solid clay. From this a 1-piece pour mold can be made.

down. In Chapter 9 we shall see how drain molds are made from shapes like these.

Molds can be made from plaster models as well as from clay models. We saw, in Photo Series 24, how plaster of Paris can be shaped by turning it when it is going through its cheese state, before it becomes hard. Designers who plan shapes for factory production usually turn them in plaster of Paris. A heavy-duty power wheel is necessary for this kind of work.

There are other ways of turning plaster shapes. One of these, called a sled, is shown in the sketch. It consists of a wooden post fastened into a board. A pin in the top of the post (a nail with the head filed off) serves as a pivot. The sled, made of two pieces of wood, has a bent piece of sheet metal with a hole in it fastened at the end. This fits over the pivot pin in such a manner that it rests on the post while the sled stands level on the board. A removable metal template (this may be sheet metal or a piece of tin can flattened) is cut to form the profile of the shape to be turned. The cut must be made carefully and the edges filed smooth so that the model will have a good surface.

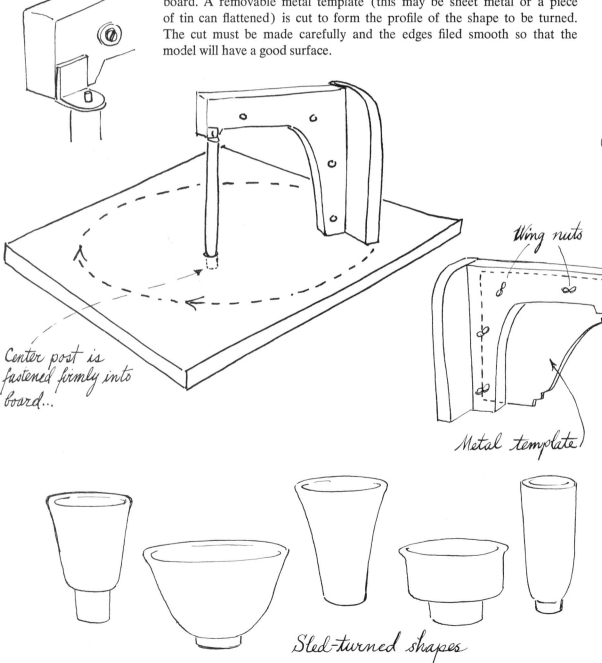

Center post is fastened firmly into board...

Wing nuts

Metal template

Sled-turned shapes

The turning sled

Before using the sled, the potter must make preparations as follows. The board on which the sled is to rotate must be thoroughly coated with size. The wood portions of the sled must be given a coating of size also. The metal template should be wiped with oil or Vaseline and then wiped clean. The post should have a protective collar of clay built around it so that the final model can be lifted off easily.

When these preparations are completed, plaster is mixed in a bowl in the proper proportions, namely, 2¾ lbs. of plaster for 1 quart of water.

The plaster is allowed to slake for one or two minutes, after which it is stirred for a short period. Then a portion of the plaster is dipped out into a second bowl. This second bowl is left untouched while the stirring of the first bowl continues.

When the plaster starts to thicken and reaches the consistency where a spoonful of plaster will retain its shape in about the same manner that a spoonful of whipped cream would when dropped on a table, the potter begins to pile plaster around the clay which was used to protect the post.

As he piles plaster around the center post, the potter gives the sled a turn, continuing to pile plaster until the volume of the plaster becomes great enough so that the template in its path begins to shape the plaster.

After the first rotation of the sled there will be holes left in the plaster.

Spoonfuls of plaster must be dipped out and put over these holes and the sled rotated again. This process must be continued until the template has formed a shape free from cavities.

At this point the potter must remove the sled, wipe it and the template clean, wipe the excess plaster from the board, and then put the sled back again for the final splash coat.

For this final coat the potter uses plaster from the second bowl. This was not stirred and so it has remained more liquid than the other batch of plaster. This more liquid plaster can be dipped over the model and the sled rotated quickly for the final smooth surface of the plaster model.

As the last step in the forming, water is poured over the model and the sled is given a final few turns. Now the plaster is left to set hard.

The turned model lifted off the post. The edge of the rim is trimmed by hand. A pour mold will be made from this model.

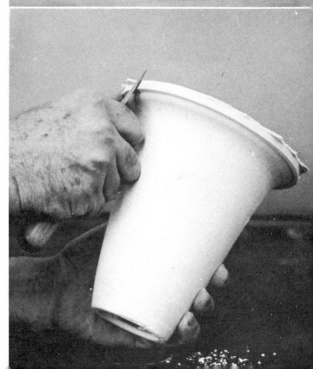

Different templates produce different models. Templates can be perforated in such a manner that they are interchangeable on the sled. This is a valuable device for design.

The turning box

Models for vase shapes can be turned in plaster by means of a fairly simple device called a "turning box." This works on the same principle as the turning sled. The box has a metal rod, one end of which is bent

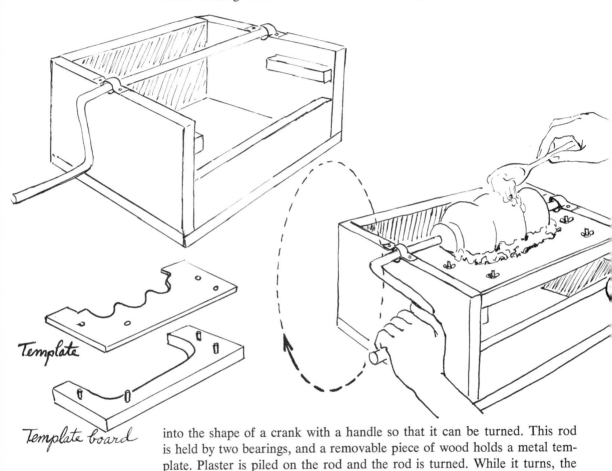

Template

Template board

into the shape of a crank with a handle so that it can be turned. This rod is held by two bearings, and a removable piece of wood holds a metal template. Plaster is piled on the rod and the rod is turned. While it turns, the template cuts the plaster to the desired shape.

With the turning box, one can turn models quickly. This allows for experimentation with profiles of vase forms, just as the sled allows experimentation with profiles of bowls.

The work we have done in this chapter has been mechanical. Mechanical forms have their place in ceramics. These forms are quite different from things made freehand, just as steel ball bearings are different from pebbles one finds on a beach. Each has its own beauty; each has its own place in design.

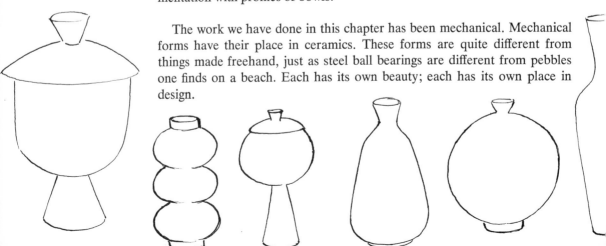

8

Press

CERAMIC DESIGN can be achieved by pressing clay into things or by pressing things into clay. Let's consider the second of these first.

A surface pattern pressed into a layer of clay will be retained in a piece that is formed over a drape mold. Here is how it is done.

PHOTO SERIES 26

Pressing and draping

A layer of clay has been rolled and a lattice design is pressed into it with a wooden stick. The drape mold that will be used is in the background.

The layer of clay in which the design was pressed has been turned upside down and flopped over the mold. The edge is trimmed.

Feet are added.

The completed piece is taken off the mold and the edge is sponged.

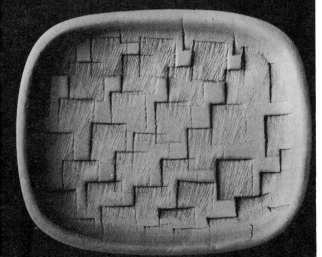

A different pattern made by pressing with the end of a stick.

Plate 16 — A decorating wheel or roulette, made of clay.

A great variety of objects may be used for pressing patterns into a layer of clay—bottle tops, cut sticks and the like. Or dies can be made out of plaster or even out of clay. A clay die can be fired and then used when it is bisque. However, firing such a die is not absolutely necessary. The clay, when it becomes bone dry, is hard enough to press with.

In the days when all pottery was handmade, potters would sometimes use a decorating wheel to roll an ornamental band on a piece that was being formed. Designs cut into the wheel produced raised decorations on the piece. Such a wheel, called a "roulette," can be made of clay. Form clay into the shape of a wheel, about 2″ in diameter and, while it is soft, press a repeat pattern into the outer rim. After the clay has dried and been fired, the wheel can be mounted on a piece of heavy wire (coat hanger wire is good) that serves as an axle. Plate 16 shows a roulette.

Wheels from toys can be used as roulettes to give an interesting variety of rolled-on patterns.

Here is another way of pressing a design into a layer of clay.

PHOTO SERIES 27

A design pressed into a plate

A pattern of a rooster has been cut out of thin cardboard. This shape is put on a layer of clay and a rolling pin is used to roll it into the clay.

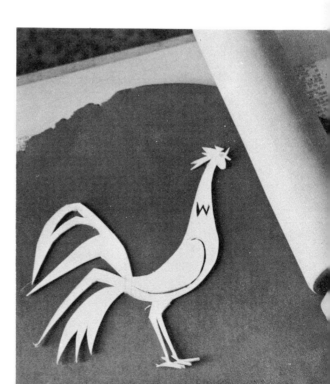

The cardboard is carefully lifted out of the clay layer. The impression of the rooster remains. (If we wish to use this design on a pair of plates with the rooster facing in opposite directions we turn the cardboard over when we roll the second layer of clay.)

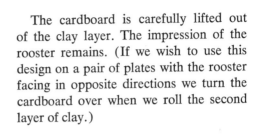

The layer of clay with the design pressed in it has been put over a drape mold, the edge has been trimmed, now a foot is added. (*Note:* This drape mold is circular and it is made to fit the head of a banding wheel. The method of making such a mold was described in Photo Series 22.)

The completed plate.

Plate 17—Rectangular platter, rolled-in design.

Plate 17 shows a rectangular dish with a fish design made by the method just described. In Plate 18 we see this same pattern used in a different way. The fish, cut from thin cardboard, was rolled into a layer of clay which was then draped over an oval drape mold. The resulting platter with the design pressed in was used to cast a second drape mold. This had the fish design in relief. From this, additional platters can be made with the fish design recessed.

Plate 18—Drape mold made from plate with rolled-in design.

Plate 19—Drape mold with a school emblem embossed on it.

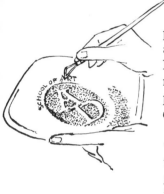

Plate 19 shows a combination of carving and draping. A rectangular plate was made over a drape mold, then a design, the emblem of a school and the school name, was carved in the plate while it was leather hard. Next, a second drape mold was cast in the leather-hard plate. By this means a drape mold with a raised pattern was produced. Layers of clay pressed over this drape mold will produce replicas of the original carved dish.

Pressing designs into layers of clay gives a unique design quality to the work. When fluid glazes are used they form pools in the depressions. Interesting effects are obtained by using two glazes of different colors. One glaze is applied to the bisque piece in the area of design, then the surface is wiped clean. After this, the second glaze, which should be transparent or semitransparent, is brushed or sprayed over the entire piece.

If, instead of using a cutout shape, we use the portion of cardboard from which it is cut, then we do not produce a design which is depressed but one which stands out with the background pressed in. This is called "island relief." An example of island relief is shown in the fish tile used with glass illustrated in Fig. 32 of the color section.

Layers of clay may be rolled on a surface that has a rough texture—a piece of burlap, for example. This gives a completely different effect in the draped piece. Or we could lay the clay on a section of metal lath and press it lightly before putting it on a drape mold. We could use the corrugated portion of a cardboard box to obtain surface pattern. The possibilities are endless—worth exploration.

Now, let's consider pressing clay into things. Suppose that instead of pressing a design in the clay before putting it over a drape mold, we had worked on the mold, carving a design into it. Then the clay form made over the drape mold would have the incised lines reproduced as ridges. This is a good method to use on certain kinds of decorative ware, where

Plate 20—Plate from Italy with a landscape in relief. Made on a drape mold with the design carved in the mold.

the raised lines on the piece will serve as walls separating areas of different colors.

A more elaborate example of this method is seen in the Italian plate shown in Plate 20 where a whole landscape in low relief projects from the surface of the dish. The design of the landscape was cut into the drape mold on which this plate was made. Such ware is not suited for table use, of course, but it is decorative and makes interesting ashtrays or fruit dishes.

In the manufacture of fine tableware, teacups are made by casting or jiggering without handles. The handles are made in press molds and attached with slip while both cup and handle are leather hard.

To make such a press mold it is necessary to make a model in plaster first. Then a two-piece mold is made from this model. No opening is left for pouring in slip. Large notch holes are made in one half of the mold so that the other half will have corresponding knobs of ample size. This will make pressing easier. After the two halves of the mold are cast, a groove ¼″ wide and about ⅛″ deep is cut in the mold around the outside of the form. When clay is pressed in the mold, the excess is squeezed into the groove.

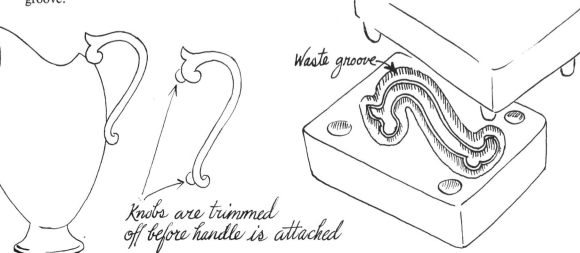

Waste groove

Knobs are trimmed off before handle is attached

A tile with raised-line design

A clay tile shown on the left was cut from a layer of clay. A bird design was made by pressing into the soft clay. After the clay dried it was pressed into another soft tile shown on the right, so that the design was reversed and every shape pressed in was reproduced as a projection.

The tile glazed and fired.

Sand casting

Sand casting is not a ceramic process, but it is another approach to design—a way of creating a sculptural form in relief by scooping out and pressing in. Here are the steps in making a sand casting at the seashore.

A sand-cast fish

We begin a design by drawing in the wet sand at the water's edge.

The shape of a fish has been scooped out.

Lines are pressed in to indicate scales. A bit of broken seashell has been placed at the mouth of the fish to make a set of teeth.

Plaster of Paris has been mixed and is poured into the depression. A spoon is held in place to receive the stream of plaster, otherwise the force of the stream would mar the design.

Pouring is completed. The plaster is beginning to set. Pieces of coat hanger are dropped into the plaster to serve as reinforcement and also to provide a hanging hook.

After the plaster has set thoroughly (one or two hours—just to be on the safe side), the casting is dug out of the sand and carried into the surf. The excess sand is washed away. The casting is completed.

Plate 21—Sand castings.

The illustrations in Plate 21 show more forms made by the same process.

Note: These castings were not made with ordinary plaster of Paris, but with *Hydrocal*. This is much harder when it sets. It should be noted, too, that even though this work was done at the seashore, it was necessary to bring fresh water for mixing. Seawater would not have worked at all.

As we said before, the product we have just made is not ceramic, but it contains design elements which can be used with clay. Here is how . . .

PHOTO SERIES 30

A mold made of sand and cement

We shall use the same method, but here, instead of working on the seashore we shall do the modeling in a cardboard box that has been lined with plastic, and instead of using sand, we shall use a mixture of sand and Portland cement (3 parts of sand to 1 of cement). The sand and cement are thoroughly mixed, dry, and then just enough water is added to make a thick mixture that is not soupy. Here the mixture of cement and sand has been put into the box and we start to press in the design, using a spoon.

Completing the design. A number of other tools were used, blocks of wood, and a knife handle. The top of a bottle was pressed in to make the eyes.

It took a few days for the cement to set thoroughly. (During this time damp cloths were kept over the box to keep the cement from drying out too rapidly.) When it was hard, clay was pressed into it to make the design relief. The negative cement mold is shown on top and the clay pressing is below.

The fired plaque.

Ceramic plaques like the one we have just made can be built into walls to serve as architectural ornaments or sections of murals. Sand castings can serve this way too, if Portland cement mortar is used in place of plaster of Paris. This type of work has interesting design possibilities, not only because of the great variety of shapes and textures that can be created but also because of the wide choice of materials that can be set in the cement. We shall say more about sand casting for architectural use in Chapter 21.

Pressings of shapes

Clay pressings can be made of natural forms or sculpture in low relief, and from these negative forms, positive pressings can be made so that the original shape becomes part of a ceramic design. An old sculptural relief can be the basis for a ceramic tile. The tile will not be an exact duplication but an adaptation of the design. Here are the steps in making a pressing from a sculptural ornament.

PHOTO SERIES 31

Making a pressing of a sculptural ornament

An angel, part of the decoration on an old iron fence. Before pressing clay against this, the angel was sponged, dried, then lightly dusted with flint.

Plastic clay is pressed against the figure.

The pressing removed. This negative is now put aside to dry. The best technique would be to fire the negative to about cone 010. (Cones are described in Chapter 17.) This would give us a press mold of bisque, hard enough to be handled freely, but soft and porous enough to have almost the absorptive quality of plaster of Paris. (In earlier days, before the manufacture of plaster was perfected, potters regularly used molds made of bisque.)

But in this case no kiln was available, so the negative was allowed to become bone dry, then soft clay was pressed in. Using an unfired clay mold for pressing is risky, of course. Too heavy pressure at any point will break the mold. But it can be done. Here is the pressing.

The finished tile.

Arretine ware, a type of red terra cotta decorated in relief, was made near the town of Arretium in Italy about 100 B.C. The potters of this region made molds for bowls out of clay. Designs were carved in the inner surface of the molds and then they were fired to bisque. Clay pressed in the molds produced bowls with raised ornaments on the outer surface.

Sprig molds were used by the English potter, Wedgwood, to produce his popular cameo-type ware or Jasper ware. The designs, usually classical figures, were modeled in clay and from these models plaster molds were made. In the production of the Wedgwood ware, the pottery form was made out of a colored clay body, light blue, pale green, sometimes black. White clay was pressed into the sprig mold, then carefully lifted out and attached to the form, thus producing a white raised ornament on a colored background. A sprig mold can be made by pressing a design into a layer of plastic clay and then letting the clay dry, and firing it.

There is another way of pressing clay into molds, a sort of reverse draping process in which a layer of clay is pressed on the inside of a shell made in plaster of Paris. A box, for example, could be made by pressing a clay layer inside a rectangular mold. The unusual planter by Lyle Perkins shown in Plate 22 was made by pressing the lower half into a plaster form that had been made especially for this piece. The upper half was then coil built on top of the supported lower section. Clay pillars were molded

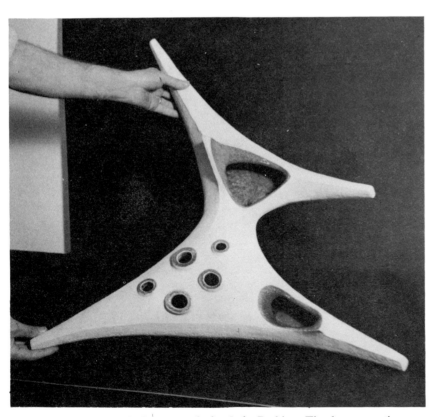

Plate 22—An unusual planter made by Lyle Perkins. The lower portion was pressed into a clay shell, the upper portion was coil built.

inside as the enclosure proceeded, to help prevent sagging during building and firing. These pillars remained as a permanent part of the form. The interior was glazed to prevent seepage of moisture; the outside surface was left unglazed.

Working with negative and positive shapes develops a fuller understanding of form. When you have scooped out a shape in some material and then made a positive pressing of it, you will be surprised at how much more you can see in that shape. Try some of the methods we have described; they are good exercises—another approach to ceramic design.

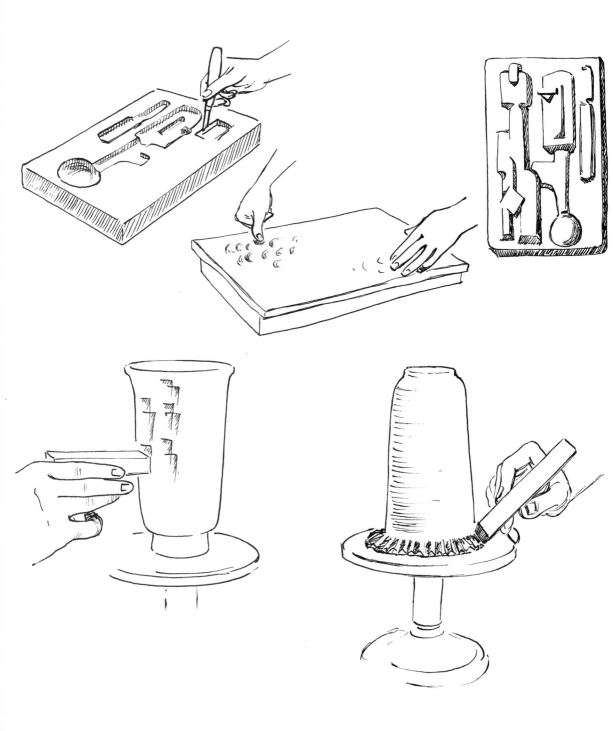

9

Pour

U P TO THIS POINT we have worked with clay in plastic form. Let's explore the design possibilities of clay in the liquid state.

As the water content of plastic clay is increased, it becomes softer and softer until it turns into a liquid which can be poured from one container into another. This liquid is called "slip." A drop of liquid clay falling onto a dry plaster slab will turn into a clay button in a few minutes, and slip poured into a hollow plaster shape will harden and produce a positive cast of that shape. It is this property of plaster which makes possible the process of slip casting in molds, a method used in most commercial production of ceramic ware.

Besides their industrial uses, molds and slip casting are of value to the studio potter. They allow him to make duplicates of his pieces when he wishes to do so. They assist him, too, in creating forms that would be difficult, if not impossible, to make in any other way.

The simplest type of mold is a one-piece drain mold for a bowl shape. Making such a mold is an exercise in working with plaster and it is a good problem in design as well.

The shape of a bowl is subtle. Slight variations in the contour and in the proportions make big differences in the aesthetic value of the bowl.

A bowl that is cast in a plaster mold will have a completely different design quality from one that is shaped on the potter's wheel or one built by the coil method. Before starting to make a mold for a bowl it is good to plan the shape by making sketches showing the profile and the type of foot. Since this is to be a one-piece mold, there must be no undercuts. Details of rim and foot should be quite simple.

After a satisfactory sketch has been made, a model of the bowl must be turned. The most efficient way of doing this is to turn the shape in plaster of Paris on a power wheel or by means of a sled as shown in Chapter 7. On the other hand, when a model is turned in clay the design can be altered during the turning process. Such alteration is frequently necessary because a flat profile sketch on paper can never give a true picture of what the bowl shape will be.

We'll make a one-piece drain mold for a bowl over a model turned on a whirler.

A one-piece drain mold

A mound of clay was turned on a whirler into the shape of a bowl upside down, using the methods described in Chapter 7. A steel scraper was used to form the continuous smooth curve of the profile. A low foot was shaped (we shall see later why in a mold of this kind the foot must be low and simple in outline). The next step will be to pour plaster over this mound. The surface of the wheel must be oiled, and a cottle must be tied firmly around the edge of the wheel. This cottle may be a strip of sized cardboard as shown in Photo Series 17 or it may be a strip of heavy transparent plastic as shown in Picture 5 of Photo Series 33. There are advantages in using plastic for a cottle—you can see what you are doing and the plastic does not need to be sized. The cottle should be tied around the wheel with a piece of twine tightened by a tourniquet.

Plaster was poured over the mound to make a one-piece mold which was then allowed to dry for several days. Here slip is poured into the mold. As the mold absorbs moisture from the slip the level will sink; slip must be added from time to time to keep the mold always full. The slip used here has been "deflocculated."

DEFLOCCULATION

At the beginning of this chapter we said that slip was clay with enough water added to it so that it could be poured as a liquid. True enough—as far as it goes. A mixture of clay and water can be used for a simple 1-piece drain mold, but for a more complicated shape it would not work. It takes too much water to make clay a liquid; there is too much shrinkage as slip dries. Any complicated parts, such as the handle or the spout of a teapot, would almost certainly break off in the mold. Even for casting a simple bowl shape we should have slip which has been deflocculated.

It is generally believed that the plasticity of clay is due to an electrical or magnetic attraction which the tiny clay particles have for one another. This causes them to flock together. If we add something to the clay which destroys or reverses this electrical charge and makes the particles repel one another instead of flocking together, then a mass of clay with 35% to 50% water, instead of being a thick sticky mud, becomes a thin, freely flowing liquid. Substances which act on clay this way are called "electrolytes." Most frequently used are sodium silicate and soda ash.

Instructions for deflocculating casting slip are given in the section on materials in the Appendix. Those who have not the time to prepare their own may buy casting slip already deflocculated from ceramic supply dealers. It is sold in liquid form or as a dry powder.

While slip is in a mold it forms a wall on the inside surface. The longer the slip remains in the mold, the thicker this wall will be. We would like to have a wall about $\frac{1}{8}''$ in thickness, so we cut in slightly at the top edge to see how the wall is building up. When a wall of the desired thickness has been formed, all of the remaining slip is poured out of the mold.

The mold must stand upside down, propped up on one edge for a few minutes until all of the slip has drained out and the shine has disappeared from the surface of the casting. After that, the mold should be turned right side up and the top edge trimmed with a knife. As the slip dries the cast form will shrink slightly and pull away from the side of the mold. If the casting sticks at one point, tap the mold on the opposite side to loosen it.

The casting removed from the mold.

Here we have a bowl with a thin wall, even in thickness throughout. Good ceramic design can be achieved through well-planned mold making and casting. In later chapters we shall see the uses that can be made of castings of this type with various methods of carving and engobe decoration.

drain casting

Solid casting

If we look at the inside of the bowl we have just cast, we will see that even though we made the foot small, there is a depression in the bottom where the foot is formed. If we want the inside surface absolutely smooth, or a piece with a larger foot or a shape thicker in some places than in others, it will be necessary to make a two-piece solid casting mold. We can use the drape mold that we made in Chapter 6 and from it make a solid casting mold in two pieces.

solid casting

⑩

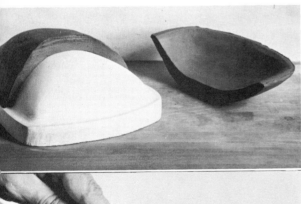

PHOTO SERIES 33

A *two-piece solid casting mold*

A layer of clay has been pressed over the drape mold, then cut in half. This gives us a chance to see the thickness of the wall. The wall must be thicker at the base than at the top edge. When the profile is satisfactory, we can put the two halves of the shape back together again.

The two pieces have been rejoined. A block of clay is welded in place on the bottom of the model. This will make an opening through which slip can be poured into the mold and it will also form the footing on the casting.

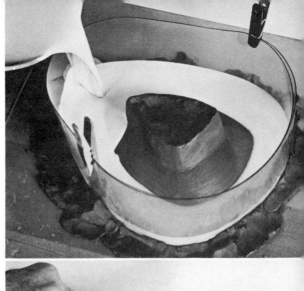

The model rests on a sheet of glass. A cottle, a strip of heavy plastic, has been set in place around it. Plaster is being poured.

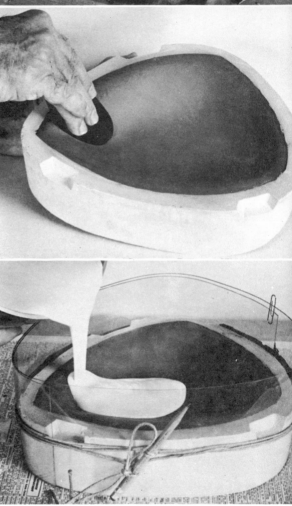

The first half of the mold has been poured. This is now turned over with the clay still in place. Notches have been cut so that the two halves of the mold will fit together properly. The edge of the first piece of the mold and the notches will have to be sized. When this is done we shall be ready to fasten the cottle in place, and pour the second half of the mold.

Pouring the second half.

Using the mold for solid casting after it has dried. The two halves of the mold are held together by heavy rubber bands.

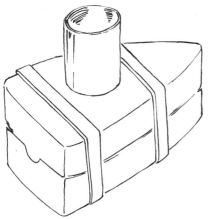

(*Note:* In pouring such a mold it is necessary to keep the pouring channel constantly filled with slip. A tin can with both the top and bottom removed can be used as a reservoir as shown in the sketch, so that it is not necessary to refill the mold frequently.)

After the slip has remained in the mold long enough to build up a solid wall between the top and bottom halves, the mold is turned over and the remaining slip is poured out. The mold is then allowed to stand upside down, one edge propped up, until the casting becomes firm enough to remove from the mold.

The completed casting. Whenever a casting is made in a two-piece mold a seam line or fettle will remain. This must be trimmed with a knife or metal scraper and then sponged. This process is called "fettling." Move the knife or scraper across the seam, not along it. This will remove all trace of the seam.

The finished piece, glazed and fired. In Plate 72 in Chapter 19 we shall see overglaze decorations tried on this piece.

There are a number of design variations possible with a mold of this type. We could incise a decoration on the inner surface of the clay model before pouring plaster for the second half. This decoration would come out as a series of raised lines in the mold and would be reproduced as an incised decoration in every casting. Or, we could carve a design into the surface of the second half of the mold. This would be reproduced as a raised-line decoration on each casting. This is effective when used with fluid glazes of different colors that fill the areas enclosed by the raised lines. The dish by Harris Strong shown in Fig. 12 in the color section was made this way.

Hollow casting

When the outside and inside profile of a dish are not the same, the shape can be made in a hollow casting mold. The process is similar to solid casting except that the original model is made considerably thicker. The mold is then made by the steps shown in Photo Series 33.

A piece poured in such a mold will have two walls with an open space between and an opening or openings in the base. These openings are usually covered with pieces of felt. Such ware is used for decorative fruit dishes, large ashtrays and the like. The pieces by Neil Harper shown in Figs. 13 and 14 in the color section are examples of hollow casting.

hollow casting

It is almost impossible when working with clay to resist the urge, now and then, to make something gay or playful. Potters of all countries in all periods of time have made pots and pitchers in the shapes of amusing people or animals. Let's make a pitcher in the shape of a bird.

PHOTO SERIES 34

A mold for a pitcher shaped like a bird

The model for this was made of solid clay rolled into a fat sausage shape to form the body; then head, beak, handle and legs were added. When the clay became leather hard the shape was more carefully finished with modeling tools, then the clay was allowed to dry and final smoothing was done with sandpaper. Before plaster can be cast against dry clay, the model must be given a coat of shellac. When the shellac has dried, the model is sized. Since there is no absorption in a shellacked model, one coat of size is sufficient.

SHELLAC

Building clay dividing walls. This mold will have to be in three parts, one for the bottom area and one for each side portion. Here clay has been used to fill the space under the tail and the legs.

A clay wall is built down the center line. The portion above the opening of the pitcher is built up in solid clay.

Ready to pour the first of the three portions of the mold. A sheet of heavy transparent plastic is wrapped around the model and its dividing walls. This will be tied firmly in place and plaster will be poured. After the first sidepiece of the mold has been poured, the clay will be removed from the other side.

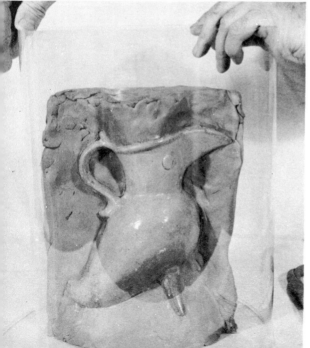

Notches will be cut in the first piece of the mold and it will be sized, then the second sidepiece of the mold will be poured. The clay at the bottom will be removed, the two sidepieces with the model between them will be turned upside down, notches will be cut in the two sidepieces, they will be sized (another coat of size will be put on the model, too) and the third piece of the mold will be poured.

Pouring the mold.

Here we see the three pieces of the mold and the casting. After the slip was poured out, a small amount of slip was poured back into each leg so that the legs are not hollow, but solid. The mold was then tipped on its side and a bit of slip was poured into the handle so that it, too, is solid.

Trimming and fettling the casting.

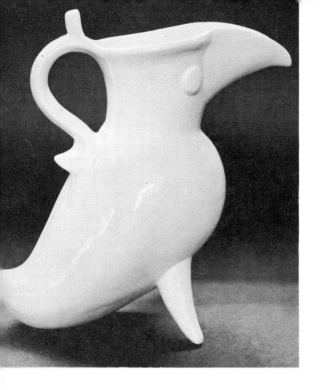

The glazed pitcher. This is another example of a ceramic form which required a plaster mold. The pitcher is thin and light. The original clay model was solid and heavy. Only by means of a mold could this model be translated into a piece of pottery light enough for table use.

Sometimes a waste mold is made of a clay shape and the shape is reproduced in plaster of Paris by pouring plaster into the waste mold (so called because it is usually destroyed). This plaster model is carefully refined with plaster tools and sandpaper, then a pour mold is made from it. Here are the steps:

PHOTO SERIES 35

A waste mold and a plaster model of a teapot

A rectangular teapot is modeled in clay. The model is not solid, there is an empty cardboard box in the center. This makes less clay necessary and the model is lighter.

The modeling continues; shapes are refined. This is the important part of the design process. Proportions of handle, lid and spout are studied.

A heavy linen thread is placed around the model on the center line. The handle was sliced in half and a thin piece of metal was slid into the cut to act as a partition or shim. This metal was given a coat of Vaseline.

The thread is in place. Plaster is mixed. When the plaster reaches a heavy cream consistency, it is poured over the model, which stands on a sheet of glass.

As the plaster thickens it can be molded with a spatula. A mound is built up over the model at least ½″ thick at all points.

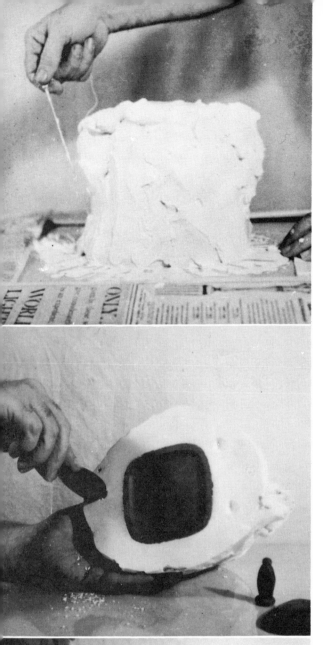

When the plaster has reached the cheese state, the thread is pulled up and out. This divides the waste mold into two parts.

The model has a footing and a depression at the base. The mold must have a third piece to form the lower portion. Here the two halves of the waste mold are kept together while notches are cut in the bottom of each half. After this the bottom surfaces will be sized.

The two pieces of the waste mold with the model in place between them are turned upside down. A clay wall is built to hold the plaster that will form the third piece of the mold. A retaining wall was also built around the lid. (The knob of the lid was removed.) Plaster has been poured over the lid and is now being poured for the third piece of the waste mold.

The three portions of the waste mold have been separated and the clay model has been removed. The inside is being sized. The mold for the lid is in the foreground.

The three pieces of the waste mold are held together by heavy rubber bands while plaster is poured in.

The plaster model has been removed from the waste mold. Additional refinement of the form is made with plaster finishing tools and sandpaper. The design cannot be changed radically at this point but the transitions between planes can be made smoother, lines can be made more rhythmic. When all the refinement of the form is completed we are ready to make the final mold.

The model has been embedded up to its center line in a block of clay.

A casting box has been set in place. We are ready to size the model and the inside of the casting box and pour plaster to form the first portion of the mold.

Casting box

The casting box consists of four pieces of wood with metal straps bent to angle form fastened to them as shown in the sketch. These four pieces are fastened together to make a box of any proportion desired.

When the first portion of the mold has been completed the work will be turned over, the clay will be removed, leaving the plaster model in the first portion of the mold. Notch holes will be cut, the surface of mold and model will be sized, the casting box will be set in place again, and the second portion of the mold will be poured. When this portion has hardened, the work will be turned so that the teapot model is upside down in place between the two halves of the mold. Notch holes will be cut in the bottom surfaces of the two portions of the mold already made. These surfaces will be sized, the casting box set in place again, and the third portion of the mold cast. When this has set, the three pieces of the mold will be removed from the model and allowed to dry.

When the mold has dried thoroughly a casting is made. The three pieces of the mold are held together by heavy rubber bands. Slip is poured into the mold and allowed to form a wall slightly less than ⅛″ thick, then all of the slip is poured out and the mold is allowed to drain upside down.

An hour later. The casting is firm enough so that the mold can be opened and the casting lifted out. Note the escape channels cut in the mold over the spout and the handle. These are to permit slip to fill every portion of the spout and the handle with no air trapped. The waste columns of clay attached to the spout and the handle will be trimmed off when the casting is fettled.

Making the mold for the lid. A knob has been made out of clay, allowed to harden, then shellacked and sized. This knob is placed in position on the plaster model of the lid. A wall dividing the lid along the center has been made of clay. Pieces of wood are being set in place for a retaining wall. A third piece of wood will be placed in the front. The plaster model will be sized and the first portion of the mold poured.

The remainder of the lid mold is made by removing the clay, keeping the knob in place, and pouring the second half of the mold in the manner described for the teapot. Notches must be cut and all plaster surfaces must be sized. When the two portions of the lid mold are finished, they must be turned upside down and a block of clay put on the underside of the model of the lid to form a flange. Retaining walls are then set in place, notches are cut in the bottom surfaces of the two sidepieces, the bottom surfaces are sized and the third piece of the lid mold is poured.

A slip casting has been made of the lid. Here it is removed from the three pieces of the mold. This casting must be trimmed and fettled before it is fired.

The finished teapot.

This teapot is a simple, rather conventional design. It is large, with an ample base—a functional form combining utility with grace. The sides are slightly convex; if they were not they would look concave. Note that the top of the spout is as high as the rim. This is an important point in designing a teapot, for if the spout were lower, tea would run out as the pot was filled.

Here we have an example of ceramic design arrived at through modeling a shape in clay and then refining the shape in plaster of Paris. The teapot is a casting, so its walls are thin and it is light. The bit of extra ornament on the handle is functional; it serves as a resting place for the thumb, and it makes the pot easier to lift. The spout is designed so that it pours well without a drip. The handle on the lid adds a touch of lightness to offset the massive simplicity of the pot. The design of the knob was arrived at by squeezing a lump of clay between the thumb and index finger, and so, as a result, the knob is comfortable, easy to grasp. The flange on the underside of the lid is deep enough so that there is no chance for the lid to fall out while the last drop of tea is being poured. A tiny hole, drilled through the lid while it was leather hard, lets air get into the pot while tea is being poured, so that the stream is smooth without any gurgling.

Interesting design variations can be tried with a mold like this. A decoration carved into one of the side portions of the mold will produce an ornament in relief on the side of the teapot. Instead of carving, a heavy casting can be made in the mold and a raised decoration modeled on one side of the casting. This should be done while the casting rests in the other half of the mold. When the modeling is completed, a new mold is made by pouring plaster against the side that has been ornamented.

With a mold containing such a decoration, casting can be done in 2 colors by pouring white slip into the portion of the mold that forms the decoration. When this slip has set partially, the edge around the decoration must be carefully trimmed, then a casting of the teapot is made with slip to which colorants have been added. This produces a type of work similar to Josiah Wedgwood's Jasper ware which was mentioned in Chapter 8.

Another design variation, interesting to try, can be made by the method of slip trailing (this is described in Chapter 19). A casting of the teapot is left in one half of the mold while a design is trailed with slip on the side of the pot. When the design is completed, another mold section is poured so that castings made in the new mold will duplicate the raised-line design. This method was used by Fantoni to make the vases with raised line decoration shown in Fig. 10 in the color section.

If the teapot just made had had a flat base, it could have been cast in a two-piece mold like the chocolate pot shown in the next series. This is a product of the Harper Ceramic Studio in Fort Lauderdale, Florida.

PHOTO SERIES 36

Removing a casting from a two-piece mold

The casting has been completed, the waste portion at the top has been removed. Here the waste over the spout is being cut off.

21. Fountain with circulating pump, the Author.

22. Bird, Jacqueline Lerat.

23. *Above*. Madonna and Child, Jean Derval.

24. *Left*. Horse, Valsamakis.

25. *Above.* Glaze tests.

26. *Left.*
Engobe
decoration.

27. *Right.*
Overglaze
decoration.

28 *and* 29. *Below.* Painting ware at Keramikos, Athens; (*left*) underglaze; (*right*) overglaze.

The casting is lifted out of the mold and placed on a plaster slab to dry.

Plate 23 shows a two-piece mold of the streamlined bird we made in Chapter 2. This mold was made by the steps described for the teapot.

The little pig by Anthony Priolo, shown in the two pictures in Plate 24, required a more complicated mold. The first illustration shows the clay pig at the top, five pieces of a waste mold, and the plaster model cast in the waste mold. In the second illustration we see the final pour mold in four pieces, with a slip casting made in the mold.

With molds, duplicates can be made of small objects like the bird, and the pig. Since slip castings are hollow, no scooping out is necessary. Castings of simple forms like these are helpful for trying out glazes and decorating techniques.

Plate 23—Plaster model of a bird and 2-piece pour mold made from it.

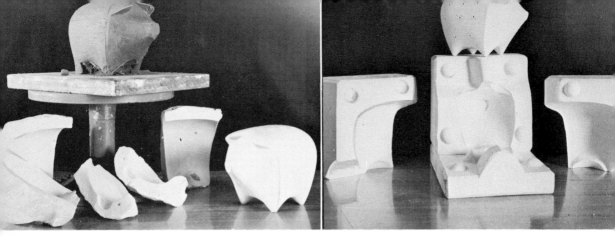

Plate 24—Pig by Anthony Priolo; clay original, waste mold, and plaster model.

Pig by Anthony Priolo; pour mold and slip casting.

Plate 25—Vases by Lyle Perkins. Cast in pour molds, the tops cut to shape.

Before we leave the subject of slip casting, let's see if a mold made in sand as described in Chapter 8 can be used for slip casting.

Slip casting in a sand mold

A wooden box has been filled with dampened sand. The box is not lined with waterproof material because we want the sand to dry out after the design has been finished and the slip has been poured. Here the surface of the sand is being smoothed.

A block of wood is used to make a depression the size and shape of a tile.

The design is pressed in with the end of a stick.

The slip is put in with care, a spoonful at a time; if it were poured, the force of the stream would destroy the design that was pressed in the sand.

The completed casting, fired. Excess sand is brushed off. The fired surface is very much like the unfired surface, with a rough sand texture in the clay.

Another tile made by the same method.

It took a long time for these castings to dry, several days as a matter of fact, but we did succeed in making tiles which fired successfully and had interesting surface textures.

When a potter shapes clay with his hands and fires it, his work bears the marks of his fingers. Things made in molds do not have a handmade look; they have a different kind of beauty, a distinctive quality of their own. Some are so light and delicate that it would be well nigh impossible to make them by hand. For the most part, we don't especially want our teacups and our dinner plates to look handmade—but we do want them to be true and beautiful, showing evidence of good design and craftsmanship. Designing with plaster of Paris for mold production is an important field for the ceramic artist.

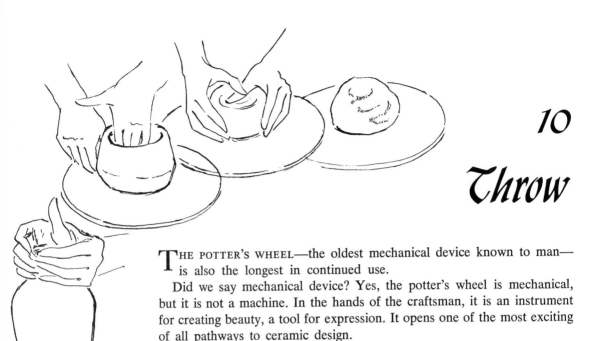

10

Throw

T HE POTTER'S WHEEL—the oldest mechanical device known to man—
is also the longest in continued use.

Did we say mechanical device? Yes, the potter's wheel is mechanical,
but it is not a machine. In the hands of the craftsman, it is an instrument
for creating beauty, a tool for expression. It opens one of the most exciting
of all pathways to ceramic design.

Shaping clay on the potter's wheel is called "throwing." The fortunate
beginner makes his acquaintance with this art by watching a skilled craftsman at work. The student stands fascinated; it looks so easy. The potter's
hands move without effort, and under them the clay seems to become
alive, rising by itself into shapes of grace and beauty. Truly, it is magic!
Then the potter moves off his bench and invites the neophyte to take his
place, to grasp a ball of clay in his hands, start the wheel in motion, and
begin to form a pottery shape.

The next few minutes bring disillusionment. The clay, so obedient a
while ago, has turned stubborn, the magic has disappeared. But if the
beginner has, deep down inside, the makings of a true craftsman, he will
not give up in despair, for he knows that he has taken the first step of a
long journey. The road has some rough spots and there will be periods of
discouragement, but at the end are the rewards of satisfaction and achieve-
ment.

It takes time and devotion to acquire skill on the potter's wheel. There
should be a good teacher at hand, too. But most of all it takes practice,
practice, and then more practice.

There are many types of potter's wheel, some, called "kick wheels,"
are turned by the potter's foot, kicking a large horizontal disc attached to
the base of a vertical shaft. At the top of the shaft is a wheel head, the
surface upon which the clay is formed. Other types of wheels are operated
by a treadle.

Most of the potter's wheels in use today are motor driven. These are
much less tiring, of course, but where the potter himself supplies the
motor power, he has more control over the process. The beginner should
start on a kick wheel, if possible, but if one of these is not available and

a motor-driven wheel must be used, there should be a device for regulating the speed of rotation by foot.

For throwing it is essential to have the right clay, one that is highly plastic, yielding and responsive, yet strong enough to hold its shape when it has been formed into a tall cylinder with thin walls. Some natural clays are excellent for throwing just as they come from the ground. Others require the addition of materials to make them more plastic or to give them greater strength. We'll say more about this in the section on clay bodies in the Appendix.

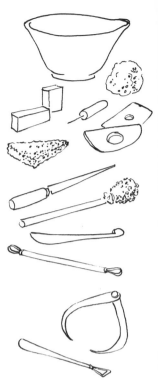

When you buy clay, get the kind that the dealer recommends for use on the wheel, a clay that has been pugged and de-aired.

Clay should always be wedged before one works with it, especially for throwing on the wheel. Cut and wedge the clay at least 20 times, then form it into balls the size of a large baseball. It is a good plan to prepare a dozen balls of wedged clay and keep them wrapped in a damp towel until they are ready to be used.

Tools

A few tools are necessary. There should be a bowl for water, a sponge, a potter's knife, a wooden modeling tool or two, and a pricker. A wooden rib is useful, and so is a kidney-shaped piece of rubber. A small sponge tied to the end of a stick is needed to remove water from the inside of thrown pieces.

Plaster bats

Lifting a shape off the wheel after it has been formed is a problem. Skilled potters who know how, can throw directly on a wheel head, then cut the shape free with a wire and lift the work off. This is difficult to do without distorting the piece. The beginner will be more likely to succeed if he works on a bat fastened to the wheel head so that the piece can be lifted off on the bat. Some wheels have heads of a recessed type with plaster bats made to fit in the recess. On regular flat wheel heads bats are attached either by smearing the bottom of the bat with slurry and pressing it firmly on the wheel head or by using wads of clay around the rim to hold the bat in place.

Plaster bat to fit recessed wheel head

We are ready to begin.

PHOTO SERIES 38

Centering

A plaster bat is fastened to the wheel head with three wads of clay. These were moistened, then pressed firmly against the bat and the wheel. Note that the wider surface of the bat is uppermost; it will be easier to lift that way.

A ball of clay has been thrown onto the center of the bat while the wheel was spinning. The left hand held against the ball on the far side presses toward the center. The right hand pushes against the clay on the other side. The right arm is braced firmly against the frame of the wheel. The hands and the clay must be kept wet. The wheel turns at maximum speed.

The left hand pulls inward while the right hand presses downward.

Excess clay at the base is removed by holding a block of wood against it.

Nothing can be made on the wheel unless the ball of clay is perfectly centered at the start. Plenty of water must be used. Some potters hold a sponge in one hand as they center and squeeze it over the clay to keep it constantly wet. When a ball of clay has been perfectly centered, it will look, while spinning rapidly, as if it were standing absolutely still.

We'll begin with a simple exercise, a bowl shape. We shall not use a plaster bat, but will work directly on the metal wheel head.

Throwing a bowl

A ball of clay, thoroughly wedged, has been thrown on the wheel while the wheel was turning.

The ball centered.

Opening. The two thumbs are held together and pushed downward into the center of the ball.

The thickness of the bottom is important. The potter's fingers must go down far enough so that there will not be a thick mass of clay at the base, and yet they must not go down too far so that the bottom becomes too thin. A pricker, a needle driven into the end of a short piece of wooden dowel, is used to measure the thickness of the clay at the bottom. The tiny hole made by the pricker is unimportant, it will close as soon as work is resumed.

Making the wall higher and thinner. The wheel turns at half speed.

Shaping the bowl. The two index fingers do the work.

Using a block of wood as a rib to secure better shape on the side.

Shaping the rim. The wheel is turning slowly.

Using a rubber kidney for smoothing the inside.

A wooden tool is used to finish the base. The form is completed. Now we are ready to lift the work off the wheel and put it aside. But . . .

5)

. . . we said this was only practice and so we cut it in half to study the thickness of the wall.

The bowl shape is the simplest form to throw on the wheel. The beginner will be able to make satisfactory bowls long before he succeeds in throwing tall cylindrical or vase shapes. Throwing bowls develops skill. Throwing lots of bowls will enable one to appreciate the design qualities that come about through subtle changes in the profiles of shapes. Make bowls and cut them in half to study the thickness of the walls. Keep practicing until you can throw a bowl with walls ¼″ thick throughout.

After practicing on bowls we are ready to start making cylinders. We'll watch the ceramist Gib Strawn as he makes a tall cylinder on a foot-operated kick wheel.

PHOTO SERIES 40

Throwing a tall cylinder

A large ball of clay has been thrown on the wheel and centered. The thumbs were pushed down in the center of the ball to open it. Now the wall is being shaped between the thumbs and index fingers of both hands.

Raising the wall. The clay is squeezed between the index finger of the left hand and the knuckle of the index finger of the right hand and is drawn upward. The left thumb touches the right hand. The wheel turns more slowly during this operation.

Pulling up. The two hands start at the bottom; as they press toward each other the wall is made thinner and a roll of clay is formed above the fingers. The potter brings his two hands straight up, coaxing the roll of clay to the top of the cylinder. The part of the wall below his hands is thinner, that above is thicker. When he has brought his hands up to the top, the wall will be the same thickness from top to bottom and the cylinder will be taller. (*Note:* If the potter were planning to make a bulging shape he would leave extra thickness at the midportion.) The process of pulling up must be repeated three or four times to get the cylinder to its full height.

Using a rib to make the sides straight and smooth.

Cutting the cylinder from the wheel with a wire. (This wire, fastened to the ends of a bent reinforcing rod, is the same tool we saw being used in Chapter 5.)

Making tall cylinders takes a lot of practice. Start with balls of clay as big as a grapefruit and work with them until you can make a cylinder 9″ tall. Look out for flare at the top. If the centrifugal force of the turning wheel makes the top start to spread, bring it back to cylindrical shape by putting both hands around it at the base, then, holding them in the same position, bring them up to the top.

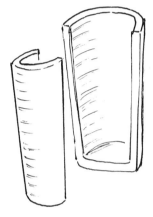

Don't save any of these practice cylinders—cut them in half and study the cross section.

Now for more complicated shapes. We'll look over the shoulder of another ceramic artist, Joan Jockwig Pearson, and watch the steps in making a tea set.

PHOTO SERIES 41

Throwing a tea set

The potter is using a motor-driven wheel with a recessed head and a plaster bat to fit it. A ball of clay has been centered; now it is being opened. The left hand is on the outside of the ball, the right hand rests on the left, and the fingers of the right hand press downward. Note the mirror that has been placed on the other side of the wheel. This gives the potter a different view of what is going on. A good idea.

The potter uses both hands to make the clay wall taller and thinner. At this stage a shape may become too wide. Both hands press from the outside to make the diameter of the cylinder smaller.

Narrowing the top. Left hand inside, right hand holding a wooden rib.

Trimming the top. At this stage in throwing, the top edge of the piece is often rough or uneven. Holding the pricker in the right hand the potter presses inward until the needle goes completely through the clay wall, then lifts off the clay strip which has been cut from the top rim.

A wooden rib was used to shape the top rim, making a seat for the lid to rest on. Excess clay at the bottom of the wall is removed.

Starting to make a lid. A smaller ball of clay is used. This is centered and then flattened.

A knob shape is formed on the lid. A pair of calipers is used to measure the top of the lid to make sure it will fit.

Trimming the base of the lid.

A spout. A smaller ball of clay has been thrown into a narrow cylinder shape.

Completing the spout

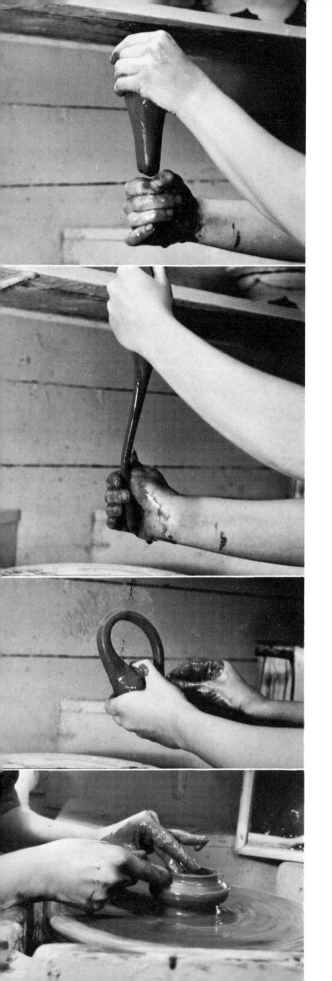

Pulling a handle. The potter holds a lump of clay in the left hand and with the right hand pulls and coaxes the clay with a kind of milking action . . .

. . . until it forms a long thin strip.

The strip bent into a loop. This loop will be set aside until it is leather hard, then it will be cut and attached to the pot which will also be leather hard. In making a handle this way the potter takes advantage of the natural fluidity of the clay which, of its own accord, forms a rhythmic loop.

Another lid. Just to make sure she has a lid exactly right, the potter makes a second. The first lid was made right side up. The potter was able to form a knob but could not make a flange at the bottom of the lid. In this case the potter is working upside down and will form a flange, leaving enough thickness at the base so that a knob may be cut later. (The flange is measured with calipers.)

30. Glass Tests on Tiles.

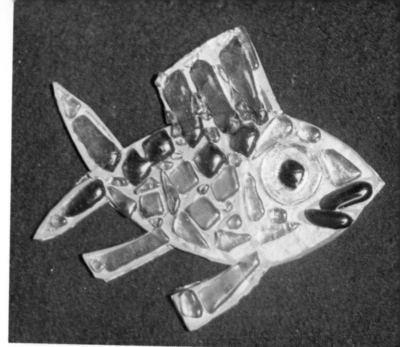

31. Glass Fish.
By the Author.

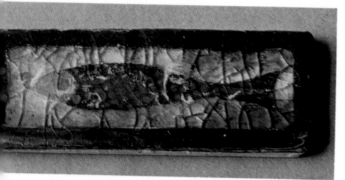

32. *Above.* Tile, "island"
type of design, glazed,
glass on top. By the
Author.

33. Lapel Pin. Glass on ceramic base
with raised lines. Italy.

. *Right.* Fish, pierced
aque with glass inset. By
e Author.

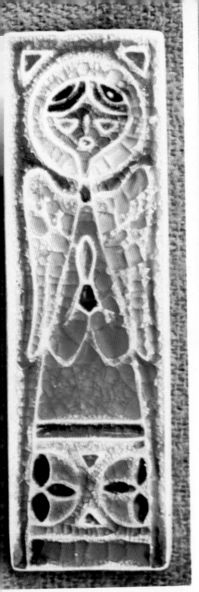

35. *Above*. Glass landscape. By the Author.

36. *Left*. Angel, glass on ceramic base with raised lines, Italy.

37. *Lower left*. Rooster, pierced plaque with glass inset. By the Author.

38. *Above*. Princess, pierced plaque with glass inset. By the Author.

Removing the excess water inside the piece with a sponge tied to the end of a stick.

Making a pitcher. The potter followed the same steps used in making the teapot, but started with a smaller lump of clay. The index finger of the right hand pushes against the shape from the inside so that it is forced out into a spout shape between the thumb and index finger of the left hand.

Making a sugar bowl. The rib is used to form the rim.

Using the calipers to measure the inside of the sugar bowl rim.

Completing the sugar bowl lid.

Pulling clay again. This time the potter is thinking of a bamboo handle, held on the pot by two clay loops. The clay that is pulled here . . .

. . . is formed into a pair of loops.

The work must harden for a while before spout and handles are attached. The potter has put coils of clay around the bases so that they will not get too dry and separate from the bats. The work has been carried outdoors to dry in the sun for about an hour. This shows the advantage of the recessed-head type of wheel. Each piece of work will be perfectly centered when its bat is put back on the wheel.

Completing the teapot lid. Both pot and lid are leather hard, so the lid can be put in place without danger. The knob is cut with a loop tool.

The knob is completed. The spout is removed from its bat. The base of the spout must be trimmed so that it will fit against the side of the pot.

The outline of the area of attachment has been marked with the point of a wooden tool. The wall of the teapot is being perforated.

Preparing the spout for attaching. The edge of the spout and the place where it will join the pot have been coated with slurry.

Pressing the spout in place.

A handle. The strip that was pulled, bent, and then allowed to become leather hard is cut . . .

. . . and held at the side of the pot. The potter studies the form and decides that she prefers the other type of handle, and so . . .

134

. . . attaches the two loops that will hold a bamboo handle.

The completed set. Plate 26 shows a similar set by the same artist. This set has an engobe decoration made while the pieces were spun on their sides on a wheel.

Plate 26—Tea set by Joan Jockwig Pearson. Slip decoration made as pieces were spun while lying on their sides on the wheel.

Turning a foot

Joan Jockwig Pearson's tea set was finished with flat bases. The pieces were made light enough and the bottoms were thin enough so that this treatment was satisfactory.

Usually a thrown piece requires turning at the base to remove a bit of weight and to form a foot. This must be done when the clay is leather hard. The piece is put on the wheel upside down, centered, and fastened in place with keys of clay. As the wheel spins, a metal turning tool is held against the piece to smooth the profile if necessary, and to cut a foot. The hand holding the tool must be placed on an armrest. Wire loop tools

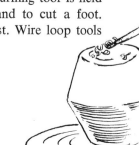

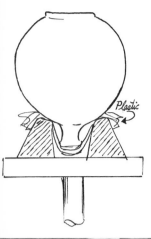

can be used for turning or strips of steel with bent ends like those shown in the sketches.

Shapes with narrow necks cannot be stood upside down on the wheel. It is necessary to construct a clay cradle for such pieces by centering a ball of clay on the wheel and opening it just enough so that the walls will support the piece to be turned. Thin plastic is then placed inside the clay cradle so that the clay does not stick fast to the leather-hard piece while it is being turned.

There is a limit to the size of a piece that can be thrown on the potter's wheel, but bigger pieces can be made by throwing two or more separate shapes and then joining them.

PHOTO SERIES 42

A piece thrown in two sections

Let's watch Gib Strawn again. The cylinder we saw him make in Photo Series 40 was not a finished piece; it was intended as the top half of a ceramic shape. The cylinder is grasped with the hands reversed so that it can be turned over easily. (We did not tell you at the time, but this cylinder has no bottom.)

 136

Here the larger bottom section has been shaped.

The first cylinder has been turned upside down and placed in position on top of the second shape. The potter seals the joint on the outside and on the inside.

Shaping a neck.

Excess clay has been removed from the base. The tall form is completed.

Now let's watch the artist Lyle Perkins as he makes a large vase form out of three shapes thrown separately.

A piece thrown in three sections

Two large bowls were thrown and allowed to stand for several hours. Stoneware clay with heavy grog content was used. The bowl shapes are now firm enough to be handled, but not yet leather hard. The one in the back is a regular bowl with a bottom and a base. The one in the foreground has no base, but is open at the bottom. This portion will be lifted, turned over, and placed on top of the other. The potter is applying a thick coating of slurry to the joint.

The two pieces in position. The joint is sealed, both outside and in.

A cylinder has been thrown for the third section, which will be the neck. The diameter at the bottom of the neck is measured with a pair of calipers.

Preparing the rim where the neck is to be joined. A pricker is used to cut the opening to exact size so that it will fit the base of the neck. The cut is made slanting inward at a 45-degree angle. The strip of clay cut off is removed.

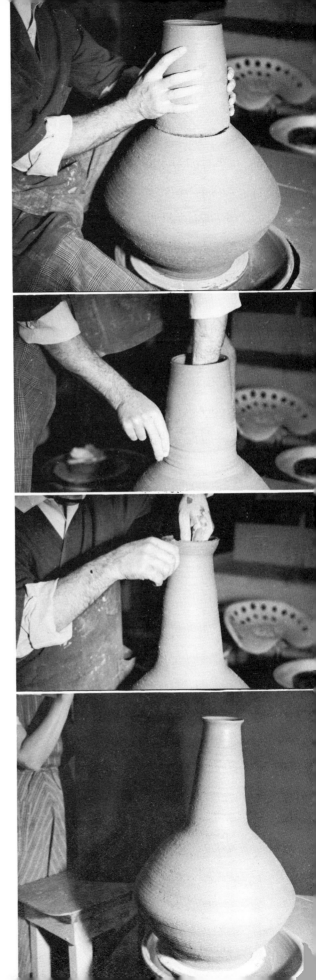

Putting the neck in place. This was cut from the bat on which it was thrown, with a cut also at a 45-degree angle.

Joining the cylinder to the body of the vase. The potter must stand on the frame of the wheel in order to reach inside. Note that the potter is continuing the throwing process on the cylinder, for as he joins it he also changes its shape.

Continuing to shape the neck, making it narrower and taller and forming a lip.

The completed form. Later, knobby projections were pressed against the surface and the potter added a high base cut to form four legs with knobs on the insides. The final piece is shown in Plate 27.

Perkins had to stand on the frame of the wheel in order to reach inside the neck of the tall piece he was shaping. Jean Lerat, a potter who lives and works in Bourges, France, has solved this problem by having his wheel head at floor level with the motor beneath the floor. He starts throwing seated on a block of wood 6″ high. As the work grows he shifts to higher and higher stools until, at the end, he finishes standing up.

We have watched a number of gifted ceramic artists working on the potter's wheel. Great skill is required for work like this. Yet skill on the wheel can be acquired by anyone who loves handling clay and is willing to devote the many hours needed for practice.

Forms created on the wheel have a design quality that cannot be achieved in any other way. Even if one's interest is in forms that are not round, ability to work on the wheel is necessary to experience complete fulfillment in ceramic design.

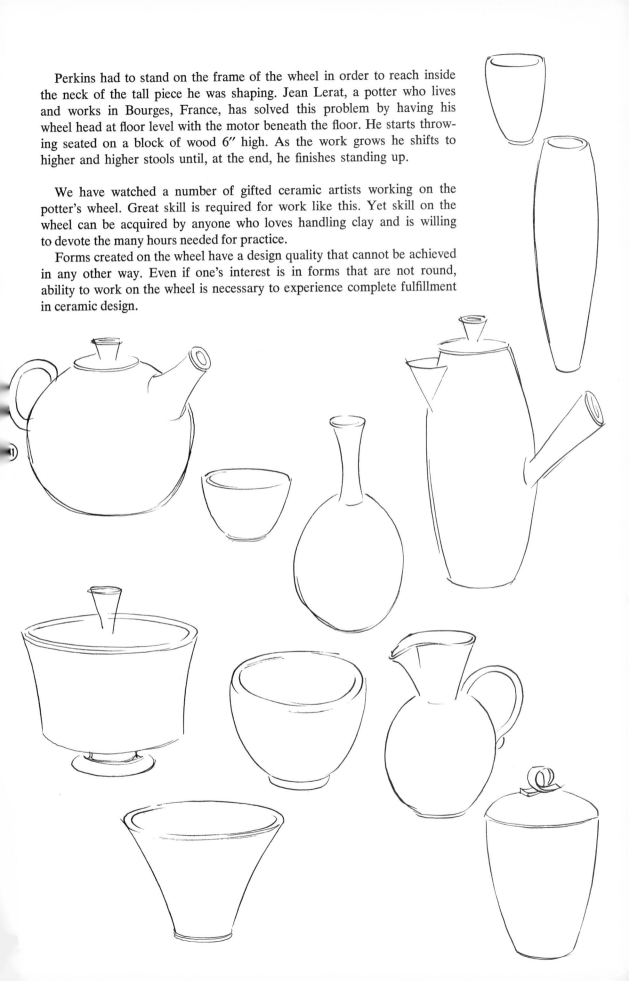

11

Combine

A METHOD of ceramic design that uses wheel-thrown shapes, cutting, squeezing, and combining them with other shapes, either wheel-thrown or slab-built, is a new direction in ceramics, one that has great appeal for many contemporary artists.

We will watch the ceramist Dorothy Perkins.

PHOTO SERIES 44

Throwing a sculptural flower holder

A ball of clay has been centered on the wheel and opened. The wall is being raised.

The top has been narrowed. A pricker is used to cut a strip off the top to make it even.

The form that has just been thrown is on the right. This is being cut to fit on top of another shape, shown at the left, which was thrown previously. The areas to be joined are cut at an angle.

The two pieces put together. Slurry was put on the edges of the joint; now the joint is being welded.

Another pair of pieces of the same shape has been thrown and joined. The top portions have been bent slightly.

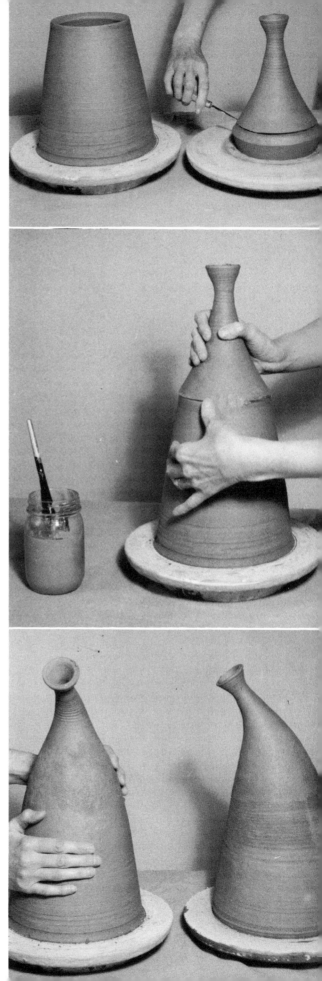

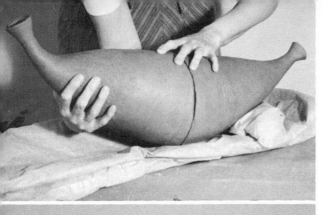

Completing the joining of all four pieces.

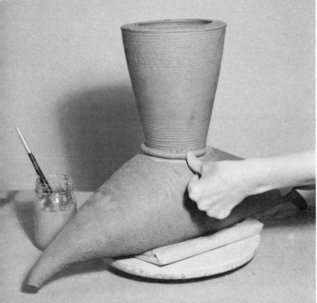

A fifth thrown piece is attached as a base. A thin coil of clay is worked into the joint.

Attaching a number of small spouts. These were thrown separately. After they are attached, openings will be cut through the spouts into the body of the piece.

The finished piece is shown in Fig. 51 in the color section. This example of ceramic design is functional, made to serve a purpose; it is a container for flowers. But function is secondary and the container is more important than the things contained. What we see is a piece of sculpture, complete in itself with or without flowers.

Now let's watch another ceramic artist, Robert Sperry.

Creating a figurine on the wheel

The artist started with a ball of clay. It was centered, opened, and raised into what looks like the beginning of a classic vase form.

The top is made narrower.

Beginning to shape a head.

Closing the top of the head. This portion of the work is finished. It will be trimmed at the bottom, cut off the wheel, and set aside for a while.

The artist starts again. This time he plans to make a small piece to serve as an arm for the figurine, but he is using a large mass of clay. At the top of this mass he shapes what looks like a small vase.

The form that will be an arm is closed at the top. It is cut off of the mass of clay with a wire.

Drying the parts of the figurine (two arms and a body) under an infrared lamp. A piece of damp paper towel has been put over the head of the figurine to keep that portion from drying out more rapidly than the rest.

Attaching the arms. Long thin strips of clay have been put on as hair.

Adding the final details.

Robert Sperry does some interesting things with shapes thrown on the wheel. More of his work is shown in Plate 28. The illustration in Plate 29 shows another figurine created on the wheel, a little clown by Sim Wilson

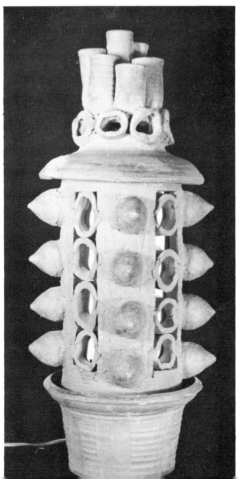

Plate 28—Top left. Garden lantern by Robert Sperry. Wheel-thrown shapes, cut, carved and combined. *Top right*. A group of fireplace figures by Robert Sperry. These highly original creations are of glazed stoneware. They are made of wheel-thrown shapes, carved and textured. They remain in the fireplace while a fire burns. Interesting patterns of light are cast on their surfaces and fascinating patterns of shadow are made on the fireplace wall. *Bottom right*. Flower container by Robert Sperry. Made of many wheel-thrown shapes, cut and combined. *Left*. Ceramic lamp by Robert Sperry. Made of wheel-thrown shapes, cut, carved and combined.

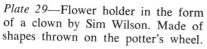

Plate 29—Flower holder in the form of a clown by Sim Wilson. Made of shapes thrown on the potter's wheel.

Humorous flower holder by Mary Lindheim. Details of features and collar were added to a wheel-thrown shape.

which stands on its head to serve as a flower holder. Strips of clay have been added to suggest features, a ruffled collar, a fancy belt.

Now we shall watch the creation of another type of ceramic design, one where the idea of function has been discarded in the search for form. This is Peter Voulkos at work.

PHOTO SERIES 46

Sculpture on the wheel

This artist works with large masses of clay, often weighing more than 30 lbs. These are too large for a wedging board, so he wedges his clay by kneading it on the studio floor.

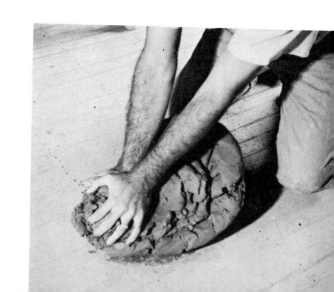

Centering. With a mass of clay this size, centering requires great strength.

Opening. The artist has forced his fist down into the center of the clay.

Shaping the wall.

Narrowing the top.

Making the top still narrower until the form is completely closed. The top portion is squeezed off.

The large balloon-like shape has been trimmed at the base and cut off the wheel head with a wire. The artist lifts it off the wheel and sets it aside to harden.

Throwing a second shape.

The second shape, a flaring form open at the top, has been completed. The bottom is being trimmed. This too will be cut from the wheel and set aside to dry.

At this point, the artist throws another piece similar to the one just completed and two more pieces of cylindrical shape. All of these are put on the studio floor and left to harden overnight.

The next day. The cylindrical piece that will serve as a base is on a modeling stand. The top edge has been roughened with a knife and coated with slurry. The balloon-like form is opened at the bottom. The edge of this will also be roughened and coated with slurry.

Putting the two pieces together.

Getting ready to attach a third piece. Before this is put in place, an opening will be cut in the main body of the construction and edges that are to be joined will be roughened and coated with slurry.

Adding the fourth piece.

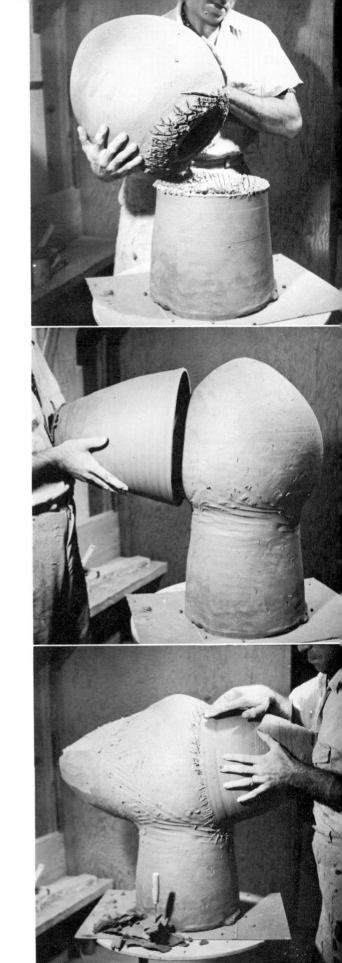

The piece has been paddled into the desired shape. An opening has been cut in the top and a fifth piece is attached.

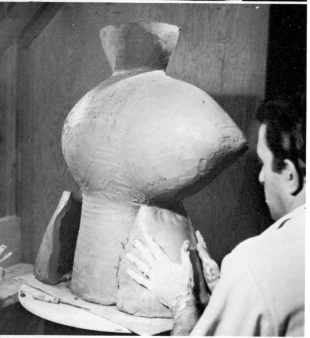

Two more pieces cut from a wheel-thrown shape are added at the base.

Completing the form.

Plate 30—A pair of flower containers by Jacqueline Lerat. These amusing figures are made of wheel-thrown shapes combined with slabs and with textures added. High-fire stoneware, salt glazed. *Photograph by H. Malvaux.*

The free-standing sculptural form we have watched in the making is the work of a pioneer. Peter Voulkos' ceramics have tremendous force and vitality and a massiveness reminiscent of the rocky forms of the mountains in our Western states. He has had a strong influence on potters throughout America.

Other pieces of work made by combinations of thrown shapes and slabs by different artists are shown in Plates 30 and 31.

The artists whose work we have seen in this chapter have great skill. All of them reached positions of eminence in the field of ceramics through

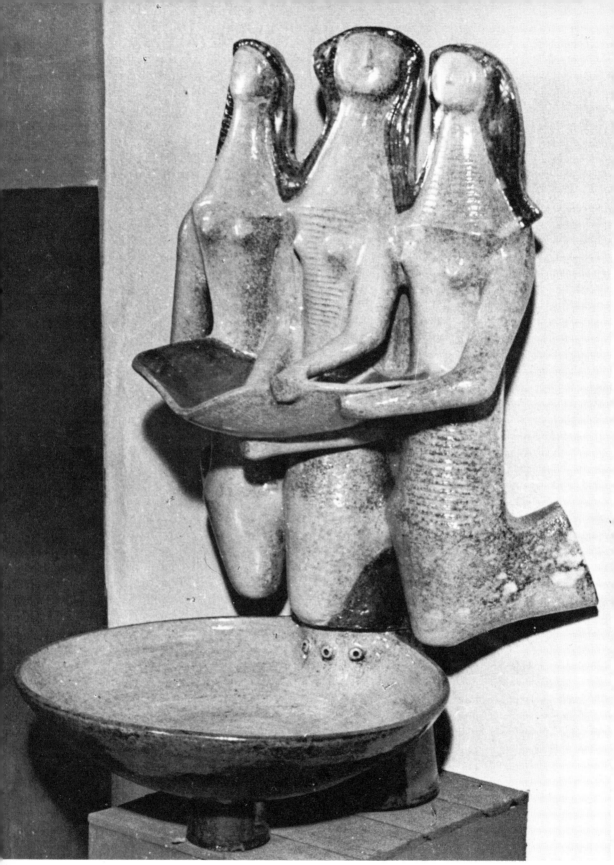

Plate 31—Fountain by Jean Derval. Made of thrown shapes and slabs.

work of more conventional form before they started exploring new directions. Their work is daring, thrilling—sometimes shocking.

We must be aware of the danger of trying to emulate work like this. Some beginning ceramists may be tempted to look upon it as a shortcut, a quick way to achieve results in the field of modern ceramic design. Not so! Good design can never come from the mere mutilation of clay. Before attempting any construction similar to those shown in this chapter, the techniques of the wheel must be mastered; one must be familiar with clay, able to throw large shapes with ease. When that degree of skill has been acquired, then exploration can begin.

Constructions need not be extremely large. One may experiment with pieces of a size that can be thrown without difficulty. Yet there is almost no limit to the size of shapes that can be made by combinations of thrown pieces, other than the size of the kiln. Even this is not an absolute limitation, for pieces can be made and fired in sections, then joined after they come out of the kiln.

The contemporary ceramists who work in this vein have pushed away limitations, have opened new paths. It is as if the potter has emerged into a world which beckons and which holds out an exciting promise. Those who have the courage to explore this new world may find themselves creating new forms.

Plate 32—Folded vase by Peter Voulkos. 24″ high, blue, green, white, black, and brown.

12

Carve

C LAY when it is plastic is shaped by squeezing or throwing or pressing. When it starts to dry and reaches its nonplastic state it can no longer be modeled but it can be shaped by cutting or carving. This can be done when clay is bone dry, but it is much easier when the clay is leather hard.

In Photo Series 19 the artist Rolf Key-Oberg made a bowl over a plaster drape mold. In the final picture of that series, we saw how the artist added interest to the form by carving the outline at the top and cutting circles in the ends.

We spoke earlier of the need to hollow out any mass of clay more than 1″ or 2″ in thickness. This suggests a method of working with clay by building solid masses, then cutting them in half and scooping out the insides. Sculptors sometimes do this when they make portrait heads. In the creation of abstract forms the method allows more freedom to the artist. He can pound, push, squeeze the mass he is working on to his heart's content, concentrating on the design without concern for the thickness of the wall. When he has achieved the shape he wants, the work is allowed to dry just enough so that it is no longer plastic. It is then cut in two and the inside is scooped out so that all portions of the wall are the same thickness. The two parts are then luted together, the joint fastened with slurry and carefully sealed.

Carving is more than a way to make pieces hollow—it is another approach to design. Clay shapes cut with a knife have a character of their own. Let's make a hanging planter by cutting a clay form.

PHOTO SERIES 47

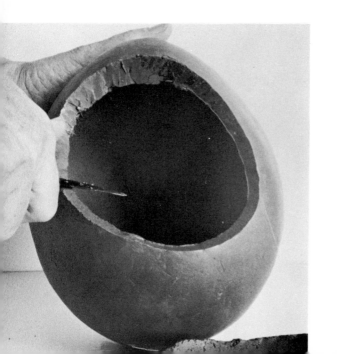

Making a hanging planter

A globe form made over a toy balloon is carved. Openings are made on 3 sides.

Carving is completed. A toothed steel scraper has been used to give surface texture.

The planter in use. The inside was glazed, the outside was left in the natural color of the red clay.

The ceramic sculptor Ellen Key-Oberg makes most of her pieces by a combination of modeling and carving. Here she is at work.

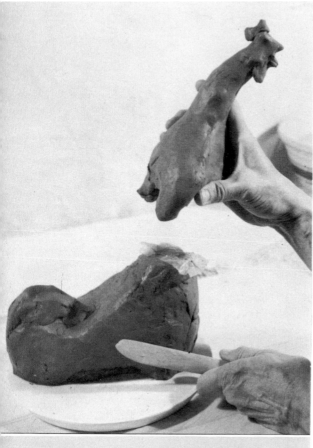

Modeling and carving a rooster

This sculpture will be in several parts. A shape for the body is modeled. Head and neck are modeled separately.

A third part has been modeled and put in place.

Shaping.

Hollowing out.

Carving.

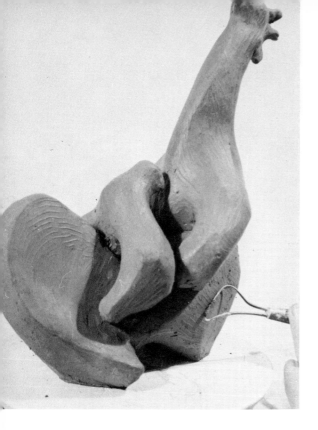

Refining forms with a wire loop tool.

Plate 33 shows Jean Derval at work carving a relief for an architectural ornament, and in Plate 41 there is an illustration of a carved sculptural composition by Edris Eckhardt.

Carving is a method of surface decoration that can be used on pottery shapes that have been thrown on the wheel or slab built or made in molds. The plate shown in Plate 34 was made in the factory of Keramikos in Greece. It was jiggered. Despian, an artist on the staff of this factory,

Plate 33—Carving a bas-relief for an architectural ceramic frieze. Jean Derval.

Plate 34—Carved dish from the factory of Keramikos, Athens. This ware is carved by an artist-craftsman, who works with greenware that has been jiggered.

takes greenware from the production line before it becomes thoroughly dry, and carves it. His themes are classical and traditional but the pieces he makes are all individual—no two exactly alike.

Ceramic pieces can be pierced like the sculpture by Frank Eliscu shown in Plate 35. This shape was made in a mold. Pierced ware like this makes interesting lighting fixtures or candle lanterns for use in the garden.

In Plate 36 are shown three carved lamps by Rita Sargen. The two tall lamp bases were cast from the same mold; carving makes them completely different. In Plate 37 there are examples of the work of Marguerite Wildenhain; these were thrown on the wheel and then carved.

Plate 35—Head, a piece cast in a mold, carved by Frank Eliscu, 15″ high.

Plate 36—Two column lamps by Rita Sargen. 36″ high. These two lamps were cast in the same mold. They illustrate the variations in design possible through different methods of carving and texturing cast shapes.

Ellipse lamp by Rita Sargen. 25″ overall height, carved.

Photographs courtesy of Rita Sargen Ceramics.

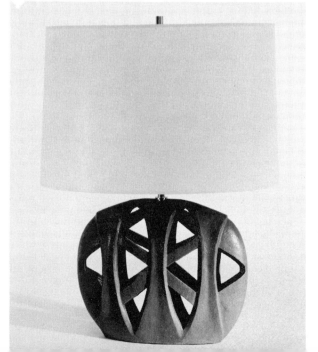

Incising is another form of carving, a process in which a decorative design or pattern is cut into the surface of the piece. Here the carving does not alter the form, it merely puts a decorative design within the larger design of the work. Sometimes designs are carved in a piece and then a clay of contrasting color is pressed into the lines. This type of inlay decoration is called "Mishima."

Any type of cutting tool may be used for carving clay. Wire loop modeling tools are good for low relief designs. Plaster carving tools with serrated edges and toothed scrapers are useful for making patterned backgrounds and textures.

Decorating clay by carving offers interesting possibilities. Try an exercise in relief carving, a design with the background cut away. Make a rectangular bottle shape by slab building. Make a foot and a neck by turning. On the body of the bottle draw a series of rectangular areas in an interesting arrangement, then cut away the background around these areas so that they stand out $\frac{1}{8}$". Carve a repeat pattern in these areas.

Another exercise—carve an "island" relief. This is made by cutting away a portion of the surface around a design that is left in relief so that the design forms an island within the cut-away area.

Don't overlook the value of extremely simple carving; lines, either regular or haphazard, which give a fluted effect to a vertical piece. Do this on pieces thrown on the wheel and on pieces cast in molds. Try some more elaborate exercise by carving the sides of pieces with figures or abstract designs.

Make some simple cylindrical shapes by slab building and pierce them. These are a few of many possible solutions to design problems by carving clay.

7—Assortment of wheel-thrown vases by Marguerite Wildenhain. Carved, slipped, and cut. *Photograph by Otto Hagel*

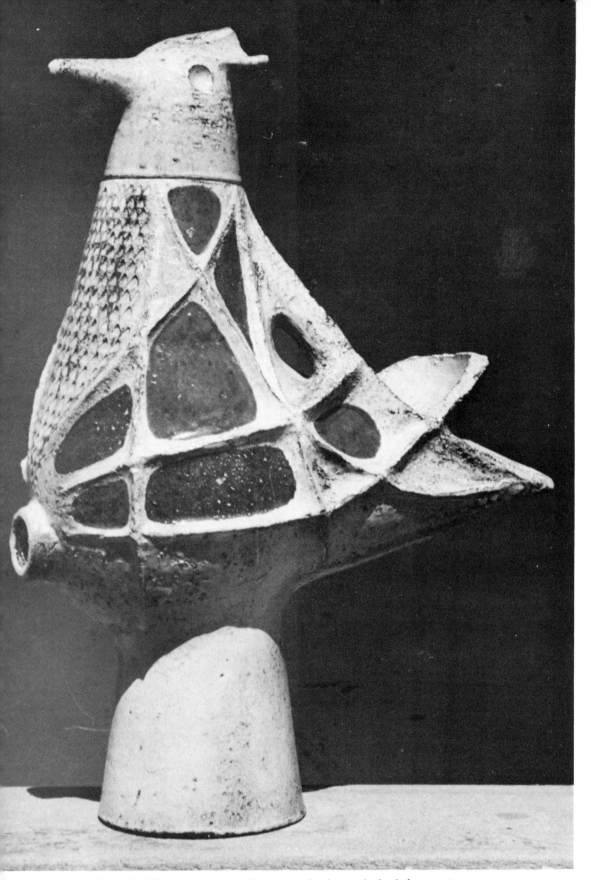

Plate 38—Wine server by Jean Derval, made of carved wheel-thrown shapes.

13
Sculpture

Why HAVE a chapter on sculpture when we have been discussing this subject throughout the book? Because we must take a moment or two to consider some of the special features of ceramic sculpture, the things that make it different from sculpture in stone, or metal, or wood.

First of all, obviously, ceramic sculpture is made of clay and so all of the problems of forming clay affect ceramic sculptural design. The selection of the clay to be used affects design also, for clays that are coarse give a surface to sculpture different from that given by finer grain.

Texture, a most important factor in ceramic sculpture, comes not only from what the sculptor does to clay with his hands and his tools, it comes also from the clay itself and from things the sculptor puts into the clay.

Most important of all, ceramic sculptural design is affected by the fact that pieces must be fired. This means that whatever method is used to shape the clay it must end up as a hollow shell.

Ceramic sculpture can be formed as a solid mass, then hollowed out, or it can be built hollow. Sculpture can be made out of clay shaped into tubes, by being rolled into cylinders over cores of newspaper. These cylinders can then be bent and joined to make hollow sculptural forms. The Haniwa figures found in ancient Japanese tombs were made of hollow cylinders, coil built, smoothed on the outside. The horse by Valsamakis shown in Fig. 24 in the color section was made of hollow cylinders also. Or sculpture can just be modeled and hollowed out as the piece takes shape. Let's watch the making of a fountain figure by this method. This is a figure 21″ high intended for the edge of a garden pool.

PHOTO SERIES 49

A figure for a fountain

A number of clay sketches have been made. These show a figure pouring from a jar held in different ways.

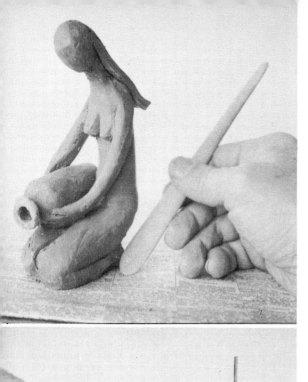

A sketch is selected and finished a little more carefully.

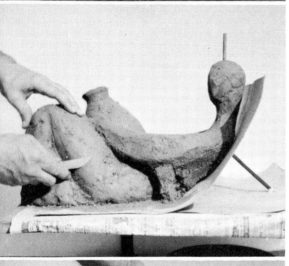

 Starting on the larger figure. Clay walls are roughed out with the figure reclining on a cardboard cradle.

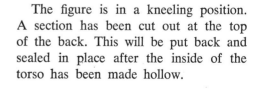

The figure is in a kneeling position. A section has been cut out at the top of the back. This will be put back and sealed in place after the inside of the torso has been made hollow.

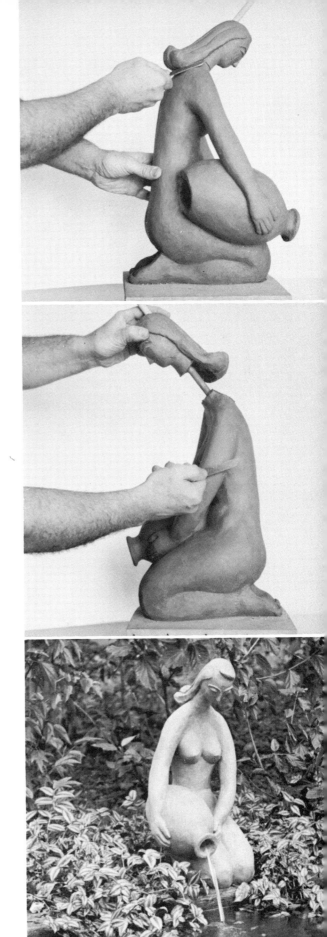

The modeling is completed. This figure is too tall for the kiln available so it must be fired in two pieces. Here the poor girl is undergoing decapitation.

The head is lifted off. Care must be taken to secure a clean, even cut so that the head can be sealed back on without a visible seam after the work has been fired.

The completed figure in place. A hose from the water inlet has been passed through the figure so that water flows into the pool from the jug she holds. More fountains are shown in Plates 39 and 40.

Plate 39—Fountain with circulating pump, 22″ high, mat green glaze with rutile, by the author. The bowl is the one made in Photo Series 6.

In making clay sculpture we have the problem of supporting the clay while it is too soft to stand alone. All sorts of temporary supports can be used for this. The figure we just watched in the making rested in a cardboard hammock in the early stages until the clay was firm enough to permit the piece to stand upright. In Chapter 2, when we made the clown and the ballerina we used wires as temporary supports. These wires were withdrawn before the pieces were fired. Where a temporary support like this or a dowel stuck in a block of wood is used, there is no problem.

But there are other approaches to ceramic design in which the sculptor's aim is the more realistic portrayal of figures in action; for these, an armature like the one shown in the sketch is needed. Such an armature permits the modeling of a figure, with delicate proportions, in any position, but when it is completed the figure cannot be fired because the armature is inside. It is necessary to make a plaster of Paris mold in which the piece that will go into the kiln may be pressed or poured.

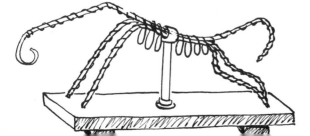

Plate 40—Fountain by Jean Derval, made of wheel-thrown shapes and slabs.

Plate 41—Divertissement, sculpture carved from a single large block of clay. By Edris Eckhardt. *Photograph courtesy of The Cleveland Museum of Art.*

Waste molds

Often the sculptor adds another step and makes a waste mold from the clay model. In Chapter 9 we saw the steps of making a waste mold of a teapot. To make a waste mold of sculpture, plaster must be poured or thrown over the model in somewhat the same manner as that illustrated in Picture 4 of Photo Series 35. Usually shims are used instead of thread.

Shim metal is thin and flexible brass, easily cut with a pair of scissors. A sculptor making a waste mold places shims along the center line of the model, dividing it into two halves. He then mixes plaster and when the plaster has reached a creamy consistency, throws cupfuls against the model until every portion has been covered. As the plaster thickens he builds up a shell over the whole piece about 1″ thick. When the plaster has set, the two halves of the waste mold that have been separated by the shims are taken apart, all of the clay is removed, the inside sized, the two halves of the mold are fastened together, and plaster to form the plaster replica of the model is poured in.

To reduce the weight of the model, it is not cast solid. Plaster is poured into the mold and the mold is tipped and tilted in all directions so that plaster is able to reach every part of the inside of the mold, then all the plaster that is still liquid is poured out. A thin shell of plaster remains on the inside surface of the mold. After a few minutes the process is repeated so that the shell inside the mold becomes thicker, and this continues until a shell about ½″ to 1″ thick has formed. Strips of burlap soaked in plaster are sometimes pressed into the shell inside the mold to give extra strength.

When the plaster inside the mold has set hard, the waste mold is chipped away. The plaster of Paris replica of the sculptural form is then used to make piece molds for pouring or pressing. This requires careful consideration of "draft," that is, directions in which pieces of a mold may be drawn away from the model without being held in place by undercuts. Pieces must be planned, too, so that they are notched into one another and can be held together when clay is to be pressed or poured into the mold.

The steps in making a waste mold and a plaster model of a monumental piece of ceramic sculpture will be demonstrated in Chapter 21.

Shims

Ceramic sculptors today make use of many materials besides clay, combining them in the final design of their pieces. Wooden blocks, metal and glass tubes, wire, metal lath, even rubber balls are used in contemporary ceramic sculpture.

The tall thin rooster shown in Plate 42 is made with a thin metal rod concealed in the leg. This does not show, but it is obvious from the shape of the piece that the rod is there. By contrast, the bird by Jacqueline Lerat in Fig. 22 of the color section has legs which are frankly made of metal,

Plate 42—Rooster, 16 tall. By the author.

Plate 43—Ceramic sculpture designed for a patio; clay shapes threaded on metal rods. Work of Antonio Prieto, member of the staff of Mills College, Oakland, California.

and so do the two birds on the lawn of the Pacetti Ceramic Factory in Albisola, Italy, shown in Fig. 76 of the color section. In any combination of clay with other materials it is necessary, of course, to fire the clay separately and join the two materials after the clay has come out of the kiln.

Here is a good exercise to try for small pieces of sculpture, especially of bird shapes. Bore a hole in a block of wood large enough to hold a piece of brass tubing, and model some forms to stand on the tubing. The tubing should be wrapped in several thicknesses of newspaper so that when the clay shape has been formed it can be taken off the tube, hollowed out and allowed to dry. When the clay shrinks it will still fit over the tubing, once the newspaper has been removed.

Grog

Don't overlook this important ingredient. Clay sculpture of any size should be made of a coarse clay with medium or coarse grog added to it. The best way to add grog to clay is to have them both dry, weigh out the quantities, mix them dry, then add water and prepare the clay in the usual manner. However, if you must add grog to plastic clay without

Plate 44—Elephant, ceramic sculpture by Raty.

Plate 45—Owls, ceramic sculpture by Raty. *Photograph by Andre Villers, Vallauris.*

drying it, judge proportions by volume, thoroughly wet the grog and knead it into the clay.

Grog is sold in grades of coarse, medium, and fine. On a large piece, coarse grog gives pleasing texture. Note that in order to see the grog the work must be sponged or scraped before it is fired, otherwise the grog will sink below the surface and the piece will look as if it had no grog in it at all. Using a coarse grog and then scraping with a toothed scraper when the clay is bone dry produces a pitted surface.

Organic materials

Organic materials such as oatmeal, sawdust, or coffee grounds can be added to clay of which sculpture is made so that during the firing the organic material burns out leaving voids within the clay wall and a pitted surface. The sculpture by Maria Wishner shown in Plate 50 was made with coffee grounds in the clay.

Color in sculpture

This is a problem. Small pieces can be glazed and decorated with colored glazes without much danger of losing their design quality. On large sculpture this method is quite apt to produce things that look like oversize painted dolls. In ceramic sculpture the artist must make as much use as possible of the natural color of the clay. Where contrasting areas of color are required, these can be obtained by adding colorants to the clay or by using engobes. These are more fully described in Chapter 14.

Plate 46—Horse and rider, ceramic sculpture by Raty.

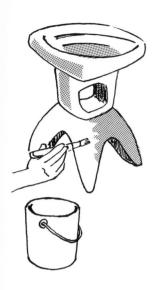

The natural color of clay is enhanced by waxing. This gives the surface a gloss without the high shine which comes from glaze. Automobile wax can be used. It should be put on the sculpture immediately after it comes out of the kiln, while it is still warm. Apply the wax with a brush or a cloth, rub it all over the surface, then use another cloth to rub off the excess. Pigments such as red iron oxide or burnt umber can be added to the wax before it is rubbed on. Powdered soapstone or talc can be used to polish terra cotta in the same way.

A piece of terra cotta soaked in milk overnight, then dried and polished with a soft cloth, will have a surface similar to that obtained with wax. Linseed oil can be brushed on terra cotta. Sometimes ceramic sculpture is painted with pigments mixed with linseed oil and turpentine, brushed on thin. For small pieces, artist's oil colors can be thinned with turpentine then rubbed over the surface with a cloth. Large garden sculpture can be painted with cement base paint.

Cement base paint is a material useful for coloring terra cotta that is to be placed out-of-doors. This type of paint protects the work from damage by the weather and reduces the likelihood of efflorescence.

Cement base paints are sold under a variety of trade names: Rocktite, Medusa, and others. They come in dry powder form in several colors. These paints must be mixed with water and applied to porous surfaces; they cannot be used on terra cotta which has been glazed. The terra cotta must be soaked with water for 1 or 2 hours beforehand, then the surface

Plate 47—Mother and child, ceramic sculpture by Raty. Made of wheel-thrown shapes.

39. *Above; 40, 41 Left.* Drawings by students in the ceramics classes of the Instituto d'Arte, Florence, Italy.

42. *Below.* Portion of a ceramic studio, Instituto d'Arte, Florence.

43. Sculptural plaque, Marguerite Wildenhain.

44. *Above*. Rain, Capacci.

45. *Left*. Flight into Egypt, Lucerni. Figures in full relief stand out from a curved ceramic background.

46. *Below*. Butterflies, Lucerni.

47. *Below*. Mermaids, Valsamakis. The design is in raised lines.

Plate 48—Les Kinsling constructing a pair of musicians from wheel-thrown forms.

water must be allowed to dry off. The first coat should be made with paint mixed with water in the ratio of 1 lb. of paint to a pint of water. It is important not to mix more paint than can be used at one time, for after 2 or 3 hours the paint sets and becomes useless. After the first coat has been completed, the work should be sprayed and kept damp for 24 hours, after which the second coat (slightly thicker than the first coat) can be flowed on with a wide, soft brush. The second coat should also

Plate 49 — Faun, garden sculpture by Portanier, Vallauris.

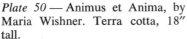

Plate 50 — Animus et Anima, by Maria Wishner. Terra cotta, 18″ tall.

Garden sculpture by Maria Wishner. Gray stoneware with ebony manganese and coffee grains for texture, 24″ high.

be sprayed with water and the work must be kept moist for at least 48 hours.

Brushes must be cleaned immediately after using paint of this type. It is advisable also to wear rubber gloves to protect the hands.

The size of the piece, the purpose for which it is made, the place where it will stand, all must be considered in determining what texture and color are best for clay sculpture. Larger work should not be smooth, pieces to be decorated should not be rough.

The sculptor's work is done mainly with his hands, but from time to time he needs the help of tools. Most artists who work with clay have a favorite tool—a chair leg, or a block of wood, something with which to roll or pound clay into shape. The design of sculpture seems to be

Plate 51—Family, ceramic sculpture by Rosemary Zwick.

Plate 52—Flight, the spirit of air travel suggested by a trio of slender, graceful ceramic statuettes; in Alitalia ticket office in New York City. By Milotti. *Photograph courtesy of Alitalia Airlines.*

Plate 53—Is this sculpture or a bowl? A combination of shapes thrown on the wheel. Jean Derval.

improved when it is pounded or paddled. A teacher, well known to students of sculpture a generation ago, used to make his students drop their work on the floor while the clay was still plastic. It was surprising how, in most cases, such a fall improved the shape. (Sometimes the student had to start over again, but that made the work better, too.) Pounding has the advantage of making clay walls more compact, better able to stand the stress of the fire.

Cutting tools are needed—a wire loop modeling tool and a knife. A modeling stand is convenient, but if your studio doesn't possess one, a banding wheel makes a good substitute. Cut a board 12″ square and nail three cleats to the underside spaced so that they fit snugly around the head of the banding wheel. These cleats will keep the board centered. Have a portable light that can be used to light the work from different angles while it is in progress.

Ceramic sculpture can be made to suit all tastes from the extreme abstract shown in Chapter 11 to the realistic and classical shown in Chapter 21. In between is the variety illustrated in the pieces by Maria Wishner, the whimsical garden sculpture of Portanier, the ebullient musicians by Les Kinsling, the imaginative birds and animals by Raty.

There are no rules to hamper you when you make ceramic sculpture, no conventions that must be followed. Be courageous, willing to try anything. Explore. Make things which interest you—do the kind of work you take pleasure in doing. In that way you will develop your own method of expression.

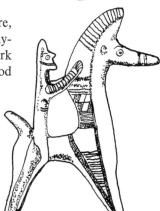

14
Color

THE PRIMARY SOURCE of color in ceramics is the clay itself and the best results in design are achieved when a ceramist makes some use of the natural color of his clay. He can do this either by leaving a portion of the clay uncovered, or by permitting some of its color to show through whatever glazes are put on it.

No two clays are exactly alike in color. When we speak of the color of a clay we mean, of course, its color after firing. When it is dug from the ground, clay may be some shade of yellow, gray, red, or blue, but that means nothing; if it comes out of the kiln red, it is red clay. Even here there are variations, for the same clay fired in different ways becomes different colors. A red clay, for example, may be a pale pink when fired to about 1700°F. or cone 08, and a deep reddish brown when the temperature of the kiln goes to above cone 1—2100°F. In a reducing fire, the same red clay would probably come out black.

Natural clays most often fire some shade of brick red or buff. A few clays fire black. Very rarely does one find a natural clay which fires white. The things that make clay different colors are the oxides of iron, manganese, calcium, and other minerals present. We call these things impurities, although they are, after all, what one expects to find in natural clays.

Metallic oxides may be added to clay to change its color as follows:

Red iron oxide

Added to a buff clay, 2% to 4% of red iron oxide will make it brick red. Added to a red clay this oxide will make the clay darker red or brown. Red iron oxide is an extremely powerful colorant, a nuisance to use, for the hands, the tools—in fact, the whole studio—are apt to become brick red. Rather than add this colorant to clay it is better to try to find a clay that fires red in the first place.

Black iron oxide

This is coarser than the red oxide and gives a more pleasing, speckled effect in fired clay. It will produce the same color changes as red iron oxide. An advantage of using black iron oxide instead of red is that it doesn't stain everything.

Iron chromate

One to 2% of iron chromate gives buff clay a warm gray color.

Manganese dioxide

About 2% of this material added to a buff clay will make it a gray-brown. Added to red clay it will make it dark brown or black. It has a pleasing speckled effect, especially pronounced when granular manganese is used.

Oxides of cobalt, copper, chromium, and other metals are valuable sources of color in glazes. They could be used for coloring clay bodies also, but it would be much too expensive. Ilmenite, an ore containing both titanium and iron, produces effects somewhat similar to those obtained from black iron oxide. When used in granular form it produces specks in clay bodies.

All of the oxides we have mentioned make clay darker. It is not possible to add anything to clay to make it lighter; if we want a light-colored clay we must start with a white body.

A number of commercially prepared white clay bodies that fire in the low temperature range from cone 06 to cone 04 are available. These contain a high proportion of talc. Talc is a valuable ingredient in a low-fire body; it makes a good hard product somewhat like china, and glazes fit the ware well. Most commercially prepared talc bodies contain 50% or more of talc.

White clay can be tinted with prepared body stains. These come in shades of pink, blue, green, yellow, gray, brown, or black. From 3% to 10% must be added, depending on the depth of color desired. A good pink body can be made by adding 2% to 3% of red iron oxide.

Color can be put on the surface of clay as a coating, that is, by applying a layer of colored liquid clay or slip. Slip used this way is called "engobe." Engobes can be applied in any number of ways: painted on with a brush, poured on, sprayed, dipped, or dabbed on with a sponge.

Some of the earliest pottery, made long before the secret of glaze was discovered, was decorated with designs painted on in clay of contrasting color. Decorative motifs developed by these early potters have a beautiful simplicity. Among them are geometric patterns and stylized natural forms used in such a way that they enhance the shape of the pots they are on. Throughout the world, primitive potters have achieved the same fine aesthetic results, proof, it would seem, that good design develops wherever there is honest and direct use of the material.

In Plate 54 there is an illustration of a piece of contemporary Mexican pottery, a plate made of buff clay, with a red clay slip floated on top of it. A design was painted with buff slip on top of the red. Strokes of green were brushed on with a soluble salt of copper. Ware of this type, decorated with simple bird and animal motifs, has a special charm. More will be said about engobe decoration in Chapter 19.

Engobe is clay and the surface to which it is applied is clay also, and so we have the problem of shrinkage. Unless both the clay of the piece and the engobe shrink the same amount and at the same rate, the engobe

Plate 54—Mexican plate decorated with engobe.

will fall off. When a buff clay is used as an engobe on red clay, the latter must be moist and soft.

Here is a recipe for a white engobe to use on moist clay.

China clay	25
Ball clay	20
Flint	30
Feldspar	17
Whiting	2
Magnesium carbonate	6

These ingredients should be weighed out, mixed dry, then ground with enough water to make a liquid of the consistency of heavy cream. A tablespoonful of gum tragacanth may be added to make application easier. Before using this engobe, rub it through a 60-mesh screen.

The engobe given above can be colored as follows:

For Blue, add	Cobalt carbonate	1
Blue-green	⌈ Copper oxide	3
	⌊ Cobalt carbonate	0.5
Green	Copper oxide	4
Yellow	Vanadium stain	10
Tan	Iron oxide	2
Brown	Iron oxide	5
Light gray	Iron chromate	1
Violet	Manganese carbonate	4
	⌈ Manganese dioxide	2
Black	⌊ Cobalt carbonate	3
	⌊ Iron oxide	3

Other colors can be made by adding underglaze pigments in quantities ranging from 10% to 30%.

Plate 55—Forms by Antonio Prieto. Red clay, built up in thrown sections, decorated with various colored engobes, fired to cone 5. Left 40″ high, right 45″ high, top section removable.

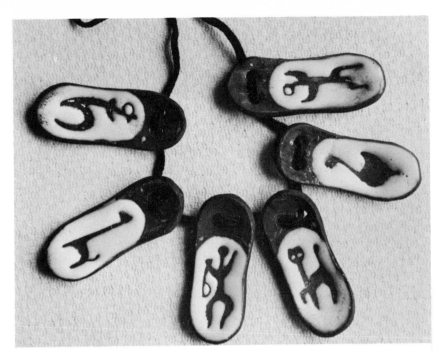

Plate 56—Necklace by Maurel of Vallauris, France. White engobe on black clay, sgraffito design.

It is much easier to apply engobes to clay that is leather hard or bone dry. Things must be added to the engobe to reduce its shrinkage so that it will fit on such clay. Here is a pair of recipes for use on dry clay and on bisqued ware.

	Dry	Bisque
China clay	15	5
Ball clay	10	10
Calcined clay	20	20
Ferro frit 3124 *	15	15
Talc	10	20
Zircopax	5	5
Borax	5	5
Flint	20	20

* For a description of frits see page 192.

The above two recipes are for vitreous engobes. That means that glass-forming ingredients have been added. In a sense, these engobes are almost glazes. Colors may be added to these in the same manner as those listed for the first recipe.

Grog is a source of color as well as a texture. Sometimes using grog whose color contrasts with clay gives an interesting effect—buff grog in red clay or vice versa. Grog purchased from dealers is usually buff, but you can buy porcelain grog which is white, and you can make your own colored grog if you wish to do so. Grinding up a brick or a scrap of red clay that has been fired will produce a red grog. An easier way to do it is to take some bone dry red clay and pound it into small pieces, then put it in an unglazed dish and fire it in your kiln. After the fired ground clay has been screened you will have a red grog. Other colored grog can be made by the same method.

A line blend

A good way to conduct experiments with pigments is by means of a line blend. Suppose, for example, you have a natural clay which fires buff and you wish to try the effects of adding various amounts of black iron oxide. Start with the clay in dry powder form and weigh out a series of small batches (50 or 100 grams each). To the first batch add 1% of the oxide, to the second 2%, and so on until you have made five different batches, the last one with 5% of the oxide added. Put just enough water in each batch so that it can be worked into plastic state and form it into a tile. Then let the tiles dry and fire them. Fire another tile also, one made of the clay with nothing added. After all 6 tiles have been fired, arrange them in order in a line—you now have a line blend which will tell you a great deal about what happens when this oxide is added to your clay.

The addition of colorants to clay bodies and to engobes offers design possibilities to the ceramist. Some experimentation with pigments is well worthwhile.

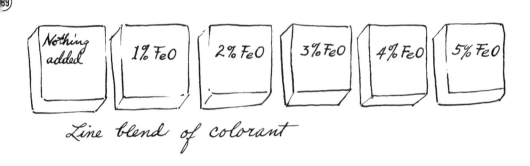

Line blend of colorant

Glaze

Glaze, the thing that gives pottery its brilliant tones, that fills the pores of bisque ware to make it waterproof and washable, that makes ceramic sculpture endure the ravages of wind and weather, is a coating of glass formed on clay while it is being fired. Glaze is made by mixing together a number of finely ground minerals and earth materials. These are mixed with a vehicle (water) and a gum that acts as a binder to hold the mixture in place on the ware.

Every glaze has three main ingredients, namely: (1) a glass-forming substance; (2) alumina to give the glaze body and make it stay on the ware (regular glass would run off like water); and (3) a flux, a melting agent to make all of the ingredients melt and fuse together.

The glass-forming substance is sand or silica. This comes from flint. It also comes from clay and feldspar. Alumina is supplied by clay which also provides silica. Fluxes come from many sources: lead, borax, sodium, potassium, calcium, and more. These are added as oxides. Fluxes work at different temperatures producing glazes for low-fire work (lead), for high-fire (feldspar), for stoneware (feldspar and zinc).

In addition to the three main ingredients listed above, glazes require ingredients to provide color—the oxides of the metals that were mentioned in Chapter 14: copper, cobalt, manganese, and others.

Ingredients can be added to glazes for special effects—tin and zirconium to make them opaque, rutile for crystals, ilmenite for specks.

Glazes are usually classified according to the flux they contain. Thus we speak of lead glazes, alkaline glazes, feldspathic glazes.

Lead glazes

Lead is an active flux frequently used in glazes for low-temperature work, from cone 010 to cone 02. At the lowest temperatures, lead can be used alone as a flux but most glaze recipes use two or more fluxes for better results.

An important drawback in the use of lead is its poisonous nature. Care must be taken when handling lead glazes to make sure that the hands are carefully washed and that no food is ever eaten in the studio. It is advisable to eliminate raw lead completely from classroom work with young children.

Here is a recipe for lead glaze.

Transparent lead glaze, cone 06

White lead	46
Whiting	12
Feldspar	20
Clay	7
Flint	15

These numbers are percentages by weight. Instructions for weighing and mixing glazes are given later in this chapter.

The glaze recipe given above will produce a colorless transparent glaze. For color, the following may be added.

Glaze colorants

For Blue, add	Cobalt oxide	0.5
Dark blue	Cobalt oxide	1.5
Green	Copper oxide	2
Tan	Iron oxide	2
Iron red	Iron oxide	8
Yellow	Antimony oxide	3
Gray violet	Manganese carbonate	2 to 3
Gray green	Chromium oxide	1
Gray	Nickel oxide	2
Black	Manganese carbonate	6
	Copper oxide	2
	Cobalt oxide	3

In addition to the above colorants, any prepared underglaze colors can be used to color a glaze. As a rule, it requires from 10% to 30% for satisfactory results. No exact quantities can be given here, experimentation is necessary.

The above glaze can be made white and opaque by adding 10% of tin oxide or 20% of zircopax, a commercially prepared oxide of zirconium. This makes a good glaze for majolica. Opaque colored glazes are made by adding colorants as well as tin.

Alkaline glazes

Glazes that use soda, borax, and potassium as fluxes and which contain no lead are called "alkaline glazes." Glazes of this type were the first glazes ever used. The secret was discovered by the Egyptians many thousands of years ago. They first used these glazes, not on pottery, but on forms carved out of steatite or soapstone. Copper in an alkaline glaze produces the beautiful turquoise color we call Egyptian blue. Here is a recipe:

Alkaline glaze, cone 06

Soda ash	28
Whiting	10
Feldspar	50
Flint	12

Two percent of copper carbonate added to this glaze will produce Egyptian blue, provided that the glaze is used over a white body. Two to 3% of manganese carbonate produces a rich purple. The other colorants listed for the lead glaze give similar colors in this glaze.

Soda ash, like the other alkaline ingredients of glazes, is soluble in water. So, in mixing an alkaline glaze, it is important not to use an excess of water. The ingredients should be ground in a mortar with just enough water added to make a thick creamy paste. This should have gum added to it and then be applied to the ware immediately.

A note of caution: the bisque on which alkaline glazes are to be applied must be fired high enough so that it is not porous. If the bisque is too absorbent, the soluble fluxes in the glaze will soak into the body of the ware. This can cause serious trouble even to the extent of causing pieces to split.

Egyptian paste

While we are on the subject of alkaline glazes, let's consider another discovery of the Egyptians, a method of making small objects—ornaments, figurines, and jewelry—out of a mixture of clay and soda with oxides of copper added. This is not really a glaze, but it is an interesting thing to experiment with. Here is a recipe:

Feldspar	36
Flint	36
Clay	12
Sodium bicarbonate	5
Copper carbonate	3
Dextrine	8

These materials must be mixed with just enough water to make a workable paste. This should be done on a glass slab with a spatula. Small objects modeled of this paste should be allowed to dry, then fired to cone 07.

Frit

A frit is a glaze or glass made by firing silica and fluxes in a crucible. When the ingredients have fused, the molten glass is dumped into water where it shatters into minute particles. These are then ground into a powder.

A studio potter can make his own frits if he wants to, but it is a great deal of trouble and hardly worthwhile. Commercial frits for industrial use are manufactured by a number of companies. These cannot be purchased from the manufacturers by studio potters, unless the purchases are in large amounts, but retail dealers in ceramic supplies carry them in stock. A list of commercial frits useful for studio potters is given in the Appendix.

There are many advantages in using commercial frits. The soluble ingredients in alkaline glazes become insoluble when they are fritted. The toxic effect of lead is reduced when lead is used as an ingredient in fritted glaze. Glazes compounded of raw materials contain substances which must burn out during the firing. These go up the chimney as waste. When glaze has been fritted, all these raw materials are burned out during the process of manufacturing the frit and the potter is spared one source of trouble. Another advantage for the studio potter, an important one, is that when he relies on commercial frits for most of his basic glazes, he is relieved of the need to buy and store many raw materials. And finally, commercially prepared frits are reliable; they behave the way they are supposed to behave all of the time.

Some frits can be used as glazes just as they are, provided a small quantity of clay is added. The clay is necessary to make the liquid glaze behave like a slip and adhere to the ware. Other frits must be combined with additional ingredients in glaze recipes.

Here are some recipes for fritted glazes. These use the products of the Ferro Enamel Company, Pemco, and O. Hommel. Most ceramic supply dealers carry these products.

Low-fire transparent lead glaze, cone 012 to 06
Pemco frit Pb-461 71
Pemco frit Pb-41 18
Ball clay 11

Low-fire opaque white lead glaze, cone 012 to 08
Pemco frit Pb-545 75
Ball clay 10
Zircopax 15

Transparent lead glaze, cone 08 to 02
Ferro frit 3304 90
Ball clay 10

Transparent lead glaze, cone 08 to 02
Pemco frit Pb-742 46
Pemco frit Pb-349 46
Ball clay 8

Opaque white leadless glaze, cone 08 to 02
Pemco frit P-64 90
Ball clay 10

Transparent lead glaze, cone 02 to 8
Pemco frit Pb-349 92
Ball clay 8

Opaque and semiopaque glazes

There are many differences in the degree of transparency of different glazes. The extent of transparency often depends upon the way a glaze has been fired. A glaze which would normally be completely clear when fired to its maturing temperature, might be somewhat cloudy when slightly underfired, or, if much underfired, would be opaque. Such glazes will become transparent if they are fired again to the full maturing point of the glaze.

Beautiful effects are achieved with semiopaque glazes, those which show some of the color of the clay body underneath them. Such glazes are good to use over underglaze decorations. The best way to make a glaze opaque or semiopaque is by adding either tin oxide or zirconium oxide. The latter is best used in the form of "zircopax," a commercial silicate of zirconium. About 10% of tin oxide added to a transparent glaze will make it white and opaque. It takes about twice as much zircopax, or 20%, to make a glaze completely opaque. For partial opaqueness use half of these amounts or slightly less than half.

Mat glaze

Another important quality in the design value of a glaze is its degree of glossiness. Some glazes are bright and shiny, others have a mat surface. If a glaze is underfired it is apt to be less shiny than it would be at maturing temperature, so that deliberate underfiring is one way to achieve a mat surface in a glaze. However, more certain results are obtained by adding such things as barium oxide or zinc oxide. About 10% of barium or 20% of zinc added to a lead glaze will give a good mat surface. Mat glazes can be made also by increasing the alumina content of a glaze, that is, by adding about 10% of china clay. Other things to try are adding whiting and increasing the flint.

Alumina mat glaze, cone 06 to 04

White lead	46
Whiting	11
Feldspar	20
China clay	16
Flint	7

Barium mat glaze, cone 06 to 04

White lead	38
Whiting	5
Feldspar	19
Barium carbonate	13
Calcined zinc oxide	3
China clay	7
Flint	15

Colemanite

Colemanite is a calcium borate which makes it possible to use boric oxide in insoluble form. It is a highly satisfactory material at temperature ranges from cone 04 to cone 2. When copper is added, it produces a beautiful greenish blue, somewhat similar to turquoise.

Colemanite or borosilicate glaze, cone 06 to 04

Colemanite	30
Feldspar	45
Zinc oxide	5
Barium carbonate	6
China clay	4
Flint	10

48. Above. Tile Table Top, Carla. Overglaze painting.

49. Right. Plaque, by Carla, four tiles incised and painted, set in plaster of Paris.

50. Left. Birds, Valsa-makis.

51. Below. Sculptured Flower Holder, Dorothy Perkins.

52. Below. Ulysses, plaque by Capacci.

53. Below. Mermaid, the Author.

54. *Left*. (Dance) and 55. *Above*. (Music). Plaques made of tiles cut to shape and mounted on plywood. Student work, High School of Art and Design, New York City.

57. *Below*. Plaque by Fantoni.

56. *Below, left*. Plaque, decorated in the style of the Island of Skiros, product of Keramikos, Athens.

Rutile

Rutile is an ore of titanium oxide which has iron oxide present also. By itself rutile gives a slightly tan or brown color to glaze. It produces mottled effects. In opaque glazes, especially those containing copper, it produces interesting streaks of color. No two pieces glazed with a rutile glaze are ever exactly alike. Rutile works very well with colemanite glazes.

Rutile glaze, cone 06 to 04
White lead	68
Feldspar	10
China clay	2
Flint	14
Rutile	6

Alkaline rutile glaze, cone 06 to 04
White lead	27
Whiting	4
Borax	18
Feldspar	18
Flint	18
Rutile	5
Tin oxide	10

These glazes produce interesting crystalline effects. Good colorants are:

Copper oxide	2
Cobalt oxide	0.5
Iron oxide	4

Bristol glazes

In the middle-temperature range from cone 2 to cone 6, zinc and magnesium can be used as fluxes instead of lead. A glaze made this way is called a "Bristol glaze." Glazes of this type were developed in England when it was discovered that lead glazes were sometimes toxic. Zinc glazes are apt to give trouble with crawling. It is a good plan when using zinc to calcine it first. Now that lead in fritted form has become available to manufacturers of dinnerware, Bristol glazes have lost much of their popularity.

Bristol glaze, cone 4 to 8
Zinc oxide	7
Whiting	10
Feldspar	68
China clay	8
Flint	7

Stoneware glazes

Stoneware, pottery fired in the temperature range from cone 4 to cone 8, has a beautiful rocklike quality. Its colors are not bright, but subtle. It has a special appeal for potters who have had the chance to work with it.

Lead volatilizes above cone 6 and so stoneware glazes must depend upon other fluxes: zinc, calcium, magnesium.

Stoneware glaze, cone 5 to 9
Feldspar	35
Dolomite	16
Whiting	6
China clay	9
Flint	34

Stoneware glaze, cone 7 to 10
Pemco frit P-586	62.8
Feldspar	12.6
Zinc oxide	3.1
China clay	11.2
Flint	10.3

Porcelain

The highest of the high-fire glazes are used on porcelain at temperatures ranging from cone 10 to cone 13. At high temperatures feldspar alone can serve as a flux. Feldspar is a kind of frit made by nature. A glaze containing 85% feldspar and 15% whiting makes a good porcelain glaze.

Porcelain glaze, cone 12 to 15
Feldspar	27
Whiting	20
China clay	20
Flint	33

Salt glazing

Salt glaze is a hard, vitreous surface produced on ware by salt which is thrown into the chamber of the kiln when the temperature is between cone 4 and cone 9. This type of glazing is best suited to stoneware. It requires a special kiln reserved for that purpose exclusively because as the salt volatilizes inside the chamber, it glazes the whole inside of the kiln as well as the pieces that are placed in it. It is hardly practical for the studio potter to try to operate his own salt-glazing kiln. However, it is sometimes possible to have work fired in the kiln of a terra-cotta factory which makes such products as salt-glazed sewer pipe.

SPECIAL GLAZE EFFECTS

Specks

Specks can be produced in a glaze by adding granular ilmenite. Specks can also be produced by spattering a glaze with another glaze of a contrasting color. In the manufacture of glazed terra-cotta building tiles at the Federal Seaboard Terra Cotta Company, they have developed a device for spraying their glazes, which uses three nozzles and three separate containers of glaze so that glazes of three different colors can be sprayed on the work simultaneously. The mottled surfaces resulting from this method of glazing are far better suited for tiles in buildings than areas of flat color would be.

Glaze over glaze

One glaze can be sprayed over another as mentioned above, or a second glaze of a contrasting color can be dabbed on with a sponge. When dabbing the second color, dip the sponge in the glaze, press it on the ware, rotate it through a quarter turn, press again, and so on, until the sponge has made a complete circle and has pressed against the ware four times.

When a fluid glaze is put on top of another which flows considerably, so that they mingle during the firing, the results are unpredictable—sometimes good.

The ashtrays by Harper shown in Figs. 13 and 14 in the color section were sprayed with colored glazes, then, before they were fired, a mixture of Ferro frit 3419, 100 parts; zircopax 20 parts; borax five parts was applied to the inside of the rim. The ingredients were mixed with enough water to make a heavy batter, a teaspoonful of gum was added, and the mixture was squirted on the pieces with a small syringe. During the firing the zircopax flowed toward the center of each piece, producing a fluid pattern of white over color.

Glazing textured ware

A piece that has a pronounced surface texture, or that has been carved, should be glazed in such a way that the glaze enhances the pattern. Some glazes which are soft and flow readily will point up a textural design by pulling away slightly from the edges. If glazing is done with glazes of two colors, it is a good idea to spray each color from a slightly different direction so that the beauty of the design is emphasized.

Crackle

A crackle in a glaze is really a defect, the result of crazing. However, on some work, especially medium-size pieces of sculpture, a crackle is decorative. A crackle is apt to occur whenever a glaze does not fit the body exactly. On buff-colored natural clays, almost any glaze is likely to produce a crackle unless the body of the piece is fired to cone 1 or higher.

Crackle can be deliberately produced by reducing the amount of flint and alumina in a glaze recipe. The beauty of a crackle glaze is increased by rubbing underglaze color over the surface of the piece so that it penetrates all of the tiny cracks. The Chinese, when producing crackleware, would deliberately underfire a piece, rub color in the cracks, then fire the piece again to a higher temperature so that all of the cracks in the glaze closed, but the pattern of the crackle remained.

Jewel glaze

This is a name given to an extremely fluid glaze used in such large amounts that it forms a pool on the inside of a piece. This pool produces a thick layer of glass which crazes and which has beauty because of its depth. This type of glaze can be used only on the inside of dishes or bowls, and any piece which is to have jewel glaze should be made extra heavy, of a clay containing grog. Here is a recipe:

Jewel glaze, cone 06
Pemco frit P-64 60
Borax 30
China clay 2
Zinc oxide 8
For color add: 3 copper carbonate for turquoise blue
1 cobalt carbonate for deep blue
2 manganese carbonate for purple

or any of the colorants listed on page 191.

The ingredients of this glaze can be mixed dry and piled in the center of the piece with a spoon.

Chromium red

Chromium oxide has a strange behavior in glazes. Depending upon the temperature, it will produce colors ranging from red through yellow to brown or green. In a low fire in a lead glaze, chromium produces a vivid orange red.

Chromium red glaze, cone 09 to 08
Red lead 67
Potassium bichromate 5
Soda ash 2
China clay 8
Flint 18

Red glazes can be made with cadmium or with selenium, but it is better to use these as commercially prepared glaze colors.

Purple

Alkaline glaze, aubergine color, cone 05
Soda ash 15
Magnesium carbonate 8
Boric acid 60
Flint 15
Cobalt oxide 2

Luster

This is a form of decoration in which a thin film of metal is deposited on the surface of a glazed piece. Lusters were developed by the early Persian potters who applied metallic salts to the ware, then fired it in a strong reducing fire. The reduction deposited the luster film on the ware. (Reduction is explained in Chapter 17.)

Another, simpler method does not require reduction in the kiln. A reducing agent (resin) is combined with metallic salts, usually chlorides or nitrates of gold, silver, copper, and bismuth. An oil (oil of lavender) is used as a medium and the mixture is sprayed or painted on the ware, which is then fired to red heat (about cone 012). The carbon formed by the reducing agent and the oil reduces the metal and creates the luster film without the need for reducing the kiln. Prepared lusters with the reducing agents added can be purchased from dealers in ceramic supplies.

Some glazes that contain manganese and iron produce a surface with a mirrorlike or lustrous quality. Here are two recipes.

Black luster glaze (mirror black), cone 04
White lead 56
Whiting 6
China clay 9
Flint 22
Cobalt oxide 3
Red iron oxide 2
Manganese dioxide 2

Brown luster glaze, cone 04
White lead 58
Feldspar 13
China clay 5
Flint 16
Manganese carbonate 5.5
Red iron oxide 2.5

Mixing glazes

The glaze recipes in this chapter give quantities in percentages. If a recipe is weighed out in grams, it will produce a total batch of 100 grams. If the numbers are multiplied by 3, the batch will add up to 300 grams, enough for a pint of glaze.

After the ingredients have been weighed out, they must be mixed. In the studios where large quantities of glaze are prepared, a ball mill for grinding glazes is a handy machine to have, but the average studio potter does not need such a piece of equipment. The ingredients may be put into a mortar with ½ cup of water and ground with a pestle for about ½ hour. After this the mixture should be rubbed through a 60-mesh sieve. Some potters find that grinding with a pestle is not necessary; it is enough to mix the ingredients with water in a bowl and pass them through a sieve two or three times. Since all commercially prepared ingredients are finely ground, simple mixing suffices.

Care must be taken in grinding alkaline glazes which contain soluble ingredients. These must be weighed, ground with just enough water to make a creamy paste, and applied to the ware immediately.

Gums

The application of glaze to pottery is made easier when gum is used. Gum tragacanth, one of the best for pottery, is prepared by stirring a teaspoonful of powdered tragacanth in an ounce of alcohol, then adding a pint of water. A tablespoonful of this solution should be added to a glaze before it is used.

CMC makes a good binder also. One ounce of this to a quart of water makes a good gum to add to glazes. Veegum T is another good gum.

The quantities of gum recommended above are for glazes that will be brushed or poured on ware. For spraying, it is advisable to use a gum solution of half strength. Gums don't keep. Mix small quantities at a time or else add a small quantity of formaldehyde to keep them from spoiling.

Settling

Some glazes, especially fritted ones, settle into hard masses at the bottom of the container they are in. To prevent this, add a teaspoonful of epsom salts to the water with which the glaze is mixed.

APPLYING GLAZE

Dipping

The simplest way of putting glaze on a bisqued piece is by dipping. The glaze is put into a large container and the piece is dipped in and out with a single motion, held in the air and tipped in different directions so that all of the excess glaze drains off from the inside as well as the outside, then it is stood on a board or on stilts to dry. The fingermarks are touched up with a brush. In commercial pottery establishments, dipping tongs are used to hold the ware while it goes in and out of the glaze. The studio potter who does much dipping would find a pair of these tongs a good investment.

The bisqued ware should be sponged slightly before it is dipped. The absorption of the bisque and the thickness of the glaze must be adjusted to one another so that a layer of glaze of the proper thickness is built up on the piece. The more absorbent the piece the thinner the glaze must be. Some experimentation is needed to get a proper relationship. Have a number of small bisqued test tiles at hand and start with a liquid glaze as thick as heavy cream. Dip the tile in and out, then check the result by scratching the layer of glaze with a pin. It should be about as thick as a postcard. If it is too thin, the glaze must be made heavier by allowing it to settle and then pouring off excess water. If the layer is too thick, add water to the glaze.

Some potters prefer to use a glaze that has a very heavy consistency. The bisque is dipped into water first until it becomes saturated. Then it is removed from the water and the surface is dried with a towel until all the shine disappears. The piece is then dipped into the heavy glaze. The advantage of working this way is that the piece may be dipped more slowly; in fact, it may go in and out of the glaze a number of times until the layer is just right.

Dipping requires a large amount of glaze, but aside from that drawback it is the quickest and the most economical way of glazing ware, for no glaze is wasted. When the glaze coating has dried, the piece must be dry footed before it goes into the kiln, that is, glaze must be scraped away from the rim on which the piece stands.

Brushing

Glazes may be painted on ware with a soft brush, a method satisfactory for small pieces. Three layers should be brushed on in even strokes in opposite directions. One coat of glaze should not be allowed to dry before the next coat is brushed over it.

Sponging

Glaze can be applied to ware with a soft sponge. This is a very easy and yet quite effective way of applying even coats of glaze.

Spraying

The most satisfactory way to get an even coat of glaze on a piece is to spray it. If a studio has a spray booth with exhaust vent and fan, air compressors and spray guns, then the problem of spraying ware is simple. The ware is stood on a tile and then placed on a turntable in the booth and turned while the spray is directed at it. It is important not to let the surface of the ware become so moist that it gets shiny. If this happens the glaze is almost certain to run and the evenness of the glaze coating will be lost. If this does occur it is best to wash the piece, let it dry, and start all over. When spraying the bottom of the piece it is usually possible to find a metal lid from a jar which is just the right size so that it can be placed over the foot of the piece that is being sprayed. This makes it unnecessary to do dry footing later on.

The ceramist who is not fortunate enough to have spraying equipment can make use of much simpler tools. A small inexpensive sprayer that works on the Aerosol bomb principle using a cartridge of compressed air, gives excellent results, and if one has to, one can make do with a Flit gun. A comparatively inexpensive portable spray booth with removable filters and an electric exhaust fan can take the place of a larger spray booth attached to an exhaust vent.

When glazes are sprayed it is possible to achieve even gradations of tone. Special effects are obtained by spraying one color over another. Spraying is a good way to glaze textured surfaces. The spray may be directed at an angle to heighten the effect of the texture, or glazes of two different colors may be sprayed from opposite directions. The one disadvantage of spraying is that it is wasteful of glaze. Fiberglass filters can be soaked so that if care is used to clean them each time, some of the glaze can be reclaimed.

Keep the nose and mouth covered with a cloth while spraying to avoid inhaling particles of glaze.

Pouring glaze

The only way to glaze the inside of a pottery shape with a narrow neck is to pour the glaze in, rotate the piece so that the whole inside surface is covered, and then pour out the excess, shaking the piece to make sure that all excess is removed. The glaze should be a trifle thinner for this operation. This method can be used for bowls too, pouring in, rotating the piece, then pouring the glaze out. The operation must be done rapidly to avoid piling up too thick a coat or an uneven one.

Once the inside of the piece has been glazed by pouring, the outside may be glazed by either spraying or brushing. It can be poured also. The piece should stand supported on two wooden strips placed across the top of a bowl or pan. Glaze is then poured over the piece so that an even coating is formed while the excess is drained off into the pan or bowl.

Glazing unfired clay

It is always safer to fire ware to the bisque state before applying glaze. However, glaze can be put on unfired clay as well. This saves all the labor involved in stacking the kiln a second time and the extra cost of the fuel needed for the second fire. Most commercial terra cotta is fired only once (the ceramic architectural sculpture illustrated in Chapter 21 and in Figs. 67 and 68 in the color section were all made with a single firing). There is another advantage, namely, that a single firing of clay and glaze produces a better, more harmonious bonding between the glaze and the piece it is on.

It is risky to dip unfired ware, but glaze can be brushed on or sprayed. Ample time must be allowed for the ware to become thoroughly dry before it is put into the kiln. Because of the soluble nature of the alkaline fluxes, a raw alkaline glaze should never be used on unfired clay. (A raw alkaline glaze is one that has not been fritted.)

GLAZE DEFECTS

Glazes do not always turn out the way we want them to. The trouble may be due to mistakes in the formula or the way the glaze was mixed or applied, or it may be due to something that went wrong in the firing. A few of the most common glaze defects are these . . .

Crazing

This occurs when a glaze shrinks more than the clay it is on. It shows up as tiny cracks on the surface of the piece. Sometimes these develop as soon as the piece is removed from the kiln; often they do not appear until several days or weeks later. Tracking down the causes of crazing is the part of glaze research that gives the ceramist most trouble. Tests must be made, increasing and decreasing the amounts of silica and flux in the glaze. Sometimes, in order to make a glaze fit, work must be done on the body. When a body is fired higher the likelihood of crazing decreases. Talc in a body reduces crazing. Some low-fire white bodies are made with more than 50% of talc. This almost eliminates crazing.

Crawling

When a piece comes out of a kiln with bare spots where the glaze has moved away from a portion, exposing the body underneath, the defect is called "crawling." Crawling may be caused by insufficient gum in the glaze so that the glaze layer cracked before it was put into the kiln. It can also be caused by dirt or oil on the surface of the piece when it was glazed, too thick an application, firing before the glaze dried or, sometimes, under-firing. Glaze sometimes crawls because the body is too porous. In this case add flint to the body or fire to a higher temperature. Crawling some-times occurs because the glaze recipe contains too much plastic clay. This clay shrinks during the firing, and crawling results. As a remedy, fire some of the clay in powder form and use it in the recipe calcined instead of raw. A piece marred by crawling can be glazed again and refired.

Blistering

Blistering is often the result of sulfur in the clay. To remedy this add 2% of barium carbonate to the clay when it is in slip form. Blisters and craters caused by sulfur will burn out when the piece is refired.

If blisters appear in lead glazes and not in others the trouble is reduc-tion. Check the burners of the kiln and examine the muffle for leaks.

Pinholes

Pinholes are usually due to air holes in the clay, especially in cast pieces. Stir the casting slip more thoroughly. They often come about from too rapid firing or too rapid cooling. Putting one glaze over another after it has dried, or painting on top of a dried glaze, will sometimes cause this trouble.

Running

If a glaze runs off a piece and pools on the shelf of the kiln, the recipe calls for too much flux or the glaze is seriously overfired. Coloring oxides such as iron and copper act as fluxes. To remedy this defect, increase the alumina and decrease the flux in the recipe.

Dryness

Dryness is the result of underfiring or insufficient flux.

Sandpaper surface

A rough sandpaper-like surface indicates that the glaze was not put on thick enough.

Shiny surface on a mat glaze

If a piece which should be mat comes out shiny the piece was fired too high.

Shivering

When sections of a glaze crack off after firing, the fault is called shiver-ing. This is the opposite of crazing; the body has shrunk more than the glaze so that the glaze is under pressure. To remedy, reduce the flint in the recipe and increase the clay.

Defects in glazes like those described above are things the potter tries to avoid at all cost. At times, however, glaze defects are deliberately pro-duced. When this is done they are not really defects but special effects, an important part of ceramic design with glaze.

The three recipes which follow were worked out by Glen Lukens, formerly Professor of Ceramics at the University of Southern California, who has been a pioneer in experimental work with glazes and glass.

This glaze will shrink during the firing and come out as a series of beads of irregular size and shape.

Glaze for planned crawling, cone 06
Colemanite 75
Powdered pumice 25

Another type of crawling comes about when a glaze is too viscous and refuses to flow evenly over the ware. This can be planned by reducing the flux and increasing the content of silica and alumina.

Viscous glaze, cone 06
O. Hommel frit 25 ⎫
  or   ⎬ 57
Ferro frit 3124 ⎭
Flint 28
Georgia clay 15

This glaze should be applied in a thick coating. If it is put on with a syringe, it can be used to produce raised lines and patterns. Four percent of copper carbonate added to this glaze produces a good turquoise.

Foam or lava-type glaze

20

Sulfur is an enemy of potters because it makes bubbles and craters in lead glazes. In the following recipe, sulfur is used intentionally to produce a foam or bubbly effect. (Note Plate 57.) Barium sulfate forms bubbles in a molten glaze and at cone 06 this glaze is viscous enough to trap the gases forming the bubbles so that on cooling, an unusual texture of pits or craters remains in the surface of the glaze. This is heightened by gently rubbing the glazed surface with a piece of carborundum stone. Colored clay slips should be brushed on the greenware, then fired to bisque. After this a rather uneven coat of foam glaze should be applied heavily with a sponge. The effect is best on the outside surface of tall vases or large bowls. The same recipe with the barium sulfate omitted is good as a glaze in the interior surfaces.

Foam or lava glaze, cone 06
O. Hommel frit 14 100
Tin oxide 1.5
Bentonite 1.0
Barium sulfate 30

For color add as follows:

Turquoise . . . . . . 2.7 copper carbonate
Celadon . . . . 1.0 copper carbonate
Mauve . . . . 1.0 manganese dioxide
Dark blue . . . . 1.0 cobalt oxide

Note that barium sulfate is a poison, but when it is fused in a glaze, it becomes harmless.

Plate 57—Figure pot by Kenneth Shores. Black lava-type glaze.
Photograph courtesy of Henry Art Gallery, University of Washington.

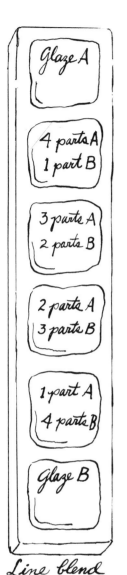

Line blend

Glaze is an element of ceramic design, not merely a coating of pigment that goes on top of a clay shape. This means that while he forms a piece, the ceramist must think of what the glaze treatment will be. Glaze is a translucent, sometimes transparent thing. Its beauty comes from the fact that we see through it and into it and sense its depth.

The chemistry of glazes is an absorbing subject, a separate science by itself. One could spend a lifetime exploring its mysteries; in fact, some ceramists have done just that.

In recent years, however, the research chemists employed by manufacturers of ceramic materials have charted most of the road. The ceramist who cannot spare the time to make his own can choose from a wide variety of commercially prepared glazes; practically any color is available to him, any special effect. Many contemporary artists feel that it is not necessary for a potter to make his own glazes, just as a painter need not grind his own pigments—something the old masters had to do because there was no other way to obtain them.

Yet there is great satisfaction in compounding one's own glazes. Even when using commercially prepared products most ceramists like to experiment and change. Glaze calculation is a highly technical process, but the ceramist who is familiar with the basic facts about glaze can do much experimenting on a trial-and-error basis, adding ingredients for special effects, blending colors, putting glaze over glaze. A good way to experiment is by a line blend. For example, if you have two different glazes, call them *A* and *B*, of contrasting colors, make a series of tests on 6 tiles. On tile 1 put glaze *A*. On tile 2 put a mixture of 4 parts *A* and 1 part *B*. On tile 3, put 3 parts *A* and 2 parts *B*. On tile 4, 2 parts *A* and 3 parts *B*. On tile 5, put 1 part *A* and 4 parts *B* and on tile 6 put all *B*. Instead of using 6 different tiles for such a line blend, you can put areas of each mixture on one long narrow strip of clay.

If you do your glaze testing on neatly prepared tiles or objects, the test results, besides being informative, will produce things of value in themselves. The simplified bird form of which we made a mold in Chapter 9 is good for testing glazes. The different surfaces allow glazes to run in different ways so that the tests are truly informative. Among many birds used as tests, some will emerge as beautiful and satisfying ceramic objects. Note Fig. 25 in the color section.

Making tests on tiles is, of course, much simpler. To get the full effect of a test it should be made on two tiles, one fired flat and the other standing on edge. Some of your tests will prove to be valuable additions to ceramic panels or tabletops. In Fig. 74 in the color section there is a mural made of shallow ceramic boxes that were originally used as tests. In these tests glazes, fragments of glass, splashes of color were used in haphazard fashion. The most interesting ones were cemented to a wall as shown in the illustration—producing an extremely pleasing mural.

When you experiment, *keep records*. Avoid the fate of a friend of mine who has made some beautiful glaze tests. The formulas are secrets—not even he knows what went into them.

16

Glass

G LASS is a ceramic material made from melted silica or sand. Silica has to be heated to over 3000°F. before it melts, and while it would be advantageous to make ordinary drinking glasses and other glass objects from silica alone, the difficulty of forming and the expense would be too great. To lower the melting point of silica, fluxes must be added, usually soda and lime. White sand, soda ash, and crushed limestone are melted in a clay crucible at a temperature of about 2500°F. and the molten liquid is then formed into shapes by blowing, pressing, or rolling.

Contemporary ceramists have become interested in designing with glass by working with sheet glass, plate glass, chunks and bits of broken bottles. Their experimentation has included combining glass with clay, bending glass, developing glass pigments, making glass pictures. Some pioneers have even tried making their own glass, mixing and fusing silica and fluxes according to their own formulas.

The science of glass is a vast subject, but even without profound technical study the ceramist who has his own kiln can explore the possibilities of glass as an element of ceramic design. Here are some things to try.

Attaching glass to clay

If we put into our kiln a flat tile that has been bisqued, then coated with glaze, and lay some fragments of glass on top of the glaze, then fire the kiln, we will find after the firing that the glass has melted, flowed into pools, and become attached firmly to the clay. This suggests possible design uses. If the tile were planned with depressions to hold pools of glass, or if design areas were outlined with slightly raised walls, it would be possible to have glass pools that were fairly deep. This could give interesting design effects.

The lapel pin shown in Fig. 33 in the color section and the tile with an angel design in Fig. 36 in the color section were formed by pressing layers of clay against plaster slabs which had grooves cut in them outlining the areas of the designs. After the pressing, both the tile and the pin had all of the design areas outlined in raised ridges. They were bisqued, given a thin coating of glaze, then fired, with fragments of broken colored glass filling all the areas of the designs. In the firing the glass turned to liquid

pools that filled each area. On cooling, the glass crazed considerably; this heightened the effectiveness of the color and the translucence of the design.

A tile with raised ridges can be made by the methods described in Photo Series 28 in Chapter 8. The tile must be bisqued, of course, because glass melts at a temperature considerably lower than the maturing point of clay. After it has been bisqued, the tile should be painted or sprayed with a low-fire glaze (Pemco frit Pb-41 or Ferro frit 3419, plus 10% of ball clay). If the tile is made of red or buff clay, in order to get the full beauty of the translucence of the glass the glaze should be made opaque and white by the addition of 10% of tin oxide or 20% of zircopax.

The glass used can be fragments of stained glass or broken bits of colored glass bottles. Beautiful colors are obtained from bottle glass—the green of ginger ale bottles, for example, the deep cobalt blue of some medicine bottles. Glass beads may be used. Colors like bright red which are hard to come by will have to be purchased as glass fragments from dealers in ceramic supplies.

The glass will need to be crushed into small pieces. This must be done with safeguards, for it can be dangerous. Glass may be put between two layers of cloth and pounded with a hammer or rolled with a piece of pipe. This should be done on a sheet of metal—any wooden tabletop would be seriously damaged. Glass bottles can be broken into small pieces by heating them in a kiln or oven until they are too hot to touch, then plunging them into a pail of water.

After the glass is crushed, fill each area of the glazed tile with the color of glass intended for it. Use a fine pointed instrument to poke the bits of glass around to cover every portion of the area. Since the chunks of glass will melt and flow, they must be piled higher than the surface desired on the finished tile. Experience will be the teacher here; it will take a few trials to see how the glass fragments should be piled for best results.

When the tile is loaded with the crushed glass, put it in the kiln. Make sure the tile is perfectly level, not closer than 2″ away from any kiln element. The tile must be placed on stilts.

Glass will melt and flow as a liquid at a temperature above 1500°F. The kiln should be turned on and fired slowly at the beginning. It is good to leave the door open for the first three hours of the firing, or until the inside temperature of the kiln reaches about 1000°F. A pyrometer on the kiln is helpful.

Fire by eye. The tile should be placed in such a way that it can be seen when the door of the kiln is opened slightly. When the temperature of the kiln has reached 1450°F. the pieces of glass will begin to soften. Look in the kiln at frequent intervals from this point on. As the temperature rises, the chunks of glass will become softer, until eventually they flow into a smooth mass. Turn off the kiln at that point. Allow the kiln to cool completely (24 hours, at least) before taking the tile out.

Filling openings in a clay tile with glass

The full benefit of the transparency of glass is obtained when the glass is put, not on clay, but in an opening in clay. Make a tile with openings cut all the way through. The glass will exert considerable pressure, so unless the tile is solidly constructed, it is quite apt to break. It must be made of a terra-cotta type clay, that is, an earthenware clay with at least 30% of medium grog, and it should be not less than 1″ thick. The outside rim of the tile should be 1″ wide or more.

The tile must be fired and glazed (this may be done in two firings or in 1). When this has been done, brush the inner surfaces of the openings with a mixture of low-fire frit (Pemco Pb-41 or Ferro 3419) and water.

Place the tile on a kiln shelf that has been given a protective coating of whiting mixed with water. This protective coating is to prevent any glass from sticking to the shelf. The whiting must be given a chance to dry thoroughly before it is put into the kiln.

Carefully spoon whiting into the openings of the tile. Use a small modeling tool to distribute the whiting so that it forms a layer about ⅛″ deep in each opening. It is important to fill the bottom of each opening completely; otherwise, during the firing, liquid glass will run out underneath the tile. Even though the whiting is put in in powder form, it will support the glass and form the bottom surface of the glass layer. There must be no shifting in the tile's position after the whiting has been put into the openings. To guard against any movement, fasten the tile to the shelf with masking tape before putting the whiting in the openings. The tape burns up during the firing with no ill effects.

Next, fill the openings with fragments of crushed glass. Glass of one color alone may be used in an opening or bits of glass of several colors may be blended. After the glass has been placed, the piece is fired in the same manner as the tile we just described. The fish tile shown in Fig. 34 in the color section and the two pierced plaques shown in Figs. 37 and 38 in the color section were made this way.

Filling openings in vertical pieces with glass

The method described above for filling openings in tiles with glass can be used for openings in vertical shapes. Use chunks of glass. Make a paste by mixing a low-firing frit (O. Hommel 5, Ferro 3419, or Pemco Pb-41) with water and paint the inside of the openings. Press chunks of glass into place in the openings as tightly as you can. Wear gloves while doing this. When the chunks are in place, preheat the kiln to 200°F., then put the piece into the kiln and fire with the door open until the temperature in the kiln climbs to about 1000°F., then close the kiln door. Continue the firing, but watch it closely. Look at the work frequently. As soon as the edges of the glass chunks have begun to round, turn off the kiln. Let it cool for 24 hours before removing the piece.

This is an interesting method to try with pierced shapes that have been thrown on the wheel or slab built or cast in molds. The clay should be heavily grogged and the walls should be thick, not less than ½″.

Glass is inexpensive and there is lots of it available. Interesting things can be done with bits of colored glass from broken bottles. Small pieces of glass fired to cone 015 will roll into balls, some of them with the beauty of jewels.

Larger bottle fragments will melt into flat layers that can be cut into smaller shapes for glass jewelry, tesserae for mosaic work, or shapes of color to be used in making glass pictures.

Melting glass fragments

Whiting is sprinkled on a tile to act as a separator and keep the glass from fusing to the tile. *Note:* Whiting used this way cannot be used again.

Fragments of bottles are placed on the tile. Care is taken not to disturb the layer of whiting.

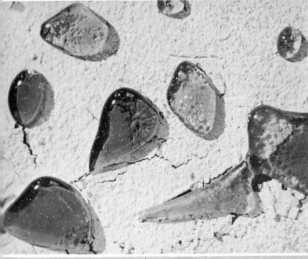

After firing to cone 015. The fragments have rounded into smooth shapes. The backs of these have a pebble surface that comes from the layer of whiting.

A pair of earrings and a pendant made by fusing bits of bottle glass to pieces of window glass. The window glass was cut into two triangles and a circle (the circle did not have to be cut accurately). Fragments of green and blue bottle glass were laid in place on the cut shapes, loops of nichrome wire (burnt-out kiln elements) were added, and the work was fired. (Other wire could be used instead of nichrome. Twenty-gauge wire would serve here; for heavier work a heavier gauge would be required.)

When glass is melted on a layer of sprinkled whiting the pebbled surface of the whiting makes a pattern on the back of the glass. If the whiting is combed into ridges with an instrument such as a fork, the back of the glass will have corresponding ridges. These irregular surfaces refract light passing through the glass, adding much to its beauty.

Glass bending

A piece of window glass heated in a kiln starts to soften at about 1400°F. or cone 017. At this point it begins to slump. If the glass is resting not on a flat surface but on a clay mold with a depression in it, the glass will sink into the depression and take the shape of the mold.

To make a glass bowl or dish, design a shape and then make a mold out of clay. The mold is made by the method described in Photo Series 9 in Chapter 4. A mound of clay is made in the shape that is wanted on the outside surface of the dish. Allowance must be made for shrinkage, so the mound must be formed slightly larger than the final dish will be. The top surface of the mound must be perfectly flat.

When the mound has been formed, it is covered with two layers of thin cloth or wet paper toweling. A layer of clay is then rolled, ½″ thick or a little thicker. Red clay is best to use for this and it should contain 30% of medium grog. When the layer has been rolled, it must be draped over the mound and gently pressed into shape. There must be a rim at least 1″ wide completely around the mound.

As soon as the clay becomes firm enough to be handled it should be lifted off the mound. The inside surface of the mold is then made smooth and the outside is trimmed. It is necessary for air to escape while glass is bending, so a hole must be made in each side of the mold. Use a thin nail to pierce the clay.

Allow the mold to become bone dry, then fire it. If the clay matures at cone 06, fire the mold to cone 08; it will work better if it is a soft bisque.

PHOTO SERIES 51

Bending glass

A mold has been prepared by sprinkling whiting on every portion of its surface. A rectangle of glass with a black and gold decalcomania design on it is being tried in position. (Decalcomanias are described in Chapter 19.)

Before the glass was actually placed, the mold was put into the kiln and preheated to 200°F., then lifted out with a pancake turner. The corners of the glass were cut off to make a more interesting design, then the glass was carefully lowered onto the mold. The mold with the glass in place was then returned to the kiln.

In firing, all of the precautions mentioned earlier in this chapter were followed. The kiln door was left open until the temperature reached 1000°F., firing was done by eye, the kiln was turned off as soon as the glass had slumped into the mold, and the door of the kiln was not opened until 24 hours later.

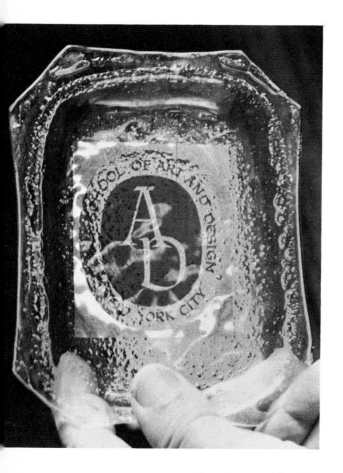

After the firing. The flat piece of glass has become a dish. The textured surface on the back made by the whiting refracts light in a pleasing manner.

The glass used in this series was double-thick window glass, best for a dish this size. For pieces under 5″ in length, single-thick glass would suffice. Glass must be clean before it goes into the kiln—use alcohol or detergent and, once it is clean, handle it only by the edges.

The illustration in Plate 58 shows two square textured glass bowls made by Glen Lukens using the method just described. Lukens has been a pioneer in exploring the possibilities of design with glass. He calls the material of which these bowls are made "desert glass" because some years ago, when he was Professor of Ceramics at the University of Southern

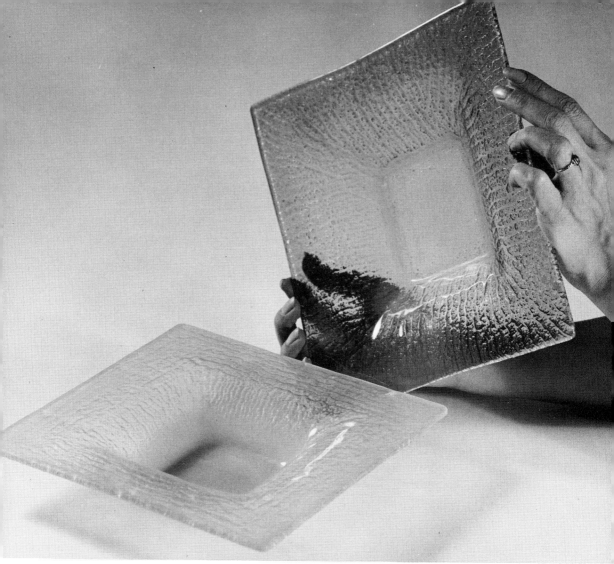

Plate 58—Two square textured glass bowls by Glen Lukens. California desert glass, one mesa blue, the other desert rose. *Photograph by Emil Cuhel.*

California, he used to make expeditions into the Mojave Desert to collect alkaline minerals for his glass and glaze work. Since the development of commercial frits, such forays in quest of materials are no longer necessary.

Cutting glass rectangles

Use a glass cutter of the wheel type with a tapping ball at the end of the handle. In cutting a rectangle out of a larger sheet of glass, cut a straight-sided piece completely off one end of the sheet of glass. This should be as wide as the rectangle desired. The sheet of glass to be cut should be placed on a tabletop that is covered with a layer of felt or some similar material. Put the pattern under the glass and score a straight line completely across the sheet of glass.

The glass cutter may be held in the fist with the thumb pressing on the ball, or it may be held like a pencil. The important thing is to score with

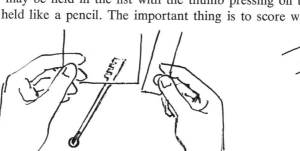

a single motion; pull the glass cutter toward you without going back over the line. Then tap along the underside of the scored line with the metal tapping ball. The glass should separate along the scored line while you are tapping. If it does not separate easily, place it so that the scored line is at the edge of the table, then press down with one hand on the portion that is on the table, hold the projecting piece in the other hand and bear down on it gently but firmly until it breaks off.

If you scored the glass well, it will break off in a clean straight line. If some rough projections remain on the edge of the piece you intend to use, these can be nibbled off with a pair of pliers.

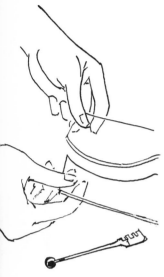

With a second scored line cut a piece from the strip that will be the size of the rectangle you want. Sandpaper or file the edges of this piece of glass to remove any excess roughness.

Cutting curves

Cutting curves is more of a problem than cutting rectangles. In cutting a free-form shape the pattern should be drawn on paper and placed under the glass from which it is to be cut in such a manner that the pattern is at least 1″ inside of any edge. Then the outline is scored with the glass cutter. When this is done, the glass is tapped on the underside along the outline of the cut. Straight cuts are made from the outside of the shape to the edge of the glass. These also are tapped on the underside so that the portion around the pattern can be broken away from the pattern in segments. It takes practice to cut glass curves successfully. The two basic curves to try are a simple convex curve and a gentle S curve.

A circle is almost impossible to cut without a special glass-cutting compass. Glass circles can be bought, however, and some commercially made circular glass plates can be used in design work.

The glass cutter used should be of the wheel type. When not in use, it should be stood in a jar with ½″ of kerosene in the bottom to keep the wheel from rusting.

Just as glass was bent into a mold in Photo Series 51, a sheet of glass can be softened while resting on a terra-cotta tile which has a carved relief design. The design must be fairly simple with no undercuts and the high surfaces of the design should project about ⅛″ above the background. Let's experiment with this technique.

PHOTO SERIES 52

A glass relief

A terra-cotta pressing has been made of the negative bird tile shown in Photo Series 28 in Chapter 8. This will be fired to cone 08, two cones lower than the maturing point of the red clay.

The fired tile has been sprinkled with whiting. (Note how the red color of the clay makes it easy to tell when the tile is completely covered.) A rectangle of glass a trifle smaller than the tile is being lowered into position.

The finished glass relief.

Glass colors

The colors used on glass are ceramic pigments. Underglaze colors and overglaze colors can both be used to color glass. Overglaze colors which are made to fire at lower temperatures than underglaze colors are more satisfactory for glass work. The dealers in ceramic supplies also sell specially prepared glass colors and stains.

Glass colors that are purchased dry should be mixed with water in the proportion of 1 teaspoonful of glass color to four tablespoons of water. A pinch of Epsom salts will prevent the color from settling. A quarter-teaspoonful of CMC gum solution works well also.

Glass colors are translucent; one can be used over another. Colors can be sprayed on glass. A type of sprayer which operates with a can of compressed gas as a propellant is good for spraying glass colors. Designs may be sgraffitoed in sprayed colors by using a piece of paper rolled so that it forms a shape like the point of a pencil.

Different colors may be dabbed onto glass with a brush in such manner that they fuse and mingle in the firing. Before color is put on glass the glass must be carefully cleaned with alcohol solvent or detergent.

The piece of glass that was bent to shape in Photo Series 51 had a decalcomania design on it. It could have been decorated with glass colors. Other things can be tried on glass that is to be bent; glass beads or droplets made by fusing bits of colored glass can be glued to the glass before it goes into the kiln.

A *glass picture*

We are familiar with the beauty of stained glass windows, constructions made out of pieces of colored glass cut carefully to shape, then fastened together by strips of lead that are *H*-shaped in cross section. Recently glass pictures have been made by fusing pieces of colored glass to sheets of clear glass. This technique, called "gemmail," has been developed in France where the paintings of Braque, Picasso, and other contemporary artists have been executed in back-lighted glass. Craftsmen cut pieces of colored glass and glue them in position on a transparent background, then fuse them in a kiln. To secure additional depth, the glass pieces are of varying thickness.

To experiment with this technique, use a piece of $\frac{3}{16}$"-thick glass. Plate glass or store front glass is good. Prepare a design on paper; place the glass over the paper, then cut pieces of colored glass to match the design. Put these in position on the plate glass. When they are in the right spot, glue them in position. These pieces of glass can be placed so that they touch each other, or where there are openings between two pieces of glass, the openings can be filled with crushed glass fragments. If you prefer to make something which is closer in appearance to a stained-glass window, glue the sections of glass onto the background, leaving $\frac{1}{8}$" space between the pieces. Use black underglaze color to outline areas of the design. After the design is complete, prepare the kiln shelf with whiting, lay the glass on it carefully, and put it into the kiln. Fire slowly with the kiln door open for the first hour, then close the door. Fire by cone or by eye. Shut the kiln off when it reaches cone 017 or when the pieces of glass begin to round at the edges. If you have trouble seeing what is going on in the kiln at the low temperature, try inserting a long sliver of wood through the peephole. It will burst into flame and it will serve as a temporary torch. When the kiln has been turned off, open the door slightly, count to 20 (10 seconds), shut the door and let the kiln cool slowly. Keep the door closed for 24 hours.

If spaces were left between the design areas, these may be filled with magnesite cement when the glass is cool.

The glass landscape panel shown in Fig. 35 in the color section was made with no space between the different portions of colored glass. The colors for this piece came from broken bottles. The design was outlined with underglaze colors. A loop made of nichrome wire was fused to the center of the top of the panel to serve as a hanging hook.

The illustration in Plate 59 shows a glass pictorial panel 27½″ × 47½″ made by Kay Kinney, another artist who has done important work exploring the design possibilities of glass. The panel was too large to fire in one piece so sections were cut and fired separately, then fastened to a sheet of base glass with Epoxy cement. This is one of a set of three panels executed in cathedral glass, all vivid and glowing. Kay Kinney's excellent book, *Glass Craft* (also published by Chilton), describes techniques of designing, forming, and decorating in great detail.

Glass designs

Pieces of glass of different colors may be arranged so that they overlap to form a design. When the design has been planned the pieces are put on a kiln shelf that has been given a coating of whiting. The pieces of glass must overlap sufficiently so that, when the kiln is fired to cone 015, the pieces will fuse together and form a solid unit. Interesting abstract designs can be planned this way, or representations of natural objects, birds, or fish like the one shown in Fig. 31 in the color section. A small loop of nichrome wire glued to one of the pieces of glass will fuse into the design and serve as a hanging loop.

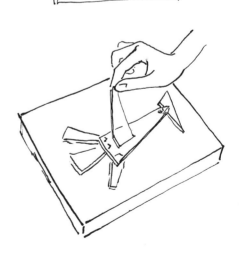

Plate 59 — Glass pictorial panel, 27½″ × 47½″, by Kay Kinney.

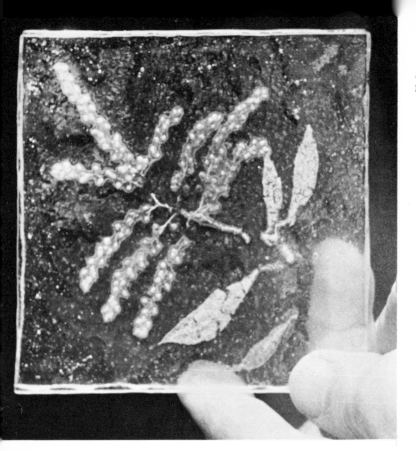

Plate 60—Lamination, a weed fired between layers of glass.

Laminating

Lamination is a process of decorating glass by using two sheets of the same size and putting color or decorative materials between the layers of glass. The designs sandwiched between the two layers may be made by using glass pigments in any of the ways described earlier in this chapter. Materials like fiberglass can be used also. Woven fiberglass dipped into pigment produces interesting results. Shapes cut out of thin copper foil can be used also.

Sections of plants, fern fronds, leaves of trees and other organic materials can be put between layers of glass and fired. The organic material burns out, of course, but it leaves an ash which sometimes produces beautiful ghostlike designs in the glass. Glass treated this way is beginning to appear in contemporary architecture.

Plate 60 shows a bit of weed fired between two glass layers. Experimentation with this technique, trying both fresh and dried plant forms, should prove rewarding.

It is only within the last few years that ceramists have become actively interested in working with glass. There is still much to be learned about the possibilities of this material. Trial and error are the best teachers. Glass has exciting possibilities, well worth the time needed for many trials; it offers a challenge to the ceramist and the designer interested in seeking out the new.

17

Fire

CLAY, when it is plastic, can be modeled into a shape, allowed to dry, broken up, made plastic again and remodeled into an entirely different shape. Once it has been hardened by fire, clay remains hard and brittle forever after.

It is interesting to speculate on how mankind may have discovered this secret—what happy accident may have tumbled some clay-lined basket into a fire where the reeds and fibers of the basket burned away, leaving the lining as a bisqued pot. So often the earliest pieces of pottery produced in primitive civilizations bear, on the outside, lines and decorations suggesting the surface of a basket—perhaps accidents like the one we have imagined occurred many times in many parts of the world.

The clay is fired in kilns that are heated by wood, gas, oil, or electricity. Coal is used, too, in some industrial plants, though rarely by studio potters. Wood-burning kilns do beautiful things to the ware. These kilns are usually of the down-draft type without a muffle; the flames go up and over a baffle wall then down through the center of the kiln and out through openings in the floor to a chimney, enveloping the work as they go. Wood ash is an ingredient of glazes (wood ashes contain potassium) and during the course of the fire a few ashes are bound to land on the ware, usually with good results.

Many of the studio potters of Europe use wood-burning kilns with chambers 30″ × 30″ × 36″ high, or larger. Wood is fed into two side fireplaces, each of which has two levels. The lower level is used for the "petit feu," or small fire, which burns for seven or eight hours. The higher level is for the "grand feu," a much hotter fire, which burns for several hours more, until the kiln reaches the proper temperature.

Wood-burning kilns are not used much in this country because of the problem of getting enough wood (it takes over a cord of wood to fire a kiln like the one just described) and because of the high cost of this fuel.

Gas kilns are efficient, especially in a region that has a supply of natural gas. These kilns may be either of the muffle type or of the down-draft type. In a muffle kiln, the ware is placed in a chamber protected from all contact with the flames. Ware can be protected from the flames in down-

Up draft kiln

Down draft kiln

Fire places

draft kilns also if the pieces are fired in "saggers," clay boxes made of a highly refractory clay called sagger clay.

Oil-burning kilns, like gas kilns, may be of either muffle or down-draft type.

Kilns that burn fuel need chimneys, something to consider in the choice of a kiln. Another thing to think of is safety; where there is fire there is danger, and where you are using gas you must beware of the hazards of explosions.

The electric kiln is the type most popular with studio potters—it needs no chimney, it is easier to operate, it is safer. For schools especially, electric kilns are the best choice because of the automatic safeguards that can be used with them; devices for turning off the kiln after a particular period of time or when the desired temperature has been reached, so that if the person watching the kiln forgets, no harm is done.

Electric kilns are heated by elements. The three most common types are nichrome, which can be used for temperatures up to 2000°F., Kanthal, which can go up to 2300°F., and Globar, which can go up to 2700°F. or cone 15, the temperature of high-fired porcelain. Nichrome and Kanthal are wires. Globar is a carborundum compound, a silicon carbide in the form of a bar. Globar kilns have a temperature range beyond the needs of most studio potters. Such kilns require special electrical installation and special transformers. Kilns with nichrome wire elements will fire most studio work satisfactorily, but there is an advantage in having a kiln with a higher range. For general studio purposes a kiln with Kanthal wire elements is the best choice.

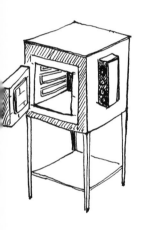

Electric kilns come in top-loading and front-loading styles. A top loader as a rule costs a little less than a front loader and is easier to stack. The choice between these two types of kilns is a matter of personal preference. A chamber 16″ × 16″ × 16″ is a good size—anything smaller wastes a lot of time in loading and unloading. A much bigger kiln is usually not necessary unless a great deal of production work is to be done. Even where more kiln space is needed, two or three kilns of medium size are apt to prove more useful than 1 enormous kiln.

Stacking

It is disheartening to have a piece of work on which one has spent a great deal of time come out of the kiln ruined—broken by an explosion, stuck fast to another piece, or hopelessly marred by fragments that have fallen into the glaze. Heartbreaking accidents like these can be prevented by care and common sense in loading and firing.

Clays mature at different temperatures, so do glazes. All of the pieces put into a kiln at the same time must have about the same maturing point.

Pieces of raw ware must be closely inspected to make sure they are thoroughly dry before they are allowed in the kiln. Anything the least bit damp must be excluded—such pieces will blow up in the firing and ruin other things in the kiln. Hold a piece to your cheek; if it feels cool it is not dry enough. Clay needs time to dry out properly and three or four days should elapse between the forming of a piece and its firing. Unfired clay

is never absolutely dry, for it absorbs moisture from the humidity of the atmosphere. It is a good plan to put such ware under an infrared lamp for one or two hours before it goes into the kiln. Any clay shape with walls more than 1″ thick should be excluded from the kiln also, unless you are sure that it contains a high proportion of coarse grog.

Pieces that are not glazed may touch each other; if stacked judiciously they may be piled one on top of another. Care must be taken, however, to avoid uneven strains that would cause a piece to break or warp, and an unfired clay shape must not be called upon to support too heavy a load. A pair of cups or bowls of the same size may be "boxed," that is, one may be turned upside down with its rim resting on the rim of the other.

A kiln must never be loaded haphazardly. Plan your shelf-loads on a table, arranging pieces of similar height on the same shelf. Room must be left for the circulation of air around pieces and nothing must be put into a kiln so that it touches an element.

Before stacking glazed pieces, examine the inside of the kiln and brush it clean. Pay special attention to the roof—brush it with a soft brush to get rid of any loose fragments of brick that might drop into glazes.

Kiln shelves and kiln floor must be given a coating of kiln wash, a mixture of equal parts china clay and flint mixed with enough water to make a liquid of creamlike consistency. Use kiln wash on only one side of kiln shelves. The reason for this is that the underside of the shelf must never contain any old kiln wash to fall off and ruin ware. It is not necessary to apply kiln wash to a shelf each time it is used, but if any drops of glaze do land on the shelf and stick fast, they must be ground off and the spots brushed with kiln wash before the shelf is used again.

Glazed pieces must be subjected to careful scrutiny. They should be dry footed—that is, glaze must be scraped away from the rim on which the piece stands. A glazed piece should not be put into the kiln unless the glaze is one which has been tested previously. This is to avoid the trouble that occurs when, through a mistake in the recipe, a glaze is too fluid and runs off the piece onto the shelf, gluing the piece and other pieces fast.

Once-fired pieces, that is, greenware to which a coating of glaze has been applied, must be examined closely to make sure that ample time has been allowed for thorough drying.

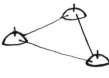

Glazed pieces that cannot be dry footed must be placed on stilts. There are many sizes and shapes of stilts—some with clay points, others with wire points. The latter are better to use for plates because they make smaller blemishes in the glaze. When putting pieces on stilts make sure they are stable, not apt to tip over and lean against something else. Kiln space should be used as efficiently as possible, but glazed pieces must not be crowded to the point where there is danger of touching. Handle glazed ware carefully, don't knock off bits of glaze, and don't let a piece brush against another at any time so that glaze rubs off one piece onto the other. Plan shelf arrangements beforehand so that glazed pieces can be put in place directly without any shifting about.

21

Temperature measurement

Kiln temperatures are measured by cones or pyrometers. Pyrometric cones are made of clay to which fluxes have been added in such amounts that the cones become soft at known temperatures. Cones have numbers stamped in them to indicate their bending temperatures. These numbers range from 022 for the lowest temperature through cone 15, the temperature of high-fire porcelain. (A table of cone temperatures is given at the beginning of the Appendix.) Most potters think of temperatures in terms of cones—they speak, for example, of a low-fire glaze as a cone 08 glaze or of stoneware clay as a cone 4 body.

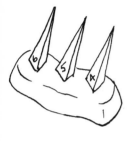

In use, cones are set in a wad of clay called a "cone pat," made of clay with coarse grog in it to keep it from blowing up in the kiln. Usually 3 cones are set in a row, slanting in the direction in which they will bend. If, for example, a potter intends to fire his kiln to cone 5, he sets 3 cones in the cone pat—numbers 4, 5, and 6. He sets the cones so that they slant to the right, with cone 4 at the right end of the row since this bends first. Cone 5 is in the middle and cone 6 at the other end.

The cone pat is placed in the kiln so that it can be seen through the peephole. As the temperature of the kiln gets close to the desired temperature, cone 4 starts to bend. This is a warning signal. The potter watches closely until cone 5 bends, and at this point turns off the kiln. If cone 6 remains standing it indicates that the kiln was not overfired.

The table of cone temperatures in the Appendix shows the color range of the kiln chamber during the firing and describes some of the things that happen in the kiln. The temperatures indicated in this table are for a comparatively rapid firing cycle or about 300°F. per hour. At a slower firing rate the cones would bend at slightly lower temperatures.

Pyrometers are devices for measuring kiln temperatures by means of a thermocouple. Pyrometers are convenient to have, especially on electric kilns where they can be combined with automatic cutoff devices which turn off the kiln when the maturing temperature has been reached.

Another automatic device that is good to have on electric kilns, especially in schools, is a timer which turns off the kiln after a set time has elapsed. This is an additional safety precaution which works if the temperature cutoff fails to operate.

The firing cycle

Plastic clay contains water of plasticity. When clay has become bone dry, it no longer has such water in it but it does have moisture that it absorbs from the atmosphere. During the first part of the firing, called the "water smoking" period, we must permit this moisture to escape. The temperature of the kiln should be raised slowly and a vent or a door should be left open so that the steam can get out. In a down-draft kiln the steam goes up the chimney. When the kiln temperature has risen to 300°F. the water smoking period has been completed. The next change in the clay comes when the chemically combined water leaves, just before the clay gets red-hot, a little under 1000°F. If the kiln has any large pieces in it, the firing should be slow up to this point. It should take well over four hours to reach complete dehydration.

As the kiln gets hotter, the chamber will start to glow at about 1100°F. and you will be able to look through the peephole and see things (electric kilns are different in this respect because the elements glow and light the inside so that you can see into the chamber of an electric kiln long before it gets hot).

A kiln loaded with only bisque pieces may be fired more rapidly above 1200°F. A kiln with glazed pieces in it must go more slowly. A kiln loaded with only glazed ware may be fired more rapidly at the beginning, but must be slower at the end. A diagram of a firing schedule for glazed ware and bisque ware is given in the Appendix.

After the proper temperature has been reached, the kiln must be turned off and the cooling process starts. In fuel-burning kilns the damper should be left open for a few minutes to permit the escape of gases, then closed tightly. With electric kilns this step is not necessary. Cooling should be as slow as possible. It should take as long for a kiln to cool as it does for it to get hot. Don't hurry. Even the smallest electric kiln should be allowed to cool overnight before the door is opened. Larger kilns take longer. *Do not* remove a piece from the kiln until it is cool enough to be picked up with the bare hands.

Reduction

Combustion is a process of oxidation. When a fuel burns, the carbon in it combines with oxygen to form carbon dioxide (CO_2). When there is an insufficient supply of oxygen, combustion is incomplete; since there is not enough oxygen to combine with all the carbon, carbon monoxide (CO) is formed and free carbon is liberated. We see this carbon as black smoke.

Carbon is a glutton for oxygen and seizes all it can lay hold of. When there is a large amount of free carbon in a kiln the mineral oxides in glazes and clay bodies are reduced to compounds of lower oxide content, sometimes to their metallic forms. In the case of iron and copper, the reduced oxide forms make drastic changes of color in the glazes, often producing effects of great beauty. Red iron oxide (Fe_2O_3), for example, in an oxidizing fire is shades of brown or tan; in a reducing fire it changes to black iron oxide (FeO) producing the delightful pale cool greens of celadon. Copper oxide (CuO) which we know as a reliable source of greens and blues, in reduction turns to cuprous oxide (Cu_2O) or to metallic copper (Cu) and produces the beautiful tones of red called "sang de boeuf," "flambé," and "peach bloom."

Other metallic oxides are not greatly changed in color by reduction, but all glazes are affected by it. High-fire leadless glazes are made more lustrous, given a more satiny quality. Low-fire lead glazes are marred by blisters. (Not always ruined, let us hasten to add—some potters deliberately produce such blistering for the rugged quality it imparts to their ware.)

Reduction changes the color of clay bodies that contain iron. Stoneware which would be brown or tan in an oxidizing fire becomes a cool gray when reduced, and red clay turns black. The bucchero ware shown in Plate 61 is an example of color produced by reduction. This vase was thrown of a common red clay, was burnished when it was leather hard by

Plate 61—Bucchero ware, made in the pottery town of Gubbio, Italy.

rubbing the surface with a smooth wooden tool. A design was made on the surface by a sgraffito technique, scratching through to the unburnished surface beneath. The vase was fired in a wood-burning kiln. When the temperature reached maturity, granular charcoal was shoveled into the kiln chamber and the dampers were closed. This reduction made the surface of the vase a beautiful satiny black, except in the area of the sgraffito design where the dull black surface of the unburnished clay made an interesting contrast. Sometimes soluble salts of silver or gold are brushed over these unburnished areas before the pieces are fired. This heightens the contrast.

It is not difficult to bring about reduction in any fuel-burning kiln—it is merely necessary to cut down on the air supply so that the flame becomes yellow instead of blue, and to close the dampers. This will fill the kiln with smoke—the kiln room as well, but that is to be expected. The point in the firing cycle where the reduction takes place is important. Sometimes the effects produced by reduction are lost when the kiln, upon cooling, oxidizes again. The manipulation of a reducing fire is something a potter learns how to do with much practice. This is where having one's own kiln is important.

Most of the work by Derval illustrated in this book shows the effects of reduction; the red in the platter by this artist shown in Fig. 11 in the color section was produced by copper in reduction. Derval puts small amounts of lead into his glazes to produce the blistering effects referred to above.

Reduction is difficult to avoid in fuel-burning kilns, especially those fired with wood. In electric kilns, on the contrary, reduction is difficult to produce. It can be brought about by introducing organic material such as pine splinters or mothballs into the chamber, through the peephole, when the temperature has reached its highest point. Such reduction in an electric kiln is interesting to experiment with once in a while, but if one plans to do much work with reduction glazes it is necessary to have a kiln that burns fuel.

Here are some recipes for reduction glazes.

Copper red glaze, cone 9

Feldspar	36
Flint	36
Calcined borax	10
Whiting	15
Tin oxide	2
Bentonite	1
Copper carbonate	0.5

Celadon glaze, cone 11

Feldspar	25
Flint	35
Whiting	20
China clay	20

Add for celadon—iron oxide 1
    for olive-green celadon—iron oxide 2
(*Note:* The addition of 10% of iron oxide to this glaze will produce a saturated iron red.)

The two recipes above require reduction in the kiln. Here is a recipe for "artificial reduction" in which a reducing agent, carborundum (silicon carbide), is put into the glaze. This eliminates the need of reducing the kiln.

Copper red glaze, cone 2 (no reduction)

Feldspar	34
Flint	17
China clay	13
Calcined borax	27
Fluorspar	6
Soda ash	1
Tin oxide	2
Carborundum 180 mesh	0.5
Copper carbonate	0.5

We spoke about salt glazing in Chapter 15 and pointed out that this must be done in a kiln reserved for this purpose. The kiln should be of a down-draft type that burns fuel. Dampened salt in paper bags is tossed into the flame while the kiln is firing. The salt volatilizes and combines with the silica in the clay to form a hard sodium silicate glaze. Salt glazing when combined with reduction produces ware of a special quality and charm. The sculpture of Jean and Jacqueline Lerat shown in this book is fired in a wood-burning kiln, reduced and salt glazed. Plate 62 shows a portion of their kiln in the process of being stacked.

Ceramists who do not have facilities for salt glazing in their own studios are able, at times, to have pieces fired for them in the salt-glazing kilns of industrial plants that manufacture heavy building products, sewer pipe and the like.

While we are speaking of sculpture, mention should be made of a type of electric kiln that is good for firing tall pieces. This is a hexagonal kiln which can be made taller by adding sectional rings.

Tunnel kilns

All of the kilns we have described so far are of the "periodic" type. That means they are loaded, fired, cooled, unloaded, then loaded and fired again. A tunnel kiln, on the other hand, operates continuously. The ware is placed on a moving platform that travels very slowly through a tunnel. As it enters the tunnel, the ware is subjected to a low heat. Continuing on its journey, the ware encounters temperatures that rise gradually until, in the center of the tunnel, the ware reaches its full maturing temperature. From this point on, the temperature decreases and the ware cools, until, as it emerges from the other end of the tunnel, the ware is cool enough to be picked up in the hands. It takes more than 24 hours, as a rule, for a piece to complete its journey through such a kiln.

Tunnel kilns are usually found only in large industrial plants, although occasionally a studio potter who produces a line of ware has found it practical to install a smaller model of this type in his plant.

In all of his work with clay, the potter must keep the fire in mind. The temperature to which he will fire his pieces must be considered when he plans their shape; for high-fired work, for example, he must design shapes that can resist slumping. The color changes produced by the fire in clays must be kept in mind, and the action of the fire on glazes.

Motor and pusher

Plate 62—Figures. Wheel-thrown sculpture by Jacqueline Lerat. *Photograph by H. Malvaux.*

The potter should work with his own kiln and fire his own ware. If someone else fires his pieces for him, part of the designing process is taken out of his hands. The potter must know his kiln intimately, be aware of all of its quirks of behavior, be able to control the temperature at all times, and bring about reduction when he wishes to do so. The fire is an important element of ceramic design.

18
Draw

ANYONE who works with clay should draw. Through drawing, the ceramist records what he sees, makes notes of ideas, shapes, and designs, and plans pieces he will make.

We often hear someone say, "I can't draw a straight line." It is not true, of course; anyone who wants to can draw a straight line, although there is no particular virtue in that. Everyone can draw much more than a straight line.

Drawing is a language, a way of conveying ideas. All of us can use it. Watch a child when he is drawing; with absolute confidence he draws a man, a house, or a tree, and we have no doubt at all what it is that he is saying to us. Why do some of us lose the ability to speak through drawing as we grow older? Is it because we are intimidated, frightened by the very finished, highly detailed, almost photographic drawings of some professional artists which we see all around us? Perhaps it is. In that case, all we need do to speak through drawing is to get rid of our timidity, get back the confidence of the child. When we wish to express an idea by means of lines on a piece of paper, all we have to do is *do it*.

Drawing is not merely copying things and it does not have to be accurate, correct in perspective, or complete in detail. A good way to begin drawing is to make quick sketches of things you see. Draw people, birds, trees, houses. Draw them simply; suggest the idea of the thing with as few lines as possible. Keep a sketchbook and use it frequently.

If you have a pet animal in your home, sketch it in different poses. Draw it in motion and then draw it again when it is asleep or sitting still. Walk around it and draw it from different viewpoints.

Practice

Facility in drawing comes with lots of practice and there are many exercises that one should try. These give strength in drawing and aid in developing acuteness of observation. The exercises are fun too.

Here are some exercises to try:

• Look at an object for a few minutes, then draw it with your eyes closed.

• Make a drawing of some familiar object without looking at it—a telephone, an umbrella, a bicycle.

• A warm-up exercise—stretch your arm out at full length and draw with your fingers in the air. Write your name in the air. Write it backward.

• Make memory drawings of people doing things; a man eating a sandwich, a child skipping rope, a musician with his musical instrument.

• Draw on a blackboard. (Every potter's studio should have a blackboard, as well as a bulletin board of some type on which ideas can be displayed.) Draw with the arm at full length. Draw large, with bold, sweeping, continuous lines. Don't make corrections; when something is not right, rub it out and do it again. Drawing on a blackboard lets you see your drawings as negatives—white lines on a black background—so that you get a different view, a different understanding of the things you draw.

• Draw with pencil. Draw with pen and ink also. Draw with a brush. Use pointed brushes of different sizes. Make brush drawings on large sheets of paper (the classified page of the Sunday newspaper is good). Practice brushstrokes. Make lines that are expressive of the shapes they outline. Use the Oriental style of brush drawing. Make a bird out of three dots (head, eye, beak) and three lines (body, wing, tail).

• Make brush drawings of trees and animals. Draw flowers by touching the brush to the paper just once to make the shape of a petal.

• Experiment with halftones. In a saucer put a few drops of water and add a drop of ink. Use this mid-tone between black and white to help in a suggestion of roundness and solidity in forms.

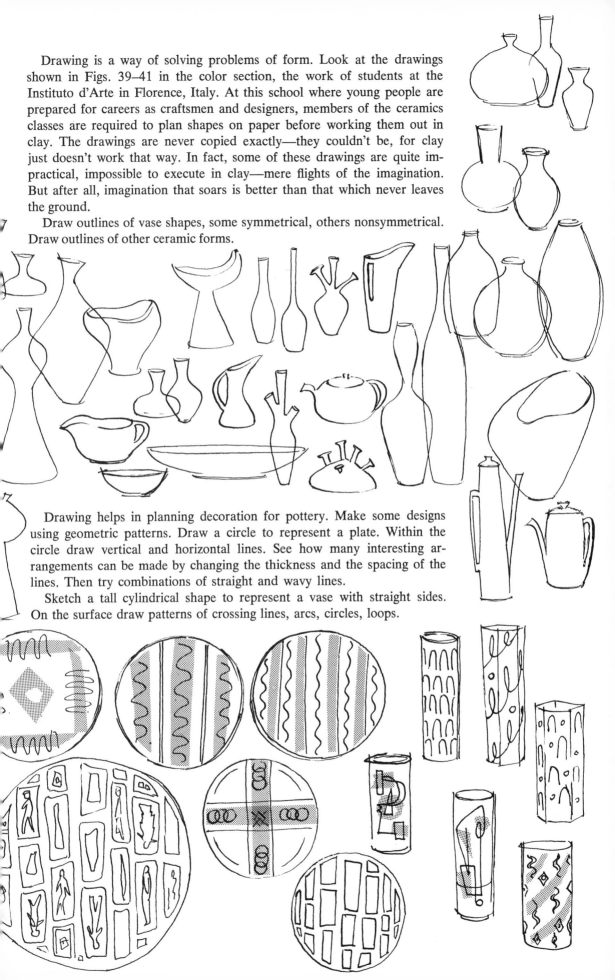

Drawing is a way of solving problems of form. Look at the drawings shown in Figs. 39–41 in the color section, the work of students at the Instituto d'Arte in Florence, Italy. At this school where young people are prepared for careers as craftsmen and designers, members of the ceramics classes are required to plan shapes on paper before working them out in clay. The drawings are never copied exactly—they couldn't be, for clay just doesn't work that way. In fact, some of these drawings are quite impractical, impossible to execute in clay—mere flights of the imagination. But after all, imagination that soars is better than that which never leaves the ground.

Draw outlines of vase shapes, some symmetrical, others nonsymmetrical. Draw outlines of other ceramic forms.

Drawing helps in planning decoration for pottery. Make some designs using geometric patterns. Draw a circle to represent a plate. Within the circle draw vertical and horizontal lines. See how many interesting arrangements can be made by changing the thickness and the spacing of the lines. Then try combinations of straight and wavy lines.

Sketch a tall cylindrical shape to represent a vase with straight sides. On the surface draw patterns of crossing lines, arcs, circles, loops.

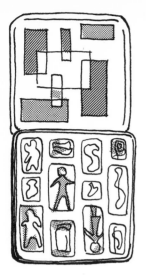

Draw a number of squares 6″ wide with slightly rounded corners to represent square plates. Within these areas make designs of rectangles of different sizes and shapes. Use contrasting areas of dark and light within some of the rectangles. Have some rectangles overlap others. Try patterns of rectangles with figures inside them. Use rectangles and circles, or elliptical shapes. Try many more varieties of shapes, some of them geometric, others the shapes of things.

Sketch more squares, this time without rounded corners. These will represent tiles. Draw a leaf in simple outline. Cut it out. Use this cut-out leaf as a stencil. Put it on the square which represents the tile, dip a sponge in pigment, and dab around the edges. Do this a number of times, moving the shape around in the square.

Take a piece of paper from which the shape was cut. Use it as a stencil, dabbing the area with a sponge.

Cut out other shapes—the outline of a piece of fruit, a flower, or a bird. Cut out some geometric patterns—squares and triangles. Use these as patterns and dab with a sponge around the edges. Make the shapes overlap. See what interesting patterns can be created by changes of tone within the overlapped areas.

Draw birds as designs. Draw real ones and imaginary ones. Birds are a fascinating subject for potters—note how many of the artists whose work is shown in this book have used birds for inspiration, and note, too, how completely individual all of their birds are. Draw bird designs inside of squares. Divide the spaces around the birds into interesting shapes. Hold the paper sidewise and upside down to judge the effectiveness of the space divisions.

Collect weeds. Draw them. Look for design patterns in their leaves and in the seed pods. Cut a seed pod in half. Make a design from it.

Collect seashells. Draw them. Draw the perfect ones that have rhythm and symmetry. Draw the broken ones too, those that startle us with unexpected shapes.

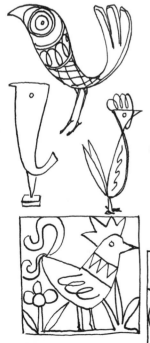

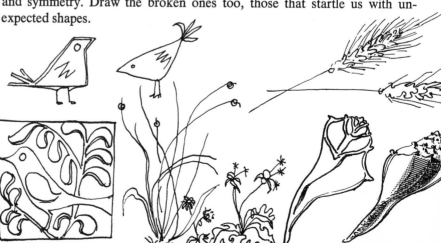

Draw animals in simple outline. How many ways can you draw a cat? —not a real cat, correct in anatomical detail, but a design-type cat. Draw other animals in a similar way.

Draw flowers realistically, then draw them in decorative, simple design. Turn the designs into abstractions. Make arrangements of flower and leaf shapes within a rectangle. Have some of the areas overlap. Fill areas with contrasting tones and patterns.

Draw people as design. Make them as nonrealistic as you can, yet recognizable as people. Draw a row of circles touching one another, then turn these into people.

Make a sketch for a design using a locomotive, or an automobile. Look at the group of cyclists by Jean Lerat shown in Fig. 20 in the color section. Imagine the sketches that were made for this piece.

Draw a series of designs for a tile using a man on horseback as your motif.

Make another series using a simple landscape, a farm scene or a house with two trees. Make a series of designs using buildings of a modern city, or buildings of antiquity.

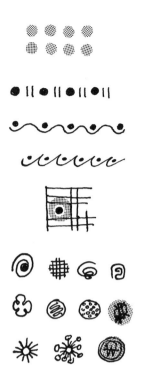

Dots are important elements in design. They do exciting things to arrangements of line and space. A dot is a point of emphasis. A dot is an eye. A dot can make a shape come alive.

Put dots on sketches of pottery forms. Use dots in combination with lines. Add dots to some of your drawings for plate and tile designs.

A way of making dots: use the eraser on the end of a new pencil as a rubber stamp, ink it on a stamp pad and press it on paper. (*Note:* When you make designs on pottery you can make a ceramic ink by mixing black underglaze color and glycerine. You can make a stamp pad with this kind of ink so that designs can be stamped directly on ware which is to be fired.)

A wandering line creates design. Touch your pencil to paper and move it about, returning to the starting place without crossing the path. The line has enclosed an area. Do this many times, letting the pencil move at times with a smooth flowing motion, sometimes with jagged zigzags. See if shapes develop that are new and interesting.

Do it again, this time crossing the line a few times before getting back to the starting point. Here are a number of patterns. Fill in some of the areas with contrasting tones.

Fill a sheet of paper, about 12″ × 14″ or slightly larger, with wandering lines. Cut an opening 3″ square in another piece of paper (use black paper and leave ample margins around the opening). Use the second sheet as a "design finder" by moving it about over the larger sheet with the drawings on it. Some of the patterns that appear in the opening may be interesting—worth keeping for use in decorating a tile. Try this again, this time filling the first sheet with intersecting rectangles of different sizes.

Draw a series of shapes inside of other shapes. Add dots to some of the shapes and areas that have been developed.

What we have done with lines is not mere doodling, it is serious exploration in design. Out of many pages filled with experiments like these will come a few original shapes good for use as ceramic forms or as ceramic decorations.

Explore the possibilities of radiating design. Make drawings that radiate from a line, the way leaves of a plant radiate from the stem. Make designs that spring from a point like the beams of a star or the rays of the sun. Try designs that radiate from a circle like the sparks of a pinwheel. Work within a rectangle, making lines radiate from a point not the center.

Experiment with symmetry. Make symmetrical designs and fill areas with contrasting tones. Draw symmetrical designs like those we see in the king, queen, and jack of a deck of cards where the lower half is the same as the upper half but inverted. Make a design suitable for an oval platter, using two fish.

In searching for symmetry, hold a small mirror edgewise against the page on which you have let your pencil wander and move the mirror about slowly. Sketch some of the symmetrical designs discovered this way.

Experiment with the kind of symmetry that is in the designs one sees in a kaleidoscope. Here an arrangement of lines and shapes, by being reversed and repeated a number of times, produces fantastic and unexpected results. Designs of this type can be made by folding a piece of paper in half, then in half again so that four quadrants are formed. Each quadrant is folded diagonally so that it becomes two triangles. A design is drawn in one of these triangles. The paper is folded on the diagonal crease, the design is rubbed on the back with a blunt tool (the handle of a knife) so that it is transferred, reversed, to the other half of the quadrant. The first quadrant now contains a design that is symmetrical about the diagonal. The paper is folded on the original fold, the design in the first quadrant is rubbed on the back and transferred to the second quadrant. The paper is unfolded and folded once again on the second crease so that the designs in the first and second quadrant can be transferred to the third and fourth

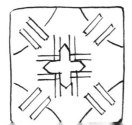

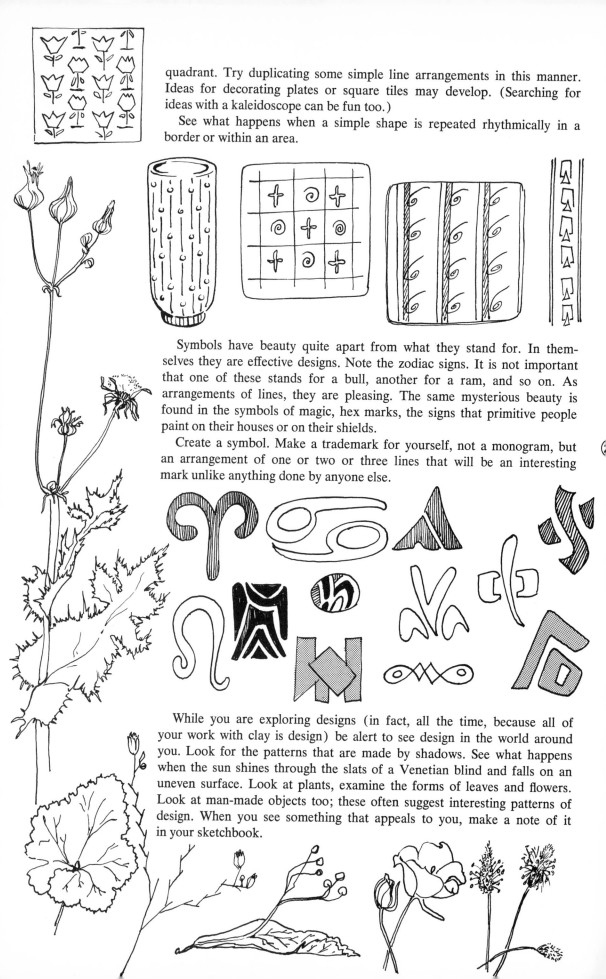

quadrant. Try duplicating some simple line arrangements in this manner. Ideas for decorating plates or square tiles may develop. (Searching for ideas with a kaleidoscope can be fun too.)

See what happens when a simple shape is repeated rhythmically in a border or within an area.

Symbols have beauty quite apart from what they stand for. In themselves they are effective designs. Note the zodiac signs. It is not important that one of these stands for a bull, another for a ram, and so on. As arrangements of lines, they are pleasing. The same mysterious beauty is found in the symbols of magic, hex marks, the signs that primitive people paint on their houses or on their shields.

Create a symbol. Make a trademark for yourself, not a monogram, but an arrangement of one or two or three lines that will be an interesting mark unlike anything done by anyone else.

While you are exploring designs (in fact, all the time, because all of your work with clay is design) be alert to see design in the world around you. Look for the patterns that are made by shadows. See what happens when the sun shines through the slats of a Venetian blind and falls on an uneven surface. Look at plants, examine the forms of leaves and flowers. Look at man-made objects too; these often suggest interesting patterns of design. When you see something that appeals to you, make a note of it in your sketchbook.

Plate 63—Ceramist Braun, sitting on the steps leading to his Paris studio, studies a page in his sketchbook. The piece made from this sketch is shown.

We speak a great deal about creativity. We urge people to be creative, but are we sure just what creativity is? Is it something that people are born with, or is it something that can be acquired? Can a person study and make himself creative?

There is no doubt that creativity is an inborn thing. Some people have more than others, but it is present to a degree in all of us. It can be encouraged. It can be developed. One thing that must be done to encourage it is to remove the blocks that stand in its way; get rid of timidity, acquire self-confidence.

Creativity does not grow by itself, it comes through doing things. Creativity in design develops with exercise. Make many, many designs.

Your sketches are for your eyes alone. Look at them frequently to see where you have succeeded in capturing the spirit of things with economy of line. Restudy the designs you made a few weeks ago, notice how your understanding of design has grown.

Take good care of your sketchbook. It is valuable. Besides giving you pleasure, it will prove a rich source of inspiration and ideas. It is your best teacher of design.

19

Decorate

Now that we have spent considerable time making drawings on paper, let's put some of our designs on clay. After all, that is the purpose for which we made them. We have spoken about methods of decorating clay during the process of forming it by carving, making textures, pressing in designs, and other ways. We are ready now to decorate with color.

Is it right to put pictures on pots? The ancient Greeks did it and the Egyptians did it even earlier. At times these artists of antiquity made their pottery serve as mere backgrounds for painting. Most of their work, however, shows a beautiful relationship between shape and surface decoration, with form and color complementing each other.

But we do not have to seek justification from the potters of long ago for decorating the things we make out of clay, nor from anyone else for that matter. If we like pictures on pots and enjoy painting them, that is sufficient.

The techniques of decorating pottery are quite simple, easily mastered. What is important is planning the designs to use. Here is where the drawings in our sketchbook prove helpful. The materials and the methods of decorating help, too, and so do the tools. Brushes, pens, cutting tools, spray guns, sponges—all of these play their parts in developing the final

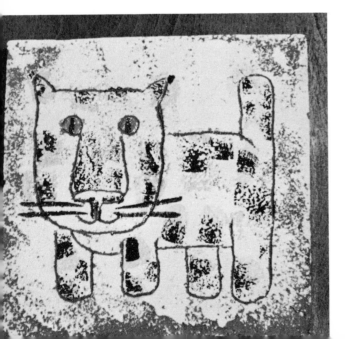

Plate 64—Tile, red clay sponged with buff engobe, dabs of color brushed on, design made by sgraffito.

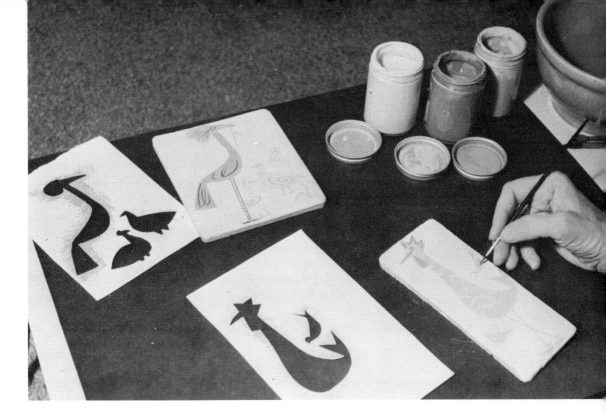

Plate 65—Using stencils. Color has been dabbed with a sponge through the openings in stencils. Details are added with a brush.

design; for decorations on pottery are never exactly like preliminary sketches made for them, designs evolve in the doing.

Let us examine some decorating techniques, starting with methods that use engobe.

Slip painting

The simplest way to decorate pottery is to paint designs on it with a slip of contrasting color. This is quite different from painting with oil or watercolors. Slip is viscous, difficult to handle with a brush; delicate thin lines are practically impossible. Designs must be planned so that they can be made with bold free brushstrokes. A few drops of glycerine will make it easier to paint.

Sponge

Instead of putting a design on with a brush, we can use a sponge. The sponge is dipped into slip and dabbed on the ware. Interesting textures can be achieved this way.

Stencils

Designs may be cut out of paper and then a sponge can be dabbed through the opening to reproduce the design on the ware.

Masks

This is the reverse of the stencil. A shape is cut out of paper and laid on the ware and then a sponge dipped in engobe is dabbed on the ware

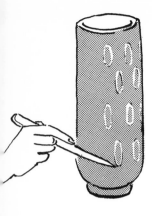

around the outline of the mask so that the portion under the mask remains uncolored. The mask should be cut out of fairly tough paper and should be dampened slightly so that it lies flat on the ware. Paper towels are good to use.

Sgraffito

This is a method of scratching designs in a layer of engobe so that the color of the clay underneath shows through. The scratching may be done while the engobe is damp or after the engobe is dry. A different quality of line results in each case. The tool used for sgraffito work may be a pen, a pointed wooden modeling tool, a nail file, in fact almost anything which you can scratch with. The selection of the tool will determine the quality of the line. It is most important to be free and bold in using the sgraffito tool. A line must be made in a single stroke and then not touched again.

Spatter

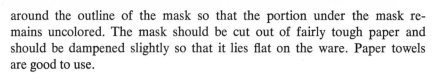

Engobe can be spattered on ware by dipping a stiff-bristle brush into the engobe and then drawing a knife blade across the bristles in a direction away from the ware. A different type of spatter can be done with a soft-haired brush. Dip it into the engobe and then shake it at the piece.

Thread

⟨238⟩

A special type of line design (see illustration in Plate 66) can be made with heavy thread. The thread is dipped in gum tragacanth or some other gum useful in applying glazes, then laid on the ware. After this, engobe is sprayed or spattered on the piece. The thread, when it is removed, leaves a thin line in the color of the body.

Another way of using thread is to dip it in a colored engobe with gum added, then put it on the ware and leave it in place when the piece goes into the kiln. The thread will burn out but the line of color will remain on the ware.

Wax resist

This technique involves painting a design with liquid wax. It used to be necessary for ceramists to heat paraffin and work with it while it was hot in order to make wax-resist designs. That was a rather difficult job which usually ruined the artist's brushes. Today, however, a wax emulsion is available for the potter. This is wax in liquid form that can be easily applied with a brush. The brush can then be rinsed with water. After the design is painted on in wax, engobe is sprayed or brushed or dabbed on the piece. Wherever there is wax the engobe will be repelled and so after the piece is fired and the wax has burned away, the design that was brushed in wax shows the color of the body while the surrounding area has the color of the engobe. A sgraffito design may be scratched through the wax before the engobe is applied so that the sgraffito line will show in the color of the engobe.

All of the techniques described above may be used with the engobe applied either to leather-hard clay or to bone-dry clay or to clay that has been bisqued. It is important to make sure that the engobe used is right for the particular kind of clay it is being applied to (see the notes on this in Chapter 14).

The techniques described above produce the best results when they are used in combination. For example, a design may be painted and then a thin line design scratched through it. The contrast in techniques will give interesting design quality. Decorations made by spatter through a stencil may be accented by brushstrokes. Designs which are a combination of brushwork and sponge with sgraffito accents are good.

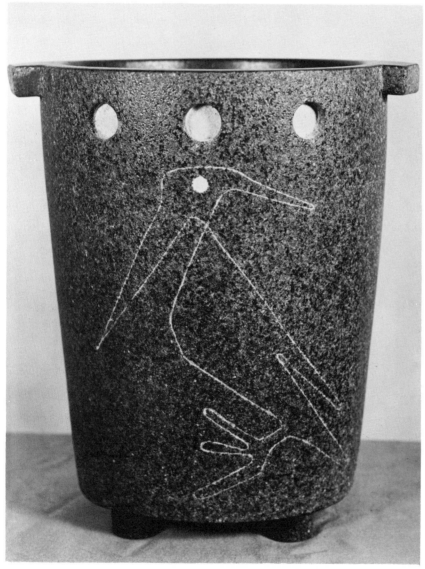

Plate 66—Vase, 21″ high, by Rolf Key-Oberg. Thread decoration. *Photograph by Soichi Sunami.*

Plate 67—Six-foot stoneware vase by F. Carlton Ball of the University of Southern California. This piece was thrown in 11 sections and fired to cone 10 in a reduction atmosphere. It weighs 125 lbs.

The piece was glazed with a white satin mat glaze. The design was then applied with wax on the unfired glaze, after which red iron oxide was applied over both glaze and wax.

Decorating a plate

Engobe is applied to a bisqued plate with a sponge.

Lines of color are brushed over the engobe.

(241)

Sgraffito. A drawing is scratched through the layer of engobe with a pointed wooden tool.

Details are added with a brush.

Mishima

This technique, mentioned in Chapter 12, is another method of engobe decoration, a type of inlay shown in Plate 68. A decoration is incised in leather-hard ware, then the line is filled with engobe of a contrasting color. Excess engobe is scraped off so that the incised line shows the color of the engobe.

Slip trailing

This method shown in Plate 69 uses a syringe to squeeze a line of engobe onto clay. Small plastic mustard dispensers are excellent for this. Slip-trailed designs are unlike any other. The design comes out as a raised line. The method lends itself to free and gay decorations.

The method of slip trailing can be used to produce inlaid designs. After a decoration has been put on a piece of clay as a raised line, the clay may be turned over on a plaster slab and pressed so that the design sinks into the surface of the clay. It is a simple matter to do this on a tile if the clay is fairly soft. It can be done also on a layer of clay which is to be draped over a drape mold or even on a layer of clay which is to be used in slab building. Here are the steps.

Plate 68—Mishima. Black clay tile with incised design, white engobe inlaid.

58. *Above*. Stairwell in a beauty salon, Florence, Nello Bini.

59. *Above*. Portion of mural on the shop of Giardini, Pesaro, Italy.

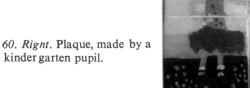

60. *Right*. Plaque, made by a kindergarten pupil.

61. *Below*. Portion of mosaic on the home of Leonardo Ricci, Florence.

62. *Right*. Plaques, raised line designs, Fantoni.

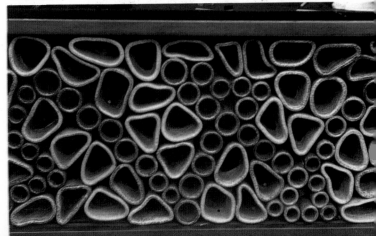

63. *Below*. Ceramic Grill under a store window, Florence, Nello Bini.

64. *Above*. Forest Children, patio wall relief, 65 inches long, Rosemary Zwick.

65. *Above*. Head, Pacetti.

66. *Right*. Figure, 60 inches tall, Lucerni.

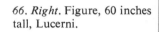

67. *Left*. Sculpture, 5×8 feet, on the Aviary, Cleveland Zoo, Viktor Schreckengost. Executed by the Federal Seaboard Terra Cotta Corp.

68. *Below*. Tile Murals, made by Rene Portocarrero, at the plant of the Federal Seaboard Terra Cotta Corp.

Plate 69—Slip trailing. Slip squeezed from a mustard dispenser makes a design on a clay layer. This will be cut to make a square tile.

PHOTO SERIES 54

Making a cookie jar with an inlaid design

A layer of clay has been rolled and cut to the proper size to wrap around the cylinder shown in the background. This cylinder is a can wrapped in several layers of newspaper. Two discs have been cut also. These will be the top and the bottom of the jar. The clay used is red clay. The mustard dispenser has been loaded with white slip.

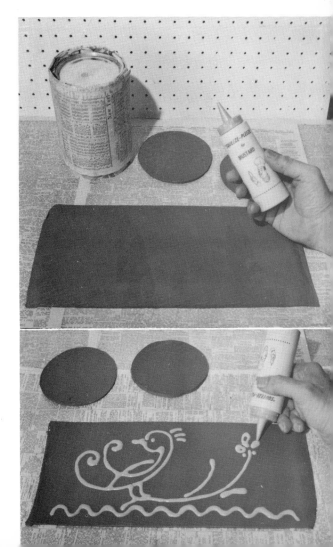

A design is trailed on the clay layer.

A design is trailed on the disc which will be the lid.

The lid is turned face down on a plaster slab and pressed. This makes the design sink into the clay. The same thing will be done with the layer of clay.

Forming the cookie jar. The layer of clay has been wrapped around a temporary support and put on the bottom disc. Sides and bottom are now being welded together. As soon as the clay is firm enough to stand alone, the support will be removed.

A flange is added to the underside of the lid. When this is completed, a loop of clay will be added as a handle.

The completed, glazed cookie jar.

Slip trailing can also be used with drain molds. If slip is trailed on the inside of a drain mold, when the casting slip (which is of a different color, of course) is poured in, it will pick up the trailed design as an inlay. The slip-trailed design should be allowed to harden for a few minutes before the casting slip is poured into the mold.

Combing

Engobe can be combed or feathered while it is wet, a method of decoration popular with the potters who made the Pennsylvania Dutch ware in this country two centuries ago. Engobe is trailed or painted on a wet clay surface and then a tool like a fork or a comb with several teeth missing, or a feather, is dragged through the wet engobe, producing haphazard patterns that are oftentimes pleasing. The method is a good one to use on layers of clay that are to be formed over a drape mold. The design must be made in the engobe while it and the layer it is on are still wet, then the layer must be allowed to dry long enough so that all of the shine disappears. A layer that has been decorated this way is easier to handle if it is formed on a piece of cloth and left on the cloth while the drape

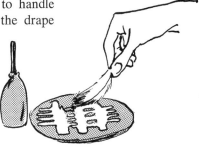

Plate 70—Wheel-thrown forms by Joan Jockwig Pearson. Engobe decoration.

mold is turned upside down and laid in place on top of it. The edges of the cloth are then lifted up so that the layer is pressed around the mold, and mold, layer and cloth are all turned over together. The cloth is carefully peeled off the layer of clay, the clay is pressed on the mold, and the edges of the shape are trimmed.

The decorating wheel

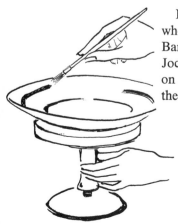

Designs can be made with engobe on pieces while they are spun on a wheel. Concentric circles and spirals can be put on plates and bowls. Bands of color can be put on tall shapes. Note the tea set made by Joan Jockwig Pearson shown in Plate 26. These pieces were put on their sides on a wheel and spirals of slip were painted on as they turned. Note, too, the work of the same artist shown in Plate 70.

Underglaze painting

As the name suggests, this method involves painting on the surface of a piece before it is glazed. The ware to be decorated may be unfired greenware or may be bisqued. Underglaze colors are used. These must be mixed with a flux and with a vehicle. The flux is needed to make the pigments fuse to the ware; the vehicle makes them work properly with a brush. You will need a piece of glass, a small spatula, and one or two small paintbrushes with good points.

With the spatula lift a small quantity of pigment onto the glass (a mound about as big as a pea will do). Then add about the same amount of flux. The flux may be a regular flux made for this purpose, or it may be some of the transparent glaze with which you will cover the piece later. Next a few drops of vehicle. For this, use glycerine and a few drops of water. With the spatula grind pigment, flux, and vehicle together until they form a smooth thick cream. Now you are ready to paint.

The piece must be clean. Your hands must be clean, also, and you must avoid handling the area on which you will paint. Work rapidly with single brushstrokes. Don't go over a line twice. It will take some practice to get just the right brushstroke, so have a number of scraps handy for trials. These scraps must be of the same material as the piece, of course. If you are working on greenware, you may find that the pigment flows better if the ware is slightly damp. Sponge it first. Some potters like to paint the greenware with a weak solution of gum before they start the underglaze decoration.

One advantage of working on greenware is that if you make a mistake you can sponge it off and start fresh. With bisque it is not so easy; once on the ware, the pigment is almost indelible, so get it right the first time.

Various kinds of background treatment are possible with underglaze painting. Before a design is painted on, the ware may be given a flat tone or one with gradations by sponging or spraying or spattering color on the piece. Backgrounds with textural patterns are made by spraying color through coarse cloth. Stencils can be used for background shapes.

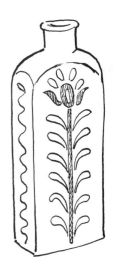

After it has been decorated, the piece must be glazed. Here you have a choice—you may fire the piece first, then apply glaze and fire again, or you may spray glaze directly over the painting and finish the piece with one firing. Firing the decorated piece before glazing seals the design on the ware. It is not necessary to bring the piece to full maturing temperature. About 1200°F. or slightly above red heat will do. This will melt the flux and make the design permanent. After this the piece can be glazed by dipping or brushing, since there is no danger of spoiling the painting.

Overglaze painting (china painting)

This is a method of painting designs on ware which has been glazed and fired. Overglaze pigments are used. These are considerably brighter than underglaze colors, but they must be fired at a lower temperature, about 1600°F., or cone 012. Since the glazed ware has already been fired to maturity, the lower temperature range of the pigments does not matter.

Plate 71—Overglaze painting. A design is made on top of a fired glazed bird.

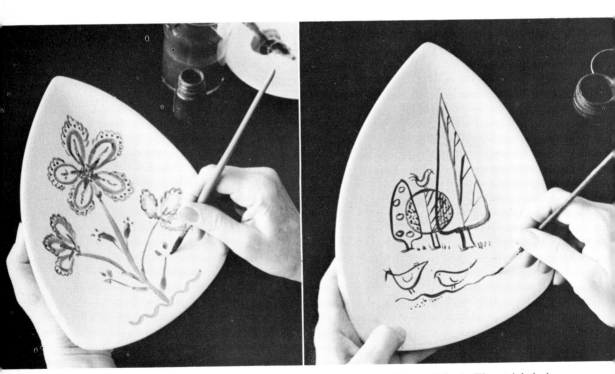

Plate 72—Overglaze decorations tried on free-form solid-cast dish. 1. First trial design. 2. First trial removed, second design painted.

The palette of overglaze colors includes brilliant reds and shades of purple difficult to obtain from other sources. It also includes gold and lusters.

Overglaze colors are usually bought ready mixed with an oil base. They are handled like oil paints, thinned with turpentine.

Majolica

This is a method of overglaze painting in which pigments are applied over a coating of glaze before the glaze has been fired. The name comes from the Island of Majorca. The glaze used is an opaque white glaze containing tin or zirconium. The pigments used must be underglaze colors because after the decoration is made the ware will have to be fired to the maturing point of the glaze. This would be too high a temperature for overglaze colors.

The ware to be decorated may be either greenware or bisque. A coating of white glaze is applied by dipping, spraying or brushing. The glaze must contain gum. To make a better surface on which to paint, it is advisable to spray or brush a thin coat of gum on top of the glaze. The underglaze pigments are then mixed with a little of the glaze and the design is painted on.

PHOTO SERIES 55

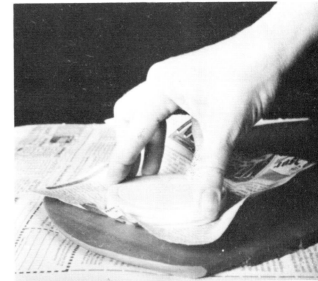

Making a series of coasters with majolica decorations

A layer of clay has been rolled. Circles are being cut from the clay. A metal jar lid is used as a cutter. Note that a sheet of dampened newspaper is placed over the clay before the lid is pressed down.

The cut for the outside ring has been made. Now a smaller jar lid (on the jar) is pressed into the center of the circle to make a depression in the coaster.

Removing the excess clay.

The coasters, trimmed, ready for glazing.

Dipping. An opaque white glaze has been put in a bowl. Each coaster is dipped in and out with one continuous motion. Fingermarks left at the edge must be touched up with a brush.

Painting designs.

The completed set of coasters after firing.

Figurines are usually decorated by overglaze painting, but the majolica method may be used as well.

Glazing and painting figurines

An opaque white glaze is applied with a brush to the pair of angels made in Photo Series 12 in Chapter 4.

Decorations are painted over the unfired glaze.

The finished fired angels.

Majolica designs can be made with other things than a brush. The method of using a sponge and stencil that was described in the section on engobe can be used here as well.

Majolica has a beautiful quality all its own which comes from the fact that the glaze matures underneath the decoration and changes the design slightly. If the glaze is one which contains borax or colemanite, it will bubble while it is maturing and this bubbling action will break through the lines of the painted decoration. An especially fluid glaze will produce an interesting effect in majolica work. If the glaze has been sprayed with a coarse spray so that tiny bumps are formed in the coating of glaze, these bumps, in melting and flowing smooth, will again affect the quality of the painted line.

Plate 73—Taurus, one of a series of zodiac tiles by Pat Lopez. Majolica decoration. The glaze used here contains colemanite which bubbles considerably during the firing. This gives a texture to the decoration.

Plate 74—Italian majolica, landscape designs painted on top of a white glaze before the glaze is fired. Designs are made quickly and in great number.

The potter who produces individual pieces that are unique may spend considerable time decorating them and some of the pieces can be quite elaborate. Some of the ancient Greek pottery as well as some of the Italian majolica produced during the high Renaissance show how elaborate pottery decorations can be.

When a potter is producing sets of ware in which the same pattern is to be repeated again and again, he is forced to simplify his designs, eliminating every unnecessary line. Through this type of simplification a special design quality with a beauty of its own is achieved. This can be seen on many types of so-called peasant ware. Note the illustrations in Plate 75.

Plate 75—Italian peasant pottery, hand thrown. Majolica-type decoration.

Plate 76 — Decorated vase, sgraffito through glaze, by Antonio Prieto. *Photograph by George A. Tagney.*

When ware is made commercially in great quantities, decorations are made mechanically. Such decorations, however, must be planned by ceramic artists. There is no reason why the craft potter cannot make use of some mechanical printing process to decorate his own handmade pieces. The English china so popular during the last century, decorated with pictorial landscapes or domestic scenes, was made by a process of copperplate engraving. The engravings were printed on transfer paper from which they went onto the ware. This method is still in use. Commercially prepared ceramic decalcomanias with stock designs, birds, flowers, and so forth, are made for industrially produced tableware. Decals are also used to print emblems, trademarks, etc., on the chinaware used by hotels, clubs, steamship companies, airlines, and the like. The designing of these emblems is usually left to commercial artists but there is no reason why that must be so. Designs created by ceramists are more apt to be right for clay than designs made by people who know little or nothing about the material.

Any line drawing can be reproduced as a decalcomania in one or in several colors (including gold). Areas of tone may be reproduced also. The drawing must be sent to a ceramic printing firm who will make the decalcomanias in ceramic pigments.

Applying a decal to a piece of ceramics is a simple process. Here are the steps.

Applying a decalcomania design

A printed decalcomania has been soaked in water so that the design has come loose from the backing paper. The design has been slid slightly off the edge of the backing paper.

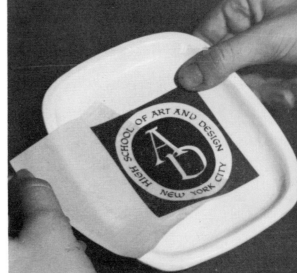

Centering the design on the dish. The dish is a fired piece covered with a white opaque glaze. When the design is in proper position, it is held with one finger while the backing paper is slid out from the back.

The design in place.

Plate 77 — Thrown stoneware by Lyle Perkins. Sgraffito through white glaze. Wax resist on central glazed areas only. Sgraffitoed sections filled with black mat by brushing repeatedly around the form.

We have explored a number of techniques for decorating pottery. They are all fairly easy. As we said at the beginning of this chapter, planning decoration is more important than the technique used. Make use of your sketchbook. When you select material from it, judge it by a number of standards. Is the design interesting? Is it original? Is it appropriate, suitable to the shape of the piece and to its use? Is it pleasing—not too busy or complicated? Finally, do you like it? Be critical here, don't accept something as good just because you made it, subject it to stern appraisal.

Designs need not be drawn beforehand; they can be made directly on the ware. Practice is needed here. Practice with a brush. Practice with

Plate 78 — Thrown stoneware by Dorothy Perkins. Wax resist on white glaze. Glaze sgraffito, then dark mat brushed over entire surface.

Plate 79—Thrown stoneware by Dorothy Perkins. Engobe pattern, covered by a semiopaque mat glaze.

sgraffito tools. Acquire dexterity so that your work is done rapidly, without hesitation. A decoration on pottery must never look labored.

Look at the decorations made by contemporary ceramic artists whenever you have the chance and study work done in the past as well. We learn from others; we need not imitate.

In the closing pages of Chapter 18 we spoke of creativity and mentioned two things needed to encourage it: one, the removal of blocks that stand in its way, and the other, exercise. There is a third important factor in the development of creativity, and that is challenge. When we are faced with a problem and seek its solution, we are forced to call upon those inner resources which are the wellspring of creativity. Planning the decoration for a piece of pottery is a challenge. To meet it we must exercise our inventiveness, our ingenuity, and above all, our imagination; and, after all, what is creativity but imagination put to use in the creation of things that have artistic merit.

Plate 80—Rectangular vase with decoration by Marc Bellaire.

20
Mural

W E HAD trouble in finding a title for this chapter. What the chapter is really about is two-dimensional ceramic design—pictures in clay, creations meant to be looked at from one direction, not things that have sides and a back. Yet, two-dimensional is not the right word, for some of the things we shall talk about are bas-reliefs which do have a third dimension, and plaques with projecting portions. "Ceramic pictures" did not seem right either as a title for a chapter that will include some sculpture. And so we chose "Mural"—a word that Webster defines as ". . . pertaining to a wall . . . ," even though some of the things we shall describe could be used as tabletops.

Ceramic murals are a form of art as old as the pyramids of Egypt. Pictures made of tiles and sculptured brick, covered with colored glazes, were used on the walls of palaces in Babylon many thousands of years ago. There is a revival of interest in this art form today. In the lobbies of hotels and office buildings, on the walls of schools and dwellings, even in industrial plants, we are beginning to see the work of the sculptor, the mosaic designer, and the ceramic artist.

A tile with a design painted on it, cemented to a wall, becomes a mural decoration. Note the tile with a stylized head by Pacetti shown in Fig. 65

Plate 81—Tile 6″ × 6″, overglaze decoration, at doorway of dress shop, Positano, Italy.

69. The Thrower.

70. The Decorator.

71. The Glazer.

72. The Kiln Loader.

Figures on the shop "Céramique Cérenne," Vallauris, France.

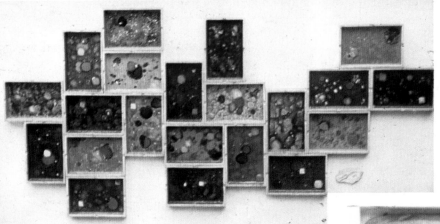

73. *Above*. Garden of the Ceramic Plant of Pacetti, Albisola, Italy.

74. *Left*. Ceramic Mural.

75. *Below*. Another view of the garden.

76. *Below*. Birds on metal legs.

in the color section. Pictures on clay have an obvious advantage over pictures on paper and canvas—they are practically indestructible. A tile tabletop remains bright and colorful no matter how often coffee is spilled on it, and a ceramic decoration on a building can endure the rigors of rain and sleet and snow, as well as summer sun. But more than that, ceramic decoration planned for a wall and actually built into it, gives a sense of unity that is often lacking when pictures are hung. A single tile decorated by any of the methods described in Chapter 19 can be used effectively for the street number of a house or for a shop. The number may be combined with some decorative motif, the homeowner's initial, or a monogram, or an emblem that tells what business the shopkeeper is in, or a trademark. (Note the tile in Plate 81.)

Recent developments in the manufacture of tile cement and mastic make it a simple matter to fasten a tile to a wall. In applying the cement, spread it on the surface of the tile and on the area of the wall where the tile is to be attached, then press the tile into position and fasten it with strips of masking tape. Allow two or three days for the mastic to set, then remove the tape, mix a grout of 1 part Portland cement and 3 parts washed white sand, and make a neat beveled edge all around the tile.

Murals can be made of several tiles that form a panel. In this case it is best to have the tiles set into the wall as the wall is built. It is so easy to put designs on commercially prepared tiles that it is surprising it is not done more frequently. In subway passages, for example, long monotonous areas of dead white tile could be relieved with murals. Certainly this would make the passages more pleasant to walk through. In Plate 82 is a portion

Plate 82—Portion of a ceramic mural at the entrance to a basement restaurant in Paris. Commercial glazed tiles were used. Overglaze painting was done on these and then a final transparent glaze was sprayed over the surface.

of a mural decoration in an underground tiled passageway leading to a Paris restaurant. The gay colorful ceramic decoration is inviting; it makes a walk to the restaurant a pleasant experience that adds to one's anticipation of a good meal. The mural was made by painting on commercially prepared glazed tiles. Underglaze pigments were used, a thin coating of clear glaze was sprayed over the painted designs and the tiles were fired again, then set into the wall. It is almost impossible to deface a mural like this; an occasional wipe with a sponge and detergent keeps it bright and fresh as new.

A portion of a mural at the entrance to the ceramic shop of Giardini in Pesaro, Italy, is shown in Fig. 59 in the color section. Giardini made the tiles for this, decorated them and set them in place himself.

Tiles for murals

The ceramist who wishes to make his own tiles may do so by cutting slabs with a taglietelle, as shown in Chapter 5, then cutting squares out of the slab. This is better than rolling clay into a layer—less likelihood of warping. In cutting tiles be sure to make allowance for shrinkage. (A shrinkage rule like the one shown in the Appendix will prove useful; make yourself one.)

Another device for making tiles is shown in the sketch. This is a paddle of plywood ½″ thick, with a square opening. The paddle is placed flat on a table and clay is put into the opening. "Put" is too mild a word—the clay is *pounded* in with force. Then a wire is drawn across the top, cutting off the excess clay. The paddle is lifted and tapped on a plaster slab so that the clay falls out onto the slab. (If there is any difficulty in coaxing the tile to fall out of the paddle, the inside edge of the paddle should be dusted with flint or talcum powder. This prevents sticking.)

The surface of a tile made this way will show the texture of cut clay. If a smoother surface is required, draw a steel knife or a spatula across the top of the tile with a kind of "buttering" motion. Do this before the tile is tapped out of the paddle.

Tiles should be allowed to dry on flat plaster slabs. They should be handled as little as possible, yet they need to be turned over frequently. A good way of turning them is to put a second slab on top, then reverse both slabs with the tile or tiles in between, then take off the slab that is on top. While tiles are face down and before they are thoroughly dry, cut three or four grooves in the back about ½″ wide and ⅛″ deep. These grooves help in drying and they also help in bonding tiles into cement.

The small plaque shown in Fig. 60 in the color section was made by a kindergarten pupil, a five-year-old. The young artist rolled and cut 4 tiles, each 4″ square. (For tiles this size, rolling works.) After the tiles were fired, the design was painted with underglaze colors, then the tiles were sprayed with a clear glaze and fired again. The completed tiles were glued to a square panel of plywood. The joints between the tiles were filled with grout and the edges were beveled with the same material.

Fig. 48 in the color section shows a panel with a fish design that was made out of 12 6″ × 6″ tiles. This panel is used as a tabletop, but it could just as well serve as a wall decoration. The frame is made of four pieces of wood rabbeted as shown in the sketch, mitered at the corners. The surface of the tiles, when they are in place, is level with the surface of the frame. A piece of plywood is used as a backing for the tiles.

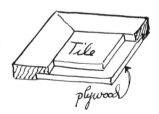

This panel is made of glazed commercial tiles. The designs were made with overglaze colors, using a combination of techniques, dabbing with a sponge, drawing with a brush, spattering, and sgraffito. If this panel were intended for use on a wall, the tiles would be fastened in place with a tile cement. However, since this is a tabletop (the legs are iron) the tiles need not be fastened, but are removable. This means that the table can have a completely different design set in place any time the owner feels like decorating and firing another dozen tiles.

In a panel like this we must not forget that the wooden frame is part of the design. Thought must be given to the kind of wood used and the surface treatment. Here the frame is of light colored maple, varnished and rubbed.

When a plaque is made of a number of tiles, the tiles may be formed individually, or they may be cut from a single large layer of clay. The latter method must be used when the shapes of the tiles are other than square, when, for example, the panel is made of shapes that fit together in a kind of jigsaw pattern. Tiles cut from a layer may be painted with designs or, either before or after the layer is cut, the tiles may be incised and modeled. Here is a method of making a large clay layer for mural work.

PHOTO SERIES 58

Making a panel of eight sculptured tiles

Two wooden guide strips ½″ thick have been fastened to a large drawing board. A strip of oilcloth just wide enough to fit between the guide strips is placed on the board, shiny side down. Terracotta clay is being pounded into a flat layer on top of the oilcloth. The pounding is done with great force so that the clay becomes a solid, compact layer.

A strip of wood is drawn along the top of the guide strips. This must be done several times in order to make the layer even in thickness with a smooth upper surface.

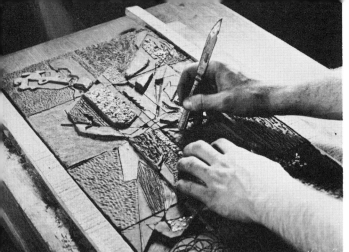

The panel has been cut into 8 6" × 6" squares. The artist has carved away some areas and built up others. Here he adds texture to part of the pattern by pressing the handle of a table knife into the clay.

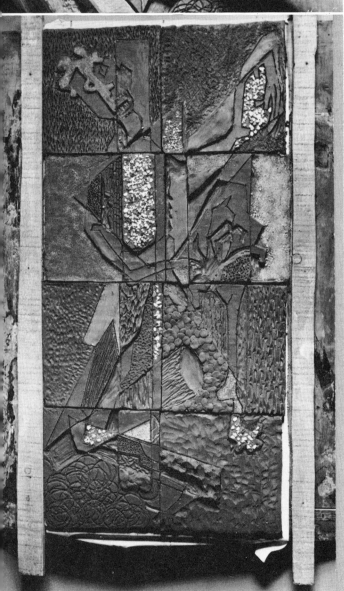

The panel of eight tiles is ready to be removed from the board. Note that coarse grog has been pressed into some areas to give variety. The portions touching the guide strips must be loosened with a knife, then the oilcloth will be drawn out carefully with tiles in place. After they have hardened for one or two hours, they will be transferred to a plaster slab where they will be covered with dry cloths and allowed to dry slowly. Then they will be fired and glazed. The finished panel is shown in Plate 83.

Plate 83—Pictorial panel, eight 6″ × 6″ tiles carved and colored. Student work, High School of Art and Design.

The student work shown in Figs. 54 and 55 in the color section was made out of pieces cut from a layer of clay prepared in the manner we have just watched. The mermaid panel shown in Plate 84 was also made from a layer of clay. A full-sized drawing of the design was made with areas to be cut outlined. In planning these shapes, thought was given to the line pattern that the joints would produce in the finished work.

The drawing was placed on top of the layer of clay, face up, and the lines were traced with a pencil; this transferred the drawing to the clay. A potter's knife, held vertically, was used to cut the sections. When the

Plate 84 — Mermaid, pictorial panel, 24″ × 36″.

cutting was completed, the panel was allowed to harden for two hours, then a second drawing board was laid on top of it and the two boards were reversed. The top board (the one with the guide strips) was lifted off and the oilcloth was peeled away from the clay; this left the cut sections face down on the second board. At this point a wire loop tool was used to gouge grooves ⅛″ deep in the backs.

The next step, an important one, was numbering. Each area on the drawing was numbered and the same number was painted on the back of the corresponding tile with marking fluid. (Marking fluid is made by mixing a bit of black underglaze color with the same amount of a low-fire frit, and adding glycerine.) The tiles were covered with cloths and left face down on the board overnight. The next day they were turned over and allowed to complete drying right side up. When the tiles were dry, they were assembled on the drawing. Wherever a tile needed to be trimmed to make a better fit, the edge was filed with a rasp.

Glazing and firing was done in one operation. After the tiles were fired, they were assembled in position with $\frac{1}{8}''$ spaces left between them. An opening the right size to receive the assembled tiles was cut in a piece of plywood with a power jigsaw. Another piece of plywood with outside dimensions the same as those of the first piece was used as a backing. These two pieces of plywood were fastened together.

The next step was cementing the tiles in place with mastic. After the mastic had set for 24 hours, a grout made of 3 parts sand and 1 part Portland cement, was worked into the joints and the surface was wiped smooth. The wooden panel enclosing the tiles was painted with a dull-finish black enamel.

Here is another type of pictorial panel made by incising a drawing in a clay slab, then cutting it into sections. Such sections, after they have been glazed and fired, could be built into a masonry wall or, as shown by Carla Kenny in the next Photo Series, set in a panel of plaster of Paris.

PHOTO SERIES 59

Woman with a bird on her hat, a panel set in plaster of Paris

A clay slab was prepared, as shown in Photo Series 58. The artist draws in the clay with a pointed stylus. When the drawing is completed, areas will be colored and glazed and the slab will be cut into four sections.

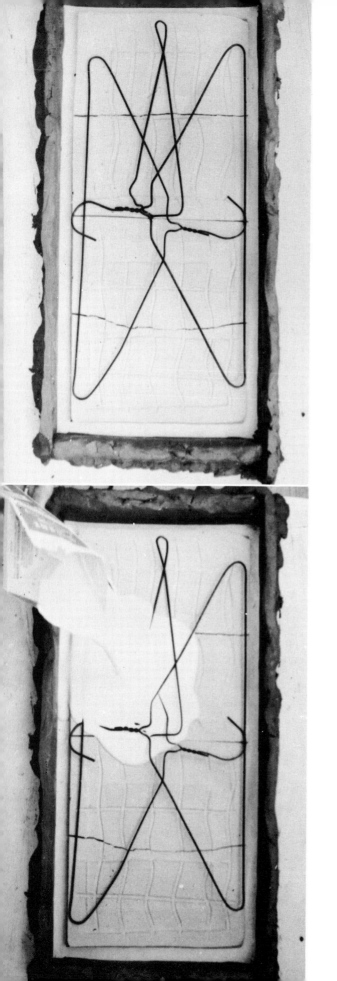

After firing, the four sections are placed face down on a large table and a wall of clay is built around them. Two coat hangers are laid in place for reinforcement and a portion of a third coat hanger is bent to form a hanging hook.

Plaster of Paris is poured. When the plaster is set, the clay retaining walls are removed and the edges are beveled. The completed panel is shown in Fig. 49 in the color section.

Here is the making of another pictorial panel by a combination of cutting shapes and modeling in relief.

Pictorial panel, an owl

A prepared clay slab has been cut into pieces, outlining the shapes of an owl and background sections. Relief details are modeled on. Indication of feathers has been made by pressing the end of a round stick into the clay.

The pieces have been fired and glazed. Here they are assembled in position.

Plate 85—Neptune and mermaid, a pair of plaques by Carla. Made in separate pieces, set in cement.

This design can be mounted on a wooden panel or set in a slab of cement. The figures of Neptune and the Mermaid by Carla shown in Plate 85 were made in a manner similar to the owl. After the sections were fired, they were assembled face down, with a retaining wall of clay around them. Reinforcing wires were set in place as shown in Photo Series 59, and a mixture of 3 parts sand and 1 part Portland cement was poured over the backs of the sections. This makes the plaques waterproof, suitable for use as decorations on an outside patio wall.

Ceramic panels can be made in one piece in sizes up to 18″ × 24″. They may be perfectly flat ceramic pictures, or have slight relief like Fig.

44, "Rain," and Fig. 52, "Ulysses," both by Capacci and both in the color section. Designs can be made with raised lines trailed on in slip, like the plaques by Fantoni shown in Fig. 62 in the color section, or modeled in higher relief with open areas, like the plaque by Marguerite Wildenhain shown in Fig. 43 and those by Lucerni in Figs. 8, 45, and 46, all in the color section. These plaques are sculpture to hang on a wall. Fig. 45, "Flight into Egypt" by Lucerni, also in the color section, has figures modeled in the round standing out from a background made of a curved slab of clay.

Making a ceramic plaque is a sculptural exercise involving building up forms, and modeling them. The sculptor Frank Eliscu demonstrates the steps.

PHOTO SERIES 61

Adam and Eve

A sketch 8″ × 10″ has been made in clay.

Working from the sketch, the artist starts constructing clay forms within a clay frame.

Continuing to build forms.

Modeling shapes.

Using a toothed wooden tool for texture.

Modeling details of features and hair.

(271) The completed sculpture. This will be allowed to dry, then fired without glazing. The clay fires a warm red.

Here is another panel made by Frank Eliscu.

PHOTO SERIES 62

Jonah and the whale

The artist makes a drawing with charcoal on a plaster slab.

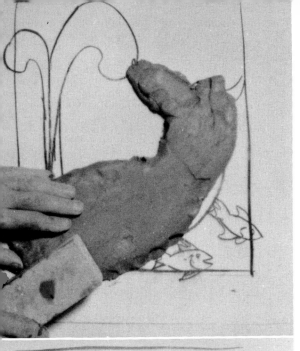

Clay shapes are built up on the outlines of the drawing.

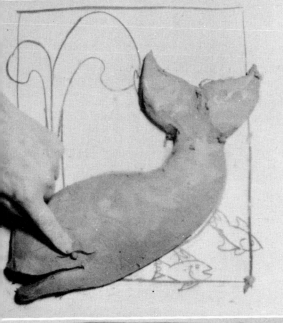

Modeling the mouth and the eye of the whale.

Jonah inside the whale is indicated by an incised line drawing.

More forms added.

Building a frame around the composition.

The completed clay panel ready to be fired.

Sometimes it is better, when making a ceramic plaque, to make a mold of the original model and then make a pressing in the mold. Here are the steps.

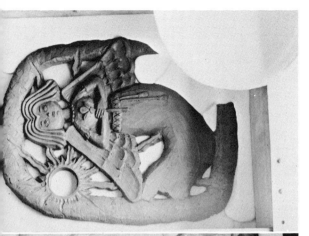

Pressing a plaque in a mold

A shape has been modeled. The casting box has been set in place around it and plaster is being poured to make a mold.

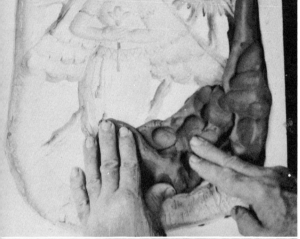

(274)

The plaster mold has set. Terra-cotta clay is being pressed in.

The fired plaque.

The next series demonstrates the steps in making a plaque by cutting a layer of clay and modeling.

PHOTO SERIES 64

Portrait of a king

A drawing has been made with brush and ink on a piece of newspaper. This drawing is transferred to a clay slab by tracing the lines with a wooden modeling tool.

Background areas are cut out.

Features and details are modeled in relief.

Gouging grooves in the back. These are to prevent warping and to make it easier to cement the panel into a wall.

The completed plaque.

Plate 86—Welcome plaque, ceramic panel for a front door. These are the people who live in the house; they are at the doorway to welcome visitors. The work of Jacqueline Lerat. *Photograph by H. Malvaux.*

A type of ceramic mural can be made of ceramic shapes mounted on a wooden panel. The work by Rita Sargen shown in Plate 89 and the girl by Rosemary Zwick (Fig. 18 in the color section) are creations of this type. In plaques like these the wood is part of the design; the selection of the wood and the type of finish must receive careful consideration.

Designing ceramics for wall decorations is a thrilling and exciting part of contemporary ceramic design. Many ceramists today devote a major part of their time to design in two dimensions. There is not the great need

te 87—Angels over the housetops, wall panel by Jean Derval. Three large tiles, carved and colored with engobes.

Plate 89—Plaque by Rita Sargen, a group of ceramic shapes of contrasting color and texture mounted on a wood panel.

for ceramic containers today that people had years ago. We no longer use amphoras to hold our grain, and our wine comes in glass bottles, not in pottery jugs. Much of our best tableware, while designed by ceramic artists, is made in factories.

On the other hand, the architects and the interior designers of modern homes are making more and more demands upon ceramists for the type of murals described in this chapter. There is opportunity and challenge for ceramists in this field.

MOSAIC

We cannot leave the subject of ceramic pictures without reference to mosaics. This ancient art merits a book all to itself—it would be impossible to give a complete description of methods and techniques in this short section. But we must mention the subject, even though briefly, because many of the materials of mosaics are ceramic, and because planning mosaic decorations offers the ceramist another, different approach to design.

Mosaics are pictures made by setting small pieces of colored stone, glass, tiles, fragments of pottery, pebbles, and other hard materials in a bed of cement. The small pieces used this way are called "tesserae" (one alone

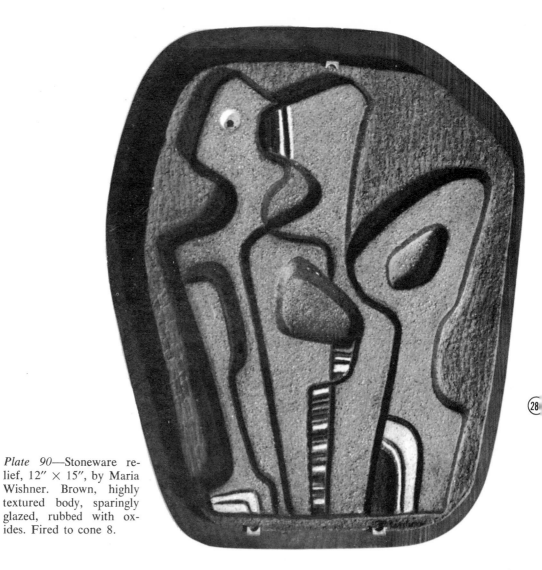

Plate 90—Stoneware relief, 12″ × 15″, by Maria Wishner. Brown, highly textured body, sparingly glazed, rubbed with oxides. Fired to cone 8.

is called a "tessera"). Tesserae can be purchased ready made; the ceramist can make his own.

Commercial tesserae

The most beautiful ceramic mosaic tiles available are imported from Italy. They come mounted on sheets about 12″ square. The tiles measure ¾″ × ¾″ and each sheet contains 256 tiles of a single color. Subtle variations in the color create a nonmechanical effect when the tiles are assembled. Tiles are also made in a wide variety of textures and patterns —marbled, brushed, or stippled effects. The range of colors available is almost unlimited.

Glass mosaic tiles are imported from Venice, the city which, over the centuries, has carried the art of glass and mosaic work to the highest state of perfection. Like ceramic tiles, these are sold mounted on sheets about a foot square. Usually each sheet contains one color, but mixed color

Plate 91—Decorative wall panel by Carla. These pieces will be set in cement wall, 12″ × 20″.

sheets are available which provide four or five shades of the same color arranged in random pattern. The colors, needless to say, have great brilliance.

Mosaic tiles of all colors are made in this country also. Both the imported and the domestic tesserae can be bought from dealers in ceramic supplies.

Making ceramic tesserae

To make small clay tiles suitable for mosaics, roll several layers of clay using wooden guide strips ¼″ thick. While the clay is still moist, brush on coatings of glaze. Ten percent of ball clay should be added to whatever

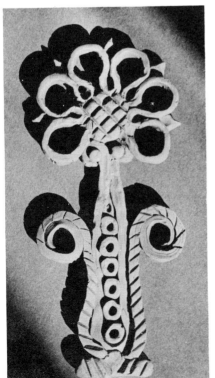

Plate 92—Flower, wall ornament, 15″ high. Made of strips of red clay.

Plate 93—Lion, ceramic wall plaque by Rut Bryk of Arabia Potteries, Finland. *Photograph courtesy of Georg Jensen, Inc.*

glaze you use because, since you are applying the glaze to moist clay, you want to increase the glaze shrinkage as it dries. This will make the glaze less likely to flake off the tesserae before you get them into the kiln. Add extra gum to the glaze also.

It is a good plan to use a basic opaque white glaze to which colors have been added. Use the colorants suggested for the transparent low-fire glaze whose recipe was given in Chapter 15, or use underglaze colors and brush each color on a different layer. After the glazed layers of clay have dried for one or two hours, cut them into small pieces. Use a potter's knife and hold it in a vertical position as you cut with it. Cut some pieces ¾″ square and cut a number of smaller pieces, some wedge-shaped, others triangular. Here is where the ceramist who makes his own tesserae has an advantage over the artist who must buy his tiles, for when he has planned his design and knows about the number of specially shaped tiles he will need, he can cut them easily before the clay is fired. After the pieces of clay have dried thoroughly while resting on a plaster slab, they are ready to be fired.

Making glass tesserae

Glass tesserae can be made by cutting scraps of stained glass into small shapes with a glass cutter. Some artists don't bother with a glass cutter, but break the glass with a hammer; the variety in the size and shape of the bits of broken glass allows more freedom in design. Colored glass bottles can be put on a kiln shelf and melted into flat layers, then cut or broken into tesserae. (The kiln shelf must be given a protective coating of whiting beforehand as described in Chapter 16.) To get the full beauty of the refraction of light from glass tesserae, they should be given a backing of aluminum leaf before they are set in a mosaic. Interesting tesserae can be made by painting one side of a sheet of double-thick window glass with oil colors before breaking it into bits (the oil paint is allowed to dry thoroughly, of course).

The mosaic shown in Plate 94 was made entirely of glass tesserae, broken with a hammer. Some of the glass fragments are stained glass, others are window glass, painted in the manner described in the last paragraph.

The two mosaic tabletops shown in Plate 95 were made with commercial tesserae. In the square one, the beauty of the design comes not only from the pattern and the flowing lines of color, but from the lines of movement in the tesserae themselves. Note here that it was necessary to cut a number of the square tesserae into smaller and different shapes. This is done with a pair of tile nippers. The tessera is held in the fingers of the left hand, the edge of the nippers is placed about ⅛″ in from the edge of the tessera and given a sharp nip.

The circular tabletop shown in the same plate was made with practically no cutting of the tesserae. The beauty of this design comes from the way in which the square tiles are set in place, moving in concentric circles, broken at random by radial lines of contrasting color. A comparison of these two tabletops with the glass mosaic shown in Plate 94 or the mosaic in Plate 96 illustrates the completely different design quality arrived at in using different types of tesserae.

Designing a mosaic

Mosaics can be made without patterns prepared beforehand, a method in which the design develops during the construction of the mosaic, but for the beginner it is better to plan by making drawings.

We could use an abstract design for our beginning project, something entirely geometric that could be executed with uncut, square tiles but since

Plate 94—Mosaic made of pieces of broken glass mounted on plywood. Student work, High School of Art and Design, New York.

Plate 95—Two mosaic tabletops by Mildred Harston.

we want experience in cutting tesserae to special shapes, let us start with a simplified pictorial pattern to be made on a rectangular panel 12″ × 16″.

Consult your sketchbook; select some motif that lends itself to the kind of uncomplicated outlines and flat areas required in mosaics. Draw the motif a number of times, either the actual size of the panel or to a smaller scale. Smaller drawings must be done within a rectangle that has the same proportions as the panel; since the panel is 12″ × 16″, the small sketches can be made in rectangles 3″ × 4″. (You can reduce or enlarge a rectangle by drawing its diagonal. Any other rectangle on the same diagonal whose sides are parallel to the sides of the original rectangle, has the same proportions.) Drawing within the rectangle is important because the problem here is to create a design that fills an area. All of the shapes within the rectangle play their part—the spaces around the motif as well as the motif itself. While you are sketching, think of color; plan a design which can be executed in a few colors or tones—not more than four or five at the most.

As soon as you have a sketch that seems satisfactory, draw it full size and outline the different color areas. Such a drawing is called a "cartoon." Next make the tesserae you will need to fill them. Make plenty—it is much better to have too many than too few. You can tell about how many tiles of each color you will need by putting the leather-hard tesserae on the drawing. If more are needed or some special shapes are required to execute the design, this is the time to cut them.

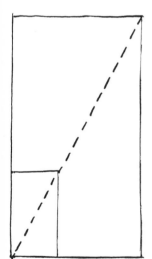

While the tesserae are being fired, prepare a panel of waterproof marine-type plywood ½″ thick, cut to proper size. Make a retaining frame around the panel out of wood edging ¾″ wide × ¼″ thick. Fasten this around the plywood panel so that the top of the edging projects ¼″ above the surface of the panel. Then give the panel and the edging several coats of shellac.

After the tesserae have been fired, arrange them in place on the drawing or on a piece of paper or cardboard the same size as the panel. Here you have an opportunity to study mosaic design. By moving the tesserae around, you can alter the sizes and shapes of the areas at will. You can try the tesserae crowded close together, or with wider spaces between them. You can study the patterns that are made by the joints between the tesserae, seeing how the arrangement of tesserae within an area can add interest to the design. If some tesserae must be cut for better fit, use the tile nippers. When the tesserae have been arranged to your complete satisfaction, the next step is to transfer them to the panel.

The direct method

Sketch a design on the plywood panel, select a small portion in the center of the design and put a layer of tile mastic on that portion. Spread the mastic evenly into a layer about $\frac{1}{8}''$ thick, using a spatula. Keep the mastic within the area you have chosen so that the rest of the drawing is not obliterated. Pick up the tesserae intended for this area and fasten them one by one in place on the panel. Start in the center. Complete one portion of the design, then put more mastic on the panel and continue working outward to the edge. This method of placing the tesserae one by one is called the "direct method."

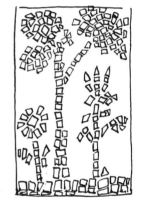

The mastic tile cement stays soft for a long time and you will be able to move the tesserae about slightly, if necessary. When all the tesserae have been put in place on the panel, set it aside for two or three days so that the mastic can harden thoroughly. Rest a drawing board on top of the panel and put a couple of heavy books on the board.

The next step, after the mastic has hardened, is filling the joints between the tesserae with grout. Grout is a thin cement mortar. You can make your own with a 1-to-3 mixture of Portland cement and fine beach sand, adding enough water to make mortar the consistency of pancake batter. Grout made of Portland cement will be gray. Keene cement used instead of Portland cement will produce a white grout, but this lacks the water-proof quality of grout made with Portland cement.

Some mosaic artists advocate adding 10% of lime putty to the mixture. Two percent of plaster of Paris added to the grout will slow its setting time. The prepared grout must be worked into the joints between the tesserae and the surface of the design wiped clean.

If you wish to avoid the trouble of making your own grout, you may purchase prepared grout in powder form.

Note: Take care in handling mastics and cement. Some mastics are highly combustible; a note on the label will warn you of this. Once mastic has hardened it is almost impossible to remove. Any mastic that gets on the surface of tesserae or any other place you don't want it, should be wiped off while it is still soft. Cement can hurt the skin; wash your hands thoroughly after working with it.

Now let's look at a demonstration of some of the steps described above.

Making a 12″ × 16″ mosaic panel by the direct method

The artist has made a number of small sketches in proportions of 3″ × 4″. One, the sketch of a cat, has been selected and redrawn full size.

Tesserae were made by rolling, glazing, and cutting clay. Then they were fired. The drawing was sketched on a 12″ × 16″ plywood panel. The artist is setting tesserae in place one by one in tile mastic which is spread by means of a spatula. Here a tessera is being "buttered."

Even when the tiles are made by the artist, it is sometimes necessary to use the tile nippers to cut a special shape.

The completed design, tiles in place ready to be grouted.

A comparison of the finished mosaic with the original sketch shows that many changes came about in the course of executing the design. This is not bad—the altered shape has a kind of freedom and interest that was lacking in the more formal original. Had it been necessary to reproduce the drawing more exactly, the artist would have put the tesserae in place on the drawing, carefully planning the execution of each area before transferring the tesserae to the plywood.

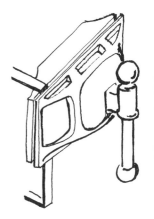

The edge of a mosaic panel is a problem that can be treated in many ways. In the work we just completed, wooden edging strips were used, but these would not serve on a panel of an irregular shape, or on a circular one. The simplest edge treatment for such a shape would be to make a beveled edge with grout. Such an edge is shown on the mermaid panel shown in Fig. 53 in the color section. The circular tabletop shown in Plate 95 has a brass edging.

Brass edging

To make a brass edging for a mosaic panel, a strip of brass binding ¾″ wide should be cut 1″ or 2″ longer than the perimeter of the panel. If the panel has square corners, the binding should be bent in a vise so that it fits snugly. Tapping the binding with a hammer while it is in the vise makes the corners sharp and square. The binding must be nailed to the edge of the panel with small brass nails. (It may be necessary to punch holes in the binding first.) The overlapping portion of the binding is cut off to make a neat butt joint.

Edge tiles

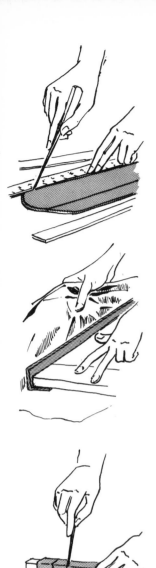

Another way of treating the edge of a rectangular panel is with specially prepared angle-shaped tiles. Such tiles can be made out of a rolled layer of clay. Cut a strip 2″ wide, lay it on a piece of oilcloth (shiny side down). Place a drawing board on the strip so that the edge of the drawing board comes in the center of the clay strip. Lift the oilcloth so that the clay is bent into a right angle on the edge of the drawing board.

Turn the drawing board on end with the bent clay strip in place, and allow the clay to harden for one or two hours, then cut the strips into a variety of different lengths, from ¾″ to 2″. Cut some diagonally as shown in the sketch; these are used for mitered corners.

After the angle-shaped tiles have been glazed and fired, they may be glued to the edge of a plywood panel where they serve as edge treatment and also as a border for the mosaic.

Edge tiles are good, too, for a type of mosaic design in which tesserae are set in cement on a panel in such a way that areas of cement are left plain. These unadorned cement areas form part of the design. An effective use of this method is an outdoor tabletop in which the central motif of tile is surrounded by a larger area of cement. To make such a table, use a piece of ¾″ waterproof plywood. Shellac it thoroughly. Plan the design by arranging the tesserae on the panel and when the design is right, glue them into position. The rest of the tabletop will be cement.

A binder is needed to hold the cement to the plywood. Galvanized screening should be fastened in this area with staples, or flat-head screws put in at frequent intervals with the heads projecting slightly above the surface of the plywood. When all the tiles are glued in place and the plywood has been prepared, a 1-to-3 mixture of Portland cement and fine beach sand is floated over the whole surface. This must be troweled to a smooth level surface, then allowed to set. While it is setting (a period of four or five days), the cement must be covered with wet newspapers or cloths so that it does not dry out too rapidly. After the cement has hardened, any areas between tiles which need to be filled with cement can be attended to.

The indirect method

A different procedure for making mosaics, the reverse of the direct method, is as follows.

After the tesserae are all arranged, face up, in a mosaic pattern either on a tabletop or on a drawing, a piece of Kraft paper is given a heavy coating of a water-soluble paste or glue. The paper is then laid, glue side down, on the tesserae and pressed gently but firmly so that every tessera adheres to the paper. A bed of cement is prepared to receive the tesserae. A plywood panel, after having been given several coats of shellac, has metal lath or galvanized wire screen fastened to it to serve as a bond for the cement. Retaining walls of wood or brass ½″ high are fastened around the panel. These walls must be given a protective covering of masking tape to protect them from the cement, after which cement is mixed and floated evenly over the whole panel. As soon as the cement has been poured,

Plate 96—White and white, mosaic panel by Florence Gurland, 16″ × 20″, made of chunks of glass, gravel, pieces of marble of different sizes, some laid flat, others projecting from ¼″ to ¾″, ceramic tesserae, and glass tubes; no grout used, tile mastic fills all spaces between the tesserae.

the paper to which the tesserae are fastened is lifted up, turned over, and pressed into the bed of cement so that all the tesserae are forced into the cement.

It is good to have the help of a friend at this point. When the paper with the tesserae attached is turned over, lay it on a sheet of cardboard. Hold the sheet of cardboard in position over the bed but not touching the cement. As your assistant holds the paper in the right position over the bed, slide out the piece of cardboard.

When the tesserae are in place, the surface of the paper must be pressed downward so that cement is forced up into all the joints. Rolling a rolling pin over the paper will help to distribute pressure over the whole area and make the surface level.

A day or two must be allowed for the cement to set, then the paper is soaked off; the surface of the design is cleaned, and any joints that need it are filled with grout.

A variation of this method is shown in the sketch. A wooden frame is made for a panel. This must be coated several times with Tungseal, allowed to dry, then rubbed with boiled linseed oil. The outside edges must be covered with masking tape for protection. The frame is laid face down on a worktable. The tiles, when fired and glazed, are arranged face up on a worktable in position so that they form the design to be made. Con-Tact paper, cut to the size of the opening of the frame, is laid on top of the tesserae and pressed so that all of the tesserae stick to the paper. The Con-Tact paper is then lifted up, turned over, and laid in the frame with the paper at the bottom so that the tesserae are all upside down. Next, cement is mixed and poured into the back of the frame to a depth of ¾″. Care must be taken in the pouring to see that the cement fills all parts of the frame evenly and flows into all of the spaces between the tesserae.

A backing of marine-type plywood, shellacked and with screws driven into it at frequent intervals with the heads of the screws projecting, is pressed into the cement, screw-side down, and fastened to the frame as shown in the sketch. After 24 hours the frame can be turned over and the cement cleaned away from the surface by scraping and sponging.

In a project like this the beauty of the wood is important. After the masking tape has been removed, the frame should be rubbed once more with linseed oil.

Here is another variation of the indirect method. Set the tesserae in place, paste Kraft paper on top of the design, allow several hours for the paste to set, then lift the paper and turn it over so that the tiles are all face down. Coat a prepared wooden panel with a thick layer of mastic and press it firmly against the back of the tiles. Put weights on the panel and allow it to stay in this position for several days. Then turn the work over, dab a wet sponge on the paper to soak it thoroughly, peel off the paper, sponge the tiles and grout the joints.

Tesserae can be set directly in cement instead of being glued to a wooden panel. Prepare a cement bed by putting either a wood or a brass frame around the edge of a wooden panel. Shellac the wood thoroughly and put a protective coating of masking tape on all parts of the frame. Fasten

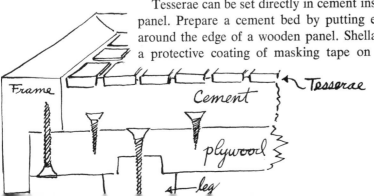

galvanized screening to the plywood to serve as a bond for the cement. Then mix cement mortar and flow it into the area enclosed by the frame.

While the cement mortar is still soft, put the tesserae in place and press them down. Have the drawing of the design close at hand. Start in the middle and work out toward the edges. When working this way it is not necessary to place the tesserae so that they are all flat on top. If some tesserae are at an angle, there is a sparkle to the mosaic when light is reflected in different ways. This is especially true of glass tesserae, for these refract the light in a more interesting way when they are set at slight angles.

A ready-made mixture of cement and sand can be purchased from dealers in building materials; some ceramic suppliers carry it and sell it in smaller quantities.

Magnesite cement can be used in place of Portland cement provided the work is not to be used outdoors. Magnesite is usually sold only in 100-lb. bags and it is not easy to store. Furthermore, when it is used for mortar it must be mixed with a strong chloride solution. It has advantages for the artist who makes mosaics on a large scale; for the ceramist who makes smaller mosaics, the special tile cement sold by dealers in ceramic supplies is more practical. This comes in 3-lb. packages, enough for one square foot of mosaics.

Mosaics intended for outdoor use are best set in cement beds, not on wood. However, I have seen a mosaic on a wood panel used most effectively on the exterior of the home of Leonardo Ricci in Florence. This panel is shown in Fig. 61 in the color section.

Coloring materials can be used in cement—such things as red iron oxide, raw umber and others. There are commercially prepared cement colorants as well. All of these must be mixed with the cement while it is dry.

There is a fascination in mosaic work, pleasure too—a happiness that comes just from handling the materials and watching designs develop, ideas take form. We said at the beginning of this section that it would be impossible to give a complete description of all methods and techniques. These few pages are offered as a suggestion, a signpost on another pathway to design. There is more to know—much more. Ceramists who wish to go farther, certainly any who plan to make architectural mosaics, will need more technical information. For these there are many books on the subject that cover it in great detail.

The craftsman familiar with clay who turns to mosaics has an important advantage—he already knows many of the materials and has facility in handling them. The fact that he can make his own tiles in any size or shape gives him greater freedom, too. After all, the pieces of a mosaic don't have to be tiny; some can be large, even sculptured. The ceramist with daring and originality can develop his own way of working, his own mosaic style.

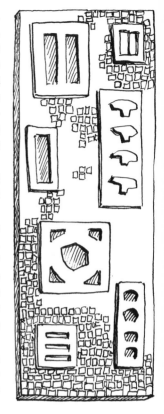

21

Architecture

MODERN BUILDINGS with their large areas of glass, their unadorned facades, their almost stark functional quality, seem to cry out for a touch of color and human warmth. Ceramics can supply this missing ingredient.

Fortunately, architects and interior designers are becoming aware of this and more and more ceramists find themselves called upon to execute commissions for both public and private buildings, civic centers, housing projects, hotels, stores. Some of these commissions are for free-standing ceramic sculpture or for sculpture attached to a wall; some are for ceramic wall plaques; others, especially those designed for stores, call for arrangements of flat tiles with designs painted on them.

On Plate 97 is a tile mural executed by Jean Derval for a Paris beauty salon. The tiles are square, cut with a taglietelle as described in Chapter 5, painted with underglaze colors. They are shown here assembled in the courtyard of the artist's studio before being packed and shipped to the client who commissioned them.

"City Skyline," a mural by Harris Strong (Plate 98), shows a different use of tiles. Here the tiles are cut to shape and set in a wall to form larger areas with open spaces around them. The open spaces are an integral part of the design. The area around Strong's "Eagle" in Plate 99 is also part of the design.

Executing murals like these involves no serious technical problems for the ceramist—the finished work is large but the pieces are small. Ceramic plaques 24″ high or less are no problem either. On the outside wall of "Céramique Cérenne" in Vallauris, France, is a series of amusing ceramic reliefs made by Francis Crociani (see Figs. 69–72 in the color section). These are of such size that one person could do all the work of forming, firing, and setting them in a wall. Oftentimes, however, architectural sculpture is large. Making such pieces requires heavy equipment and the help of several assistants. At first glance this would seem to put work of this type forever beyond the scope of the average studio potter. Not so! The ceramist who executes architectural commissions can, in most cases, work directly with the manufacturers of architectural terra cotta so that practically all of the major production problems are solved for him.

Plate 97—Ceramic mural by Jean Derval. Painting on tiles. The tiles were photographed on the floor of the courtyard of the artist's studio in Vallauris, France. The mural is now installed in a Parisian beauty salon.

Plate 98—City Skyline, a mural decoration in a club dining room, the work of Harris G. Strong. This mural is 15′ long, made of cut sections, 12″ × 12″ × ⅜″. Multicolor decorations with blues and greens predominant.

Plate 99—Eagle, a ceramic mural decoration for a lobby. 25′ long, made of cut tile. The work of Harris G. Strong.

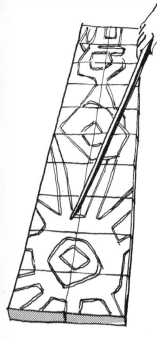

One of the illustrations in the color section (Fig. 67) shows the use of ceramics on a building in the Cleveland Zoological Park, a piece of sculpture over 5 feet high by 8 feet long. It was designed by Viktor Schreckengost and executed by the Federal Seaboard Terra Cotta Corporation at their plant in Perth Amboy, New Jersey. The artist made preliminary sketches in clay, then worked at the plant making the original model of the sculpture. This was made full size—actually larger than full size because allowance had to be made for shrinkage. Then the technicians of the plant took over, made molds from the model, and pressed clay into the molds. The pressings were glazed and fired and, after being assembled at the plant, were shipped to the site where they were installed. This is one of many sculptures in the Cleveland Zoo executed by the same artist.

Also in the color section, in Fig. 68, we see another example of cooperation between the artist and the ceramics manufacturer, a number of large mural panels made of incised and painted tiles. The tiles were manufactured at the same plant by a process of extruding. Clay with the proper additions of grog, flint, and other minerals needed to assure the best firing results, is put into a pug mill where it is thoroughly ground up and mixed with the right amount of water. A vacuum draws most of the air out of the clay and gives it good working consistency and a density that makes it fire to a hard, durable body. Under pressure the clay is forced through a die to emerge as a long, flat ribbon the right width for tiles. The ribbon is cut into the proper lengths and the tiles are formed.

When Rene Portocarrero, the Cuban artist, designed murals for the Havana Hilton Hotel, he went to the plant, where moist tiles, still soft, were arranged on the floor in the shapes of the mural panels. The artist took a long, pointed stick, walked around the panels, and drew directly in the clay. You can imagine what bold and free designs result from work like this. When the incising was done, he dabbed on areas of pigment by using long sticks to the ends of which sponges were tied (making, in effect, long-handled paintbrushes). After the tiles were dry they were fired. In Fig. 68 in the color section they are shown assembled for final inspection before shipment.

Sometimes architects rely upon the manufacturer's staff artists to design and execute sculptural ornaments. Here is a series of photographs taken at the Federal Seaboard Terra Cotta plant showing the making of a large figure for a church.

(294)

PHOTO SERIES 66

A terra-cotta statue of Saint Hedwig

Planning. The architect's plans of the church are worked on by a draftsman-designer. Terra-cotta ornament is drawn to scale. Note the drawing of the statue on the facade of the church.

A heavy steel frame is constructed to serve as an armature. The sculptor Herbert Todd works on the armature. "Butterflies," little crosses of wood, have been attached to the frame by lengths of wire. These will anchor masses of clay at the outside edges of the model and prevent them from sliding downward.

The sculptor applies modeling clay to the armature.

The central column of the armature is completely covered with clay. The butterflies hang free, ready to support clay that will be added.

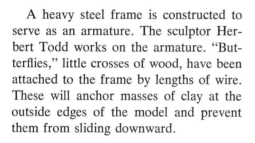

Modeling the figure. Burlap has been soaked in plaster of Paris, then draped over the head and shoulders of the figure to form the garments. After this plaster-soaked cloth has become hard, clay will be put on top of it to complete the modeling. The sculptor works on the left hand which holds a wooden board, the base of the little church.

The sculptor models the right hand. The plaster-soaked burlap has been covered with clay. The model of the church held by the left hand has been roughly blocked out.

The clay modeling completed. Much painstaking work has been done; details of crown, church, shoes, and costume have been carefully executed. This piece of sculpture cannot be fired—for one thing, it contains a heavy steel frame, and for another, the clay is so thick that it would be certain to explode—and so molds must be made of it.

Making a plaster waste mold. The clay model has been shellacked and sized. Pipe frames have been built to reinforce the two large portions of the mold that will be cast against the front and back of the figure. Brass shims are in place across the breast and down the sides. These will divide the two large sections of the mold into front and back. The portion above the breast will be cast in smaller sections. Cupfuls of plaster are thrown against the model to form the shell that will be the mold. Note how some details, the spire of the church, the cross on top of the crown, have been removed from the model.

Removing a section of the mold. The clay model is destroyed in this process.

The mold we have watched in the making is a waste mold. From this a plaster of Paris model will be made to be used in casting the final press mold. Here the portions of the waste mold that form the head have been sealed together and a workman is making a plaster cast of the head. A piece of burlap soaked in plaster of Paris is being put into the casting for reinforcement. This plaster casting will not be solid. Plaster will be built up on the inner surfaces of the waste mold with burlap reinforcement making a shell about 1½″ thick.

A section of the plaster model of the statue has been cast; the waste mold is being removed.

Where shapes are intricate, the waste mold must be chipped away from the plaster model.

Finishing the plaster model. Two of the sections have been joined together. Pipes have been passed through holes cut in the sections. These pipes are used when sections of the model are hoisted into position. After the plaster model is finished, a final press mold in smaller sections will be made.

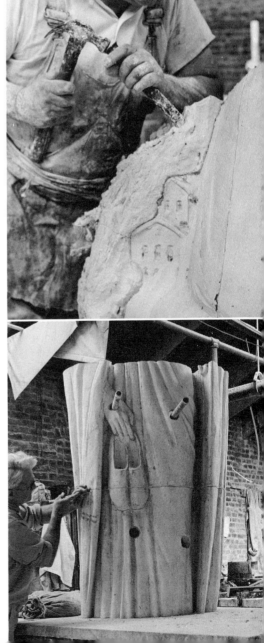

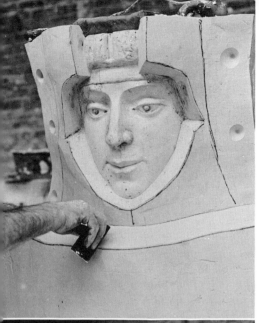

Making the press mold for the head. The portions of the press mold that form the sides of the head and the area under the chin have been completed. The sculptor is ready to cast the portion that will form the face. Note the notches.

Pressing clay into the mold. The portions of the mold that form the head are held together with metal strips tightened with wooden blocks. A workman pounds clay into the mold with his fist. The walls of the statue must be of uniform thickness, about $1\frac{1}{2}''$ to $2''$.

The pressed head is taken out of the mold. The sculptor removes seam lines and carefully finishes the surface.

Color. The pressing has not yet been fired. It is dry, glaze has been sprayed on it, pigments are being painted on the unfired glaze to give a polychrome effect.

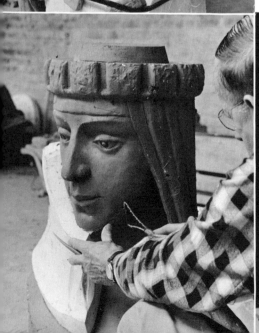

Into the kiln.

Inside the kiln. This is an oil-fired bee-hive kiln, down draft. Temperature is brought up very slowly until it reaches 2200°F. After firing, the kiln is cooled very slowly to anneal the terra cotta. The cycle of heating and cooling requires from 12 to 14 days.

The assembling room. Portions of the fired statue are put together, ground where necessary to assure proper fit, then packed for shipment. The finished statue is now in place on a church in Elizabeth, New Jersey.

Plate 100—Terra-cotta wall tile with design painted in engobe by Antonio Prieto.

The technology of terra cotta has advanced to a point where manufacturers are able to produce extremely thin yet strong panels in sizes up to 18″ × 24″. Some of these are perfectly flat while others have decorations in relief made in a number of stock patterns. Specially designed panels can be custom made to meet the requirements of architects and their ceramic designers.

Many ceramists have been able to work with unfired terra-cotta shapes obtained from commercial plants, carving and decorating them, making garden sculpture out of large sections of extruded sewer pipe, using pieces of smaller pipe to make grilles and wall dividers. In the illustration in Plate 100, Antonio Prieto displays an unfired terra-cotta wall tile on which he has painted an abstract design, using engobes and underglaze colors. When this tile has gone back to the factory and been fired, it will be used in a wall as a built-in mural.

The ceramic-walled ticket office of Alitalia in New York City is another example of cooperation between the architect and the ceramist. In planning this project, Gio Ponti the architect called upon a number of ceramic artists, among them Fausto Melotti whose work we saw in Chapter 13, and Romano Rui whose plaques are shown in Plate 101. This picture also

Plate 101—Portion of ceramic wall in the ticket office of Alitalia, New York City, with 2 ceramic plaques by Romano Rui. Architect Gio Ponti. *Photograph courtesy of Alitalia Airlines.*

Plate 102—Sand-cast mural in the lobby of the Vision Building, New York City, by George Nocito. Pebbles, crushed stones, colored gravel, and pieces of colored glass are part of the design.

Lower right: detail showing variety of materials, textures, and colors. *Photographs by Chas Nagy.*

shows some of the variety of textures and surface patterns of the handmade wall tiles.

In Chapter 8 we promised to say more about the uses of sand casting in architecture. Plate 102 shows a mural which covers one wall of the lobby of the Vision Building in New York City. This mural is much larger than the sand castings we made in Chapter 8 but the methods of construction are essentially the same. The artist, George Nocito, first prepared drawings which were approved by the client who had commissioned the mural. The next step was to construct a framework of steel angle irons on the studio floor. This framework, the full size of the planned mural, served as a form which was filled with crushed white marble (this took the place of sand). The sketch was then drawn full size directly on the crushed marble, the surface of which had been carefully leveled. After this the marble was modeled by scooping out and pressing in with various shaped objects as shown in Photo Series 29.

Upon completion of the modeling, color was added to some areas of the work by putting in chips of different colored marble. (All of this designing, of course, was done in the negative—the right side of the design became the left side of the mural, and areas pushed in became projections.)

The casting was made with white Portland cement and marble chips. It was necessary first to pour a very thin mix over the entire surface, using great care not to damage the modeling in the pouring process. The first pouring was followed by a normal mix to build up the panel to the desired thickness. The completed casting was sawed into six sections so that it could be lifted and transported. After a good brushing, the work was ready to be installed.

Visit commercial terra-cotta plants now and then—brickyards too. Such visits are bound to be interesting and they may prove to be sources of inspiration as well; they might even open doors to new opportunities.

22

Careers

A RE THERE opportunities for earning a living in the field of ceramic design? Yes, indeed; there are many, and they are good.

The art of the potter today is more than the making of pots. Ceramics have become an important part of modern living. During the past decade there has been a tremendous increase in the use of ceramic products, and people are much more aware of ceramic design than they used to be. Museums and galleries give more and more space to exhibitions of ceramic creations that range from adaptations of the classic and the traditional to the most extreme *avant-garde* sculpture, and modern homes make extensive use of ceramics in the spirit of contemporary decor.

New materials have become available to the artist-potter. Much more freedom is accepted in ceramic design; work that would have been rejected at ceramic shows 10 years ago now wins prizes.

There is recognition today of the importance of the ceramic designer and of the role he plays in industrial production, and, as we saw in the last chapter, there is recognition too of the contribution that ceramic ornament can make to modern architecture as architects and ceramists join forces to make our cities more colorful, more cheerful places in which to live. There has even been a reawakening to the value of the craftsman-potter and a new appreciation of his wares.

All of the artists mentioned in this book are professional potters pursuing careers in ceramics that are highly satisfying, not only in terms of earning a living, but in the rewards that come from doing work that is creative, that they enjoy doing, which has won recognition. The things they do cover a wide range of activities in the ceramic field.

Most of them are individual creative artists, producers of ware which they sell. The producing potter is, in a sense, a one-man industry; he does everything for himself—designs, shapes, glazes, fires. Often he digs his own clay. His plant is tiny, with just enough room for a studio and a kiln, plus storage space. The things he makes are unique. He has his own style, plans his own forms and decorations. His product may be thrown pottery shapes, decorated tiles, humorous figurines, large pieces of sculpture, or tiny ceramic jewelry; no matter what he produces, it bears his

Plate 103—Pussycat, a ceramic bell by Pat Lopez, factory produced from designs developed by the artist on the potter's wheel. *Photograph by Bob Lopez.*

personal mark. His customers are the people who come to his shop in search of his wares. They often include buyers from specialty shops and department stores.

Next larger in size is the establishment of the artist who employs two or three or a half-dozen assistants. More work is produced in such a studio, but it is still all made by hand and is the product of a single designer.

Then there are bigger pottery establishments producing the work of individual artists. Some employ as many as 50 or 100 people. In these, machinery replaces handwork; clay is prepared in pug mills, forms are cast in molds or jiggered on wheels. Decorators sit at tables painting designs on ware. Yet in spite of assembly line methods, such establishments must still be considered one-man industries, for everything that is produced is the creation of the designer, the proprietor of the plant, who in all likelihood began some years ago as a producing potter with a one-man studio. No matter how large a volume of work is turned out, it all has the touch of this artist.

Most of the ceramic industries of the type we have just described are fascinating places. Let's visit a few.

One on the Pacific coast has grown from the studio of a woman potter, who used to make wheel-thrown articles of tableware that were extremely popular. Orders came in for her pieces in such quantity that it was impossible to fill them. With the help of her husband she shifted to mechanical production methods, using the designs of her wheel-thrown pieces, modifying them slightly when necessary. The ware continued popular, the industry grew. It employs over forty people most of whom are young artists who hope some day to be in business for themselves.

Another plant makes tiles. It was started some years ago by a pair of young men who met in a television studio where they were employed as assistant producers. In the course of planning a special feature on the history of ceramics, they became interested in the art. They started to make pieces just for fun. The pieces they made appealed to others and they began selling them. Among their customers were some who wanted tiles made to order. The two young men have considerable talent and they were able to make well-designed tile murals for their clients. Business continued to expand. At present they operate a highly successful industry with tile-extruding machinery and automatic tunnel kilns.

Another organization, like the first one we described, is a husband-and-wife enterprise. The wife is a gifted sculptor, the husband a scientifically trained engineer. Through the combination of artistic talent and skilled technology in developing clay bodies of great strength, this team has built up an industry which produces ceramics for architectural use, sculptured tile for the exteriors of buildings, room dividers, interior tiles, fountains, lighting arrangements, patio sculpture, and the like.

If we were to visit pottery establishments in Europe, we would see some factories of another type, where traditional pottery is made by mass production, yet where everything is still formed by hand in the same way that it was done centuries ago. Potters sit at their wheels and throw casseroles, several hundred in a day, all identical in size and shape. Or they make pitchers, or coffeepots, or coffeepot lids. Assistants bring them clay as they need it, sometimes help by sticking on handles. The thrown pieces are placed on boards and carried out into the sunlight to harden. When leather hard they are brought back in again, put on the wheel upside down, the bottoms are trimmed, then they go out into the sun until they are bone dry. This ware is glazed and fired in enormous wood-burning kilns. This is a different aspect of the potter's art. The workers are skilled craftsmen, not designers. The ware they produce is utilitarian, the forms they shape are like those made by their fathers and grandfathers before them.

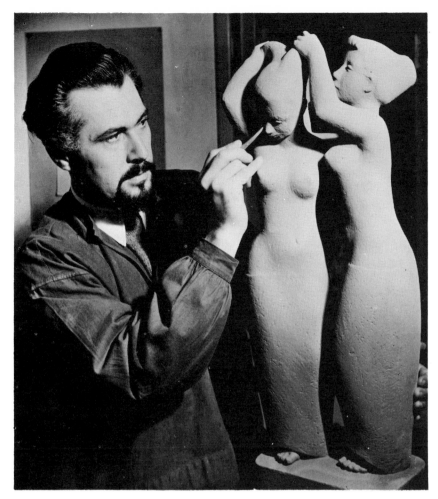

Plate 104—The sculptor Johannes Hedegaard at work in his studio. This artist is on the staff of the Royal Copenhagen Porcelain Company. *Photograph courtesy of Georg Jensen, Inc.*

A designer does not have to operate his own factory. Some have their designs mass produced for them. Others are on the staffs of industrial plants which make fine tableware of china or porcelain. The taste of the buying public is more sophisticated than it used to be; people today demand better designed products. There is a need for skilled ceramic designers.

Another ceramic industry, growing in popularity, is the small craft studio. Organizations of this type, often operated by man and wife, perform many different services. Usually the proprietors design and produce a special line of their own ware. In addition, they sell ceramic supplies and fire the work of other ceramists. They also maintain classrooms for instruction in ceramic techniques. This brings us to the last of the careers we shall mention—teaching.

Every artist is a teacher; artists learn from artists, and they in turn teach other artists. In former times this came about through an apprentice system

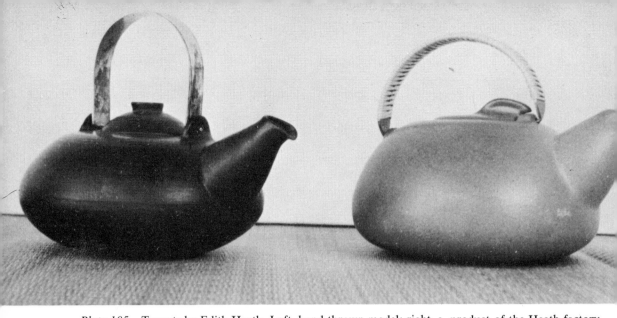

Plate 105—Teapots by Edith Heath. Left, hand-thrown model; right, a product of the Heath factory.

in which beginners started by sweeping out the studio of the master and gradually took over more important tasks until they had learned the secrets of the craft and became masters themselves, with studios and apprentices of their own.

There are few opportunities for working as an apprentice today—people who wish to study art must receive instruction in a classroom. The number of ceramics classes is increasing, not only in special art and craft schools, but in all levels of the educational system from kindergarten through college. There is a need for more ceramics teachers. The artist who enters teaching either as a full-time or a part-time career is able to continue with his own work.

The career of a teacher offers many rewards—the opportunity to work with people eager to learn, the chance to explore problems together, and above all, the privilege of giving to the world not only a number of ceramic pieces, but also the skill and the knowledge acquired while making them—of saying to someone younger, "Here is the torch; carry it high, and when it has lighted your way, pass it on to someone who will follow in your footsteps."

Plate 106—Ceramic wall surfacing, made in 12″ × 12″ × 1″ squares, and a wheel-thrown planter. These pieces were designed by the artist, Lee Rosen, and executed by Design Techniques, a firm founded by Mr. and Mrs. Rosen.

Appendix

TABLE OF CONE TEMPERATURES

Cone	Centi-grade	Fahren-heit	Color of Fire	What Happens to Clay	Type of Ware and Glazes
15	1435	2615			
14	1400	2552			
13	1350	2462		porcelain	porcelain
12	1335	2435		matures	
11	1325	2417			
10	1305	2381	white		china bodies
9	1285	2345		stoneware clays	stoneware
8	1260	2300		mature	salt glazes
7	1250	2282			
6	1230	2246			
5	1205	2201			
4	1190	2174		red clays melt	china glazes
3	1170	2138			
2	1165	2129			semi-vitreous ware
1	1160	2120			
01	1145	2093	yellow		
02	1125	2057		buff clays	earthenware
03	1115	2039		mature	
04	1060	1940			
05	1040	1904			
06	1015	1859		red clays mature	
07	990	1814			low fire earthenware
08	950	1742	orange		
09	930	1706			low fire lead glazes
010	905	1661			
011	895	1643	cherry red		
012	875	1607			lustre glazes
013	860	1580			
014	830	1526			
015	805	1481		organic matter in	chrome red glazes
016	795	1463		clay burns out	
017	770	1418	dull red		
018	720	1328			overglaze colors
019	660	1220			enamels
020	650	1202			
021	615	1139			
022	605	1121		dehydration begins	

DIAGRAM OF FIRING SCHEDULE

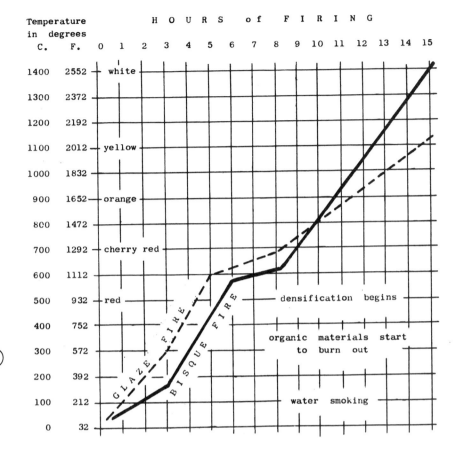

MAKING A SHRINKAGE RULE

Make a tile of plastic clay. On it draw a line and measure it. Fire the tile and measure the line again. Make a drawing as shown in the diagram.

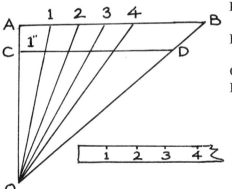

Draw line *AB* equal to the original length.
Draw line *CD* parallel to *AB* and equal to the fired length.
Draw lines *AC* and *BD;* prolong them until they meet at point *O*.
On *CD* measure 1″ distances.
Draw lines from *O* through the points laid off on *CD* and extend them until they touch line *AB*. The distance between each pair of points on *AB* shows how long a piece of clay would have to be when wet in order to be 1″ long after firing.

Mark these distances on a piece of heavy cardboard and number them *1, 2, 3* . . . This is a shrinkage rule which can be used to measure plastic clay. The reading will show what size the clay will be when fired.

CLASSIFICATION OF CLAYS

Primary or residual clay

Clay found on the spot where it was formed by the weathering of feldspathic rock; almost pure hydrous silicate of alumina; coarse, highly refractory, nonplastic, difficult to work with, fires white. Kaolin and china clay are of this type.

Secondary or sedimentary clay

Clay which has been carried great distances from its point of origin by winds, streams, glaciers. (Sometimes called "transported clay.") In its travels it has been ground to finer grain size, hence it is more plastic than primary clay. Contains many impurities and so is less refractory. Fires through a wide range of temperature. Usually fires red, buff or brown— sometimes white or black. Among secondary clays the following are the most frequently used in ceramics:

Plastic kaolin. Clay that has been transported without becoming heavily contaminated. Because of finer grain size, is more plastic than true kaolin. Fires white. Florida lake kaolin is of this type.

Ball clay. A sedimentary clay carried in a stream and deposited at the bottom of a body of water. Very fine grain, contains carbonaceous material, is highly plastic. Fires almost white. Used in porcelain and white ware bodies to provide workability.

Fire clay. A highly refractory clay, rough in texture, nonplastic. Used as an ingredient of stoneware bodies and in the manufacture of refractory brick.

Sagger clay. A type of coarse fire clay, highly refractory, used to make saggers.

Stoneware clay. Plastic clay that becomes vitreous at temperatures between cone 5 and cone 10. Usually fires light buff or gray.

Earthenware clay or common clay. Clay which contains iron and other impurities which lower the firing range. Matures between cone 08 and cone 03; most pottery throughout the world is made of common clay; also used to make bricks, tiles, and other heavy clay products.

Flint clay. A refractory clay which has been compacted into a hard, rocklike mass.

Shale. Metamorphic rock formed from sedimentary clay; nonplastic, used as an ingredient of bricks, sewer tile, and other clay products that are manufactured by extrusion.

Bentonite. A clay of volcanic origin containing colloidal matter; extremely plastic, used to improve the working properties of clay and clay bodies.

Terra cotta. A common clay of open, coarse grain structure which permits it to dry with a minimum of warping. Used in clay sculpture and in the manufacture of large building tiles.

TESTING THE PHYSICAL PROPERTIES OF CLAY

Plasticity

This is measured by handling the clay. Roll a long thin cylinder, twist it into a pretzel shape. If the clay takes the shape easily it is plastic (fat); if the clay crumbles it is nonplastic (short).

Water of plasticity

Allow clay to dry and crush it into a dry powder. Weigh out 100 grams and put on a glass slab. Put 50 grams of water in a graduate and pour it, drop by drop, onto the clay while grinding the clay with a spatula. When enough water has been added to make the clay plastic, read the graduate to determine the number of grams of water used. This number is the percentage of water of plasticity. In most clays this varies between 30% and 45%—the clays with a higher percentage are usually more plastic.

Firing range

Make draw trials. Prepare a series of test tiles $1\frac{1}{2}'' \times 6'' \times \frac{1}{4}''$; fire these with the ends resting on kiln props, placed in the kiln so that tiles may be easily reached. Fire the kiln. When the temperature reaches cone 08, remove the first tile; at 06 remove the second, and so on. Allow to cool, then examine for color and deformation, test for density, measure to determine shrinkage.

Color

The draw trials show variation in color with rise in temperature.

Deformation

Draw trials that slump are overfired. The maturing point of the clay is reached just before slumping begins.

Density

Weigh a piece of dry bisque, immerse it in water for 24 hours, weigh a second time, then calculate as follows:

$$\frac{\text{Weight wet minus Weight dry}}{\text{Weight dry}} \times 100 = \% \text{ Absorption}$$

5% absorption is satisfactory, 10% is too high—glazes will craze and ware will be too absorbent for table use.

Porosity

This is judged by examining fired tests. If pieces crack or warp badly, the clay is too "tight." There is no way for water to escape during the firing.

Shrinkage

Make a test tile, mark a distance on it exactly 6" long while the clay is wet. Allow the clay to dry, fire the tile and measure again. Calculate as follows:

$$\frac{\text{Original length minus Fired length}}{\text{Original length}} \times 100 = \% \text{ Shrinkage}$$

COLORING ACTION OF OXIDES IN GLAZES

Oxide	Percent	Color in Lead Glaze	Color in Alkaline Glaze	Color When Reduced
Chromium oxide	2%	Vermilion at cone 012 Brown at cone 06 Green at cone 02		
Cobalt carbonate	0.5%	Medium blue	Medium blue	Medium blue
	1%	Strong blue	Strong blue	Strong blue
Copper carbonate	0.5%			Copper red
	1%	Green	Turquoise	Deep red
	2–3%	Deep green	Turquoise	Red and black
	8%	Green with metallic areas	Blue-green with metallic areas	
Ilmenite	3%	Tan specks	Gray-black specks	Spotty brown
Iron chromate	2%	Gray-brown	Gray	
Iron oxide	1%			Celadon
	2%	Pale amber	Pale tan	Olive green celadon
	4%	Red-brown	Brown	Mottled green
	10%	Dark red	Black-brown	Saturated iron red
Manganese carbonate	4%	Purple-brown	Purple-violet	Brown
Nickel oxide	2%	Gray-brown	Gray	Gray-blue
Rutile	5%	Tan	Gray-brown	
Vanadium stain	6%	Yellow	Yellow	
Cobalt carbonate Iron oxide	0.5% 2%	Gray-blue	Gray-blue	
Cobalt carbonate Manganese carbonate	0.5% 4%	Blue-purple	Aubergine	
Cobalt carbonate Rutile	0.5% 3%	Gray-blue	Gray-blue	Textured blue
Copper carbonate Rutile	3% 3%	Textured green	Textured blue-green	
Ilmenite Rutile	2% 2%	Textured brown	Textured gray-brown	Spotty brown
Iron oxide Cobalt carbonate Manganese carbonate	8% 1% 3%			Black
Cobalt carbonate Iron oxide Manganese carbonate	3% 2% 2%	Mirror black		
Manganese carbonate Iron oxide	6% 3%	Luster brown		

PREPARING CASTING SLIP

1. Secure a large container; fill with desired amount of water.
2. Put electrolytes (soda ash, sodium silicate, or others) into water; stir.
3. Add body ingredients to water—plastic materials first (ball clays), nonplastic materials last (talc, grog, feldspar, flint). Weight of body ingredients should be twice the weight of the water.
4. Mix thoroughly, with a mechanical mixer (blunger) if possible. If no mechanical mixer is available, stir thoroughly with a wooden stick. Avoid getting air bubbles into slip.
5. If mixture is too dry, add small additional amounts of electrolyte, but no more than necessary to bring clay to proper consistency (casting slip should weigh about 30 oz. per pint).
6. Allow slip to age as long as possible (at least a week), stirring frequently. Keep in a warm place.
7. Screen slip through 80-mesh sieve before using.

CLAY BODIES

A mixture of 2 or more different clays or a mixture of clay and minerals is called a *clay body*. Here are some typical recipes:

White artware body, cone 06

Ball clay	33.3
Talc	66.7

Red body, cone 04

Ball clay	25
Dalton red clay	35
Talc	40

White body, cone 04

China clay	15
Ball clay	30
Feldspar	10
Talc	33
Ferro frit 3195	10
Bentonite	2

Stoneware body, cone 8

Jordan clay	20
Sagger clay	55
Fire clay	10
Nepheline syenite	5
Flint	5
Grog 40-60 mesh	5

Porcelain body, cone 10 to cone 15

China clay	17
Florida lake clay	8
Ball clay	25
Feldspar	25
Flint	25

ALTERING THE PHYSICAL PROPERTIES OF A CLAY

To increase plasticity

(a) Allow clay to age. Keep moist in a plastic bag or in a crock for several weeks. (*Note:* Aging is more rapid if clay is kept warm, about 80°F.)

—or—

(b) Add ball clay in quantities up to 20%.

—or—

(c) Add small percentage of bentonite, not over 2%.

To lower firing range

Add body flux.

To increase density

(a) Fire to a higher temperature.

—or—

(b) Add flux.

—or—

(c) Add flint.

To increase porosity

Add fine grog.

To reduce shrinkage

Add flint.

PREPARING CLAY DUG FROM THE GROUND

1. Let clay dry, break into small pieces.
2. Pour broken bits of clay into large container of water. Have twice as much water as clay.
3. Let clay slake for 3 hours.
4. Stir clay and water into a smooth slip.
5. Allow slip to stand until clay has settled to bottom of container. Pour off excess water.
6. Screen slip through 60-mesh sieve.
7. Pour screened slip into drying bats and let stand until clay is sufficiently dry to be picked up.
8. Form clay into bricks and store in a crock or in plastic bags.

DETERMINING THE PERCENTAGES OF ELECTRO-LYTES NEEDED TO DEFLOCCULATE CLAY

1. Mix together 1000 grams of dry clay and 400 grams of water.
2. Put 25 cc. of water in a glass graduate, add 3 grams of soda ash and 3 grams of sodium silicate. (To weigh sodium silicate, put the graduate containing water on a scale and weigh it. Add sodium silicate drop by drop until the total weight of container and solution increases the desired amount.) Then add enough water to bring the quantity up to 30 cc.
3. Add the solution to the clay drop by drop, while stirring the clay constantly.
4. When the clay turns into a liquid thin enough to pour, consult the graduate to find out how much of the solution has been used.
5. Calculate as follows:

$$\frac{\text{Number of grams of solution used}}{100} = \% \text{ of each deflocculent required}$$

Note 1: Don't go wrong on a decimal here. If it required 15 grams of the solution to make the clay liquid, then $15/100 = 0.15$, so it takes 0.15% of soda ash and 0.15% of sodium silicate to deflocculate the clay.

Note 2: If clay does not turn liquid, add additional amounts of water but not enough to make the total weight of water more than 500 grams (50% of clay content). If this does not work, try substituting different electrolytes, sal soda, sodium tannate, sodium alginate, or a commercial water softener such as Calgon.

Note 3: Some clays are impossible to deflocculate.

SOME COMMERCIAL FRITS USED BY STUDIO POTTERS

Leadless

FERRO ENAMEL CO.

No. 3124. Borosilicate type used in cone 3 to cone 5 glazes.
No. 3134. Borosilicate type used in artware glazes.
No. 3150. Used as body flux.
No. 3195. Used in low-temperature alkaline glazes.
No. 5301. Used for low-temperature crackle glazes.

PEMCO

P-54. Borosilicate type used in partially fritted glazes.
P-64. For low-temperature all fritted glazes.
P-626. Low-temperature barium cone 06 through cone 02.
P-930. Low-temperature strontia.

Frits Containing Lead

FERRO ENAMEL CO.

No. 3304. Good all-purpose high-lead frit for glazes cone 08 to cone 02.
No. 3419. Lead borosilicate low-melting.
No. 3466. Zinc bearing.
No. 3496. Medium lead for all fritted glazes for cone 05 to cone 02. Good as clear glaze under overglaze colors.

PEMCO

Pb-41. Zinc lead borosilicate for low-temperature glazes.
Pb-63. Low-melting high-lead frit for low-temperature glazes.
Pb-349. Used for glazes range cone 02 to cone 8.
Pb-461. Lead borosilicate.
Pb-545. Lead alumina silicate.
Pb-742. Similar to Pb-63, better for transparent glazes.

GLOSSARY OF CERAMIC TERMS

Abstraction—A work of art made without application to any particular object.

Agateware—Pottery that is veined and mottled to resemble agate.

Air floated—Sorted in particles of similar size by air separation.

Albany slip—A natural clay which melts at cone 8, used as a glaze on clay which fires at a higher temperature. Usually dark brown. Used by early American potters on stoneware and used today on porcelain electrical insulators.

Albarello—A cylindrical jar with concave sides, used for holding drugs. Decorated with majolica.

Alkali—Any substance having marked basic properties. For potters the term refers generally to compounds of sodium and potassium which act as fluxes in alkaline glazes.

Amorphous—Formless; in chemistry, without crystalline structure.

Argillaceous—Of the nature of clay or containing clay.

Armature—A framework used to support clay while it is being modeled.

Arretine ware—A red terra cotta, decorated in relief, made at Arretium in Italy, from about 100 B.C. to about A.D. 100.

Aventurine—A glossy type of glaze containing sparkling particles of copper or chromic oxide or ferric oxide.

Ball mill—A device for grinding glazes, consisting of a porcelain jar in which glaze ingredients are placed along with a charge of pebbles and water. The jar is then rotated.

Banding wheel (also **Whirler** or **Decorating wheel**)—A turntable which permits work to be rotated while it is shaped or decorated.

Basalt ware—A type of black stoneware developed by Josiah Wedgwood.

Bat—A disc or slab of plaster of Paris or fired clay, used to dry out clay or to work on.

Bisque—Unglazed fired clay.

Blanks—Pottery shapes, tiles, plates, fired but not glazed, used for applied decorations.

Blunger—A device for mixing clay slip, consisting of a container and rotating paddles.

Bone china—Hard translucent white ware containing bone ash (calcium phosphate). Originally produced in England.

Bucchero ware—A type of black pottery with ornament in relief, made by the Etruscans about 600 B.C., also called *buccero nero*. The black color was produced by reduction.

Burnishing—Producing a shiny surface on clay by rubbing it with a smooth tool when it is leather hard.

Butterfly—A small block of wood hung by a wire from the frame of an armature to support masses of clay.

Calcareous—Containing lime.

Calcining—A process of firing a material to expel volatile matter and to dehydrate it; done frequently with clay, borax and other material before they are used in glaze recipes.

Calipers—A device for measuring the dimensions of objects.

Calipers, proportional—A device for enlarging or reducing dimensions proportionately.

Cartoon—A full-size drawing for a mural.

Case mold—A mold from which other molds are made.

Casing—The process of making a case mold of a mold.

Casting—The process of pouring a liquid, either slip or plaster of Paris, into a mold where it hardens.

Casting box—A device for constructing rectangular retaining walls when making plaster of Paris molds.

Celadon—A pale green glaze produced by iron in a reduction fire.

Cheese state—The period during the setting of plaster of Paris when it has the consistency of cream cheese.

Chemically combined water—Water which is combined in molecular form with clay to make it a hydrous aluminum silicate. This water is driven off in the kiln when the clay reaches red heat (about 900° to 1000°F.).

Coefficient of expansion—the ratio of increase in size of a substance for a given rise in temperature.

Colloidal—Made up of extremely fine particles suspended in a fluid medium; gelatinous.

Cones, pyrometric—Small clay rods which indicate kiln temperatures.

Cottle—A wall set in place around a model when plaster of Paris is to be poured over it.

Crackle—Tiny cracks in the surface of a glaze.

Crawling—A glaze defect in which the glaze rolls away from areas of the piece it is on, leaving bare spots.

Crazing—A glaze defect resulting from lack of fit between a glaze and the body it is on so that fine cracks appear in the glaze.

Crystallization—The formation of crystals. This occurs in glazes containing rutile, zinc, and other crystal-forming oxides.

Damp closet—A box, usually zinc-lined, for keeping work moist.

Damper—A device for closing the flue of a kiln.

De-airing—The process of subjecting plastic clay to a vacuum so that most of the air is drawn out of the clay. This makes it better for throwing. A de-airing device is usually attached to a pug mill.

Decalcomania—A process of transferring pictures and designs from specially prepared paper to china or glass.

Decant—To pour off liquid gently without disturbing the solid material which has settled.

Decomposition—The act of separating or resolving into constituent parts; disintegration. It is the decomposition of granite rock which forms clay.

Deflocculation—The addition of electrolytes to clay slip to reduce the amount of water needed to make it pourable.

Dehydration—The expulsion of water. Clay is dehydrated when the chemically combined water is driven off at about 1000°F.

Devitrification—Recrystallization on cooling, a defect in glazes.

Dipping—A method of applying glaze to a piece of pottery by immersing it in a container of glaze.

Draft—The taper on the sides of a model which permits it to be withdrawn from a mold.

Draw trial—A piece of clay drawn from the kiln during firing to judge the progress of the fire.

Dresden china—Decorated porcelain made near Dresden in Saxony, characterized by elaborate ornamention and delicate figure pieces. Also called *Meissen ware*.

Dry footing—The process of removing glaze from the bottom rim of a piece so that it can be fired standing on a kiln shelf, without stilts.

Dunting—Breaking from strains in cooling.

Earthenware—Pottery fired to a temperature below 2000°F.

Electrolyte—An alkaline substance, usually soda ash or sodium silicate, added to a clay slip to deflocculate it.

Engobe—Clay slip, usually colored.

Epoxy cement—A strong adhesive good for attaching tiles to masonry walls.

Extruding—Process of shaping plastic clay by forcing it through a die.

Faïence—Earthenware covered with opaque glaze with decorations painted over the glaze.

Fat clay—Clay that is highly plastic.

Fettling—Removing the seams (fettles) of a cast piece.

Filler—A nonplastic material, such as flint, added to clay bodies to help drying and control shrinkage.

Filter press—A device for squeezing water out of clay slip to make it into plastic clay.

Firebox—The portion of a kiln in which the flame burns.

Fit—The adjustment between a glaze and the clay which it is on.

Flux—A substance which melts and causes other substances to melt also.

Frit—A glaze or partial glaze that has been fired and pulverized.

Frog—A device for cutting clay made by a wire stretched across two prongs.

Fuller's earth—An earthy substance resembling potter's clay but lacking plasticity, used in fulling cloth and as a filter medium. A colloidal hydrus aluminum silicate.

Fuse—To melt under the action of heat.

Glass—An amorphous substance, usually transparent or translucent, made by fusing together silica and soda and some other base.

Glass cullet—Finely pulverized glass used as an ingredient in glazes or as a body flux.

Globar—An electric element in the form of a bar, made of silicon carbide, capable of reaching extremely high temperatures.

Goldstone—Aventurine glaze.

Gombroon ware—Porcelain with pierced designs covered with flowing glaze so that no openings are left but light will shine through.

Greenware—Clay shapes that have not been fired.

Hard paste—True porcelain.

Igneous—Formed by the solidification of molten masses.

Infrared lamp—A type of electric light bulb whose light is good for drying clay.

Insulating bricks—Extremely porous, soft bricks used on the outside of kilns to reduce the loss of heat through the walls.

Jasper ware—A type of pottery made by Josiah Wedgwood, having a light-colored body with white figures and ornaments in relief.

Jiggering—The process of manufacturing pottery by means of convex molds and templates on a power wheel.

Jollying—A process similar to jiggering, using concave molds with the jigger template forming the inside of bowls and cups.

Kanthal—A metal alloy made in Sweden used as an element in electric kilns, capable of reaching temperatures of cone 6.

Kaolin—Pure clay.

Kiln furniture—Refractory shelves and posts used to stack a kiln.

Kiln wash—A mixture of china clay and flint with enough water added to make it brushable, used to protect kiln shelves from glazes that may fall upon them.

Lawn—To pass through a fine mesh screen.

Luster—A type of surface decoration made by depositing a thin layer of metal.

Luting—The process of joining two pieces of leather-hard clay with slip or slurry.

Majolica—Earthenware covered with an opaque glaze containing tin with decorations painted on top of the glaze. Named for the island of Majorca.

Mat—Dull surfaced, not shiny.

Maturing—reaching the temperature which produces the most serviceable degree of hardness. In the case of glaze, reaching the point of complete fusion.

Meissen ware—Dresden china.

Metamorphic—Changed in constitution by heat, pressure, water; said of rocks.

Muffle—A chamber in a kiln which protects ware from contact with the flame.

Nichrome—A chromium nickel alloy used as an element in electric kilns. Limited to temperatures of cone 2 and below.

Notches—Round depressions cut in one half of a mold so that the other half, when cast against it, will fit in place.

Opacifier—Material added to a transparent glaze to make it opaque; most commonly used are tin oxide and zircopax.

Organic materials—Vegetable or animal material sometimes present in natural clay.

Oxidation—The act of combining with oxygen, usually at high temperatures.

Patina—A surface appearance on objects, usually the result of age. Ceramic sculpture can be given a patina by treatment with wax, oil and other materials.

Peachbloom—A reduction glaze containing copper, with a pink color.

Peeling—A defect in which portions of a glaze or an engobe separate from the ware.

Petuntse—A type of feldspar found in China, combined with kaolin to make Chinese porcelain.

pH—The relative alkalinity or acidity of a solution.

Piercing—Cutting through the wall of a piece to create an open design.

Pinholes—A glaze defect caused by too rapid firing or by tiny air holes in the clay.

Pitchers—Porcelain grog.

Plaster of Paris—Partially dehydrated calcium sulfate, made by calcining gypsum rock. Useful for bats and molds.

Plasticity—A quality of clay which permits it to be molded into different shapes without crumbling or sagging.

Polychrome—Many-colored; a term applied especially to Greek vases made in Athens during the 6th century B.C. The ground was often white with black, white, red, and yellow colors used in the decoration.

Pooled glaze—A fluid glaze which has flowed to the bottom of a bowl or a depression, forming a pool.

Porcelain—A hard white body, often translucent, composed chiefly of kaolin and feldspar, fired to cone 12 or higher.

Porosity—The quality or degree of being porous, filled with holes, capable of absorbing liquids.

Pressing—A method of shaping clay by squeezing it into molds or between the two halves of a press mold.

Pugging—Grinding and mixing clay in a pug mill.

Pug mill—A machine for grinding and mixing plastic clay. Usually has a vacuum attached.

Pyrometer—A device for measuring kiln temperature, usually operated by an electric thermocouple.

Raku—Japanese earthenware, used in the tea ceremony, rough, with dark glaze.

Raw glaze—A glaze that contains no fritted materials.

Reducing agent—Organic material put in a glaze or into a kiln chamber during the firing to bring about reduction.

Reduction—The act of removing oxygen from metal oxides; occurs during fire when not enough oxygen is present.

Refractory—Resisting high temperatures.

Reinforcement—Materials, such as burlap or metal lath, placed in plaster or cement castings for strength.

Relief—Sculptural form which projects from a background.

Representation—A picture or piece of sculpture made in the likeness of some material object.

Retaining wall—A cottle.

Reticulation—The netlike appearance which frequently occurs when a nonflowing glaze is put on top of one that flows more freely; also occurs in glazes high in boric oxide.

Rib—A flat tool, usually wood, used to refine shapes being thrown on a potter's wheel.

Rouge flambé—A type of copper-red reduction glaze, deep red with areas of green and blue.

Roulette—A wheel of wood or bisque with recessed designs in the rim, rolled over a plastic clay form to make a band of raised decoration.

Rubbing—Burnishing.

Running plaster—A method of shaping plaster by moving templates across it while it is going through the cheese state.

Sagger—A box made of fire clay in which glazed ware is placed for protection from the flames in a down-draft kiln.

Salt glazing—A method of glazing ware (usually stoneware) by throwing salt into the firebox of the kiln when temperature is at its highest point.

Samian ware—Same as Arretine ware.

Sand casting—A method of creating form by pouring a material which will set, such as plaster of Paris, cement or clay slip, into a hollow scooped out of wet sand.

Sang de boeuf—Oxblood, a deep red copper reduction glaze.

Sedimentary—Formed by the deposit of sediment; said of rocks and clays.

Setting—The act of hardening as a result of cooling or chemical action.

Settling—A process by which materials in suspension, such as glazes, fall to the bottom of a container, often forming a hard mass.

Sgraffito—A method of decorating by scratching through a coating of engobe.

Shard—A pottery fragment.

Shims—Pieces of thin material used to separate portions of a mold.

Shivering—A glaze defect in which sections of a glaze lift off the piece.

Short clay—Clay that is not plastic.

Siccative—A drying agent.

Sinter—To harden by heat without reaching maturing temperature.

Slake—To soak with water.

Slip—Liquid clay.

Slurry—Clay of paste-like consistency.

Soft paste—An imitation of porcelain containing various materials, such as gypsum, calcium, bone, which act as fluxes, making the ware mature at a lower temperature than does true porcelain.

Spraying—A method of applying glazes with a spray gun.

Sprig—A relief decoration pressed in a sprig mold attached to ware with slip

Stacking—Loading a kiln.

Stains—Pigments used for coloring clay bodies and glazes.

Stilts—Porcelain tripods on which glazed ware is fired. Stilts for low-fire work may have points of nichrome.

Stoneware—High-fired, vitreous ware, usually gray, sometimes shades of brown or tan.

Stylization—A form of design in which objects are represented according to a convention or style rather than realistically.

Taglietelle—A device for cutting clay into layers of uniform thickness.

Temperature—Intensity of heat measured in degrees Fahrenheit or centigrade.

Template—A pattern for shaping the profile of a piece.

Terra cotta—Low-fire earthenware, usually red, often containing grog, used for sculpture.

Terra sigillata—A surface treatment, developed by the Romans, that gives pottery a hard, semiglossy surface, made by spraying on an engobe of extremely fine colloidal particles of clay.

Tessera—A small piece of tile, glass, or other hard material, used to make mosaics.

Thread separation—A method of separating the two halves of a waste mold by pulling a thread through the plaster when it is in the cheese state.

Throwing—The process of shaping clay on the potter's wheel.

Tin enamel—A type of low-fire lead glaze containing tin, used in majolica work.

Trailing—Using a tube to apply a line of slip to clay.

Translucent—Transmitting light but not transparent.

Turning—Process of shaping leather-hard clay by holding cutting tools against it as it turns on a wheel.

Turning box—A device for shaping plaster of Paris by turning it on a spindle and holding templates against it.

Turntable—A rotating platform on which work may be turned; a banding wheel.

Viscosity—Resistance of a liquid to movement.

Vitrification—The act of becoming vitreous, that is, hard, glasslike, non-absorbent.

Volatilize—To pass from solid through liquid to gaseous state under the action of heat.

Volclay—Bentonite.

Water smoking—The first portion of the firing cycle during which water is driven from the clay.

Wax resist—A method of decoration in which liquid wax is applied to portions of greenware after which engobe is brushed or sprayed over the piece. The wax repels the engobe.

Weathering—Decomposition under the action of wind, rain, heat, etc.

Wedging—The act of kneading or mixing plastic clay by cutting it in half and slamming the halves together.

Wedging board—A block of wood or plaster of Paris with a post holding a wire so that a lump of clay may be cut in half and the two halves slammed together.

Wedgwood, Josiah—The famous English potter, creator of Jasper ware.

Weep hole—A hole made in a depression in a piece of sculpture which is to be used outdoors so that rain water will not collect there.

Whirler—A banding wheel.

White body—A clay body which fires white, often at a low temperature, in which case it usually contains a high percentage of talc.

Wire, piano—Strong nonstretching wire used on wedging boards.

GLOSSARY OF CERAMIC MATERIALS

Albany slip—A natural clay which, when fired above cone 7, melts to form a deep reddish brown glaze; used on stoneware and on porcelain electrical insulators.

Antimony—A source of color, opaque white in leadless glazes; semi-opaque yellow in lead glazes.

Arsenic—An active flux, best avoided because it is extremely poisonous.

Barium—Barium carbonate ($BaCO_3$), used in clay bodies to make sulfides insoluble. Used in glazes for mat texture.

Bentonite—A highly plastic, very fine clay of volcanic origin; used in small quantities to make other clays plastic.

Bone ash—Calcium phosphate ($Ca_3(PO_4)_2$), added to china clay to produce bone china.

Borax—($Na_2O \cdot 2B_2O_3 \cdot 10H_2O$). Used as a flux in low-temperature glazes; highly soluble, almost always used fritted; produces beautiful colors, especially with copper oxide.

Cadmium—Used with selenium to produce red stains for glazes.

Calcium—An active flux used usually as whiting or calcium carbonate ($CaCO_3$) in glazes and clay bodies.

Cement—A product made by calcining and pulverizing argillaceous and calcareous materials; mixed with sand and water to form mortar.

Cement, Keene—A type of cement much like plaster of Paris, made from gypsum, used to make a white mortar. Not waterproof.

Cement, Portland—A type of cement used for exterior work; waterproof.

Ceramispar—Crushed granite used in clay bodies.

Chromium—A source of color, used as chromium oxide (Cr_2O_3). Produces shades of green in lead-free glazes. At extremely low temperatures in lead glazes produces red in an oxidizing fire. Under reduction produces yellow in high lead glazes. In conjunction with tin oxide produces various shades of pink and maroon.

Cobalt—An important color source that produces a deep blue. Usually used as cobalt carbonate ($CoCO_3$). In combination with copper, manganese, and iron, produces black and gun metal glazes. Sometimes used as cobalt oxide (CoO) which is stronger, or as cobalt nitrate, a soluble salt used to add a slight bluish cast to a glaze or a body.

Colemanite—($2CaO \cdot 3B_2O_3 \cdot 5H_2O$). A natural source of calcium oxide and boric oxide. Used in glazes (called borosilicate glazes).

Copper—An important color source used usually as copper carbonate ($CuCO_3$) or copper oxide (CuO). In a lead glaze produces shades of green. In alkaline glazes produces turquoise blue. In a reduction fire produces colors ranging from purple to brilliant red.

Cornwall stone—A material resembling feldspar. Used as a flux in glazes. As a body ingredient tends to reduce warping.

Crocus martis—A color source producing reddish brown. Contains combinations of iron, oxide, and manganese dioxide.

Cryolite—(Na_3AlF_6). A flux used in enamels and glazes.

Dextrine—A binder for glazes.

Dolomite—($CaMg(CO_3)_2$). A source of magnesium oxide and calcium oxide used to replace part of the whiting in glazes and clay bodies.

Electrolyte—An alkaline substance, usually soda ash or sodium silicate, used to deflocculate clay slip. Other electrolytes include sodium alginate, sal soda, sodium tannate, and some water softeners.

Epsom salts—Used to prevent glazes, especially fritted glazes, from settling.

Fat oil, or **fat oil of turpentine**—A vehicle used in china painting.

Feldspar—In pure form $NaO \cdot Al_2O_3 \cdot 6SiO_2$, or albite. Rarely found in nature as a pure mineral but as a mixture of several types of feldspar which contain oxides of sodium, potassium, or calcium. The most important ceramic material next to clay. Used as a flux in clay bodies and in glazes.

Flint—Silica.

Fluorspar—Calcium fluoride (CaF_2), acts as an opacifier and a flux in glazes.

Frit—A glaze which has been fired and pulverized. See special section.

Glass cullet—Pulverized glaze used as a glaze ingredient or as a flux in clay bodies.

Grog—Clay which has been fired and ground. Used in clay bodies to control shrinkage and to give rough texture.

Gums—Binders used in engobes and underglaze decorations as well as in glazes. Most frequently used are gum tragacanth, gum arabic, CMC, V gum T, and various other prepared forms.

Gypsum—A naturally occurring material, hydrated sulfate of calcium ($CaSO_4 \cdot 2H_2O$), which is calcined, to make plaster of Paris. In its pure form called alabaster.

Hydrastone—Similar to hydrocal. Sets even harder.

Hydrocal—A hard-setting type of plaster of Paris.

Ilmenite—A titanium compound ($TiO_2 \cdot FeO$), used in granular form to produce specks in glazes.

Iron—An important source of color in bodies and glazes. In clay bodies produces shades from tan to brick red. In glazes produces shades of yellow, brown, and tan. In a high lead glaze at low temperature will produce iron red. An extra amount of iron produces a gold-flecked glaze called *aventurine*. In reduction, iron produces the beautiful green glaze *celadon*. Iron has three oxide forms—red (Fe_2O_3), black (FeO), and magnetite (Fe_3O_4).

Iron chromate—($FeCrO_4$). A source of color, especially for clay bodies; produces shades of gray.

Lead—The most widely used flux in low-temperature glazes, used as lead carbonate ($2PbCO_3 \cdot Pb(OH)_2$) or white lead. Red lead (Pb_3O_4) and litharge (PbO) mixed with molasses have been used to glaze primitive types of low-fired earthenware. Lead chromate ($PbCrO_4$), a source of color, produces shades of green in alkaline glazes, yellow in lead glazes. In the presence of tin, it produces shades of pink. *Poisonous.*

Lepidolite—($LiF \cdot KF \cdot Al_2O_3 \cdot 3SiO_2$). A flux used in high-fire glazes.

Lime—*See* Calcium.

Litharge—Lead monoxide (PbO), not as much used in ceramics as other sources of lead. *Poisonous.*

Lithium—(Li). A flux, similar to sodium or potassium in glazes, not frequently used—too expensive.

316

Magnesite—Magnesium carbonate ($MgCO_3$).

Magnesite cement—A white setting cement used in mosaics and in floor construction.

Magnesium—Used as magnesium carbonate ($MgCO_3$) as a flux in high-temperature glazes.

Magnetite—(Fe_3O_4). An oxide of iron.

Manganese—A source of color in glazes and bodies; produces shades of red, brown, purple, and black. Used as manganese carbonate ($MnCO_3$) or as manganese dioxide (MnO_2).

Maroon base—A prepared ceramic pigment made by calcining chromium in the presence of tin.

Minium—(Pb_3O_4). Red lead oxide, a flux in low-temperature glazes; can be used alone as a glaze on low-fired earthenware. *Poisonous*. (The word *miniature* originally meant a picture or manuscript illumination colored with minium.)

Nepheline syenite—A type of feldspar with a low fusion point; used in place of other feldspars as a flux in stoneware bodies to lower maturing temperature.

Nickel oxide, green (NiO) or **nickel oxide, black** (Ni_2O_3)—Sources of color in glazes; in the presence of zinc, produce shades of slate blue; with calcium, shades of tan; with barium, brown; with magnesia, green. Both oxides produce similar results. Useful in crystalline glazes.

Niter—Potassium nitrate (KNO_3). A source of potassium used in making frits.

Ochre—An iron ore used as a colorant for clay bodies to produce shades of yellow, red, or brown.

Opax—A commercial silicate of zirconium; acts as an opacifier in glazes.

Pearl ash—Potassium carbonate (K_2CO_3), used as a source of potassium in glazes, usually fritted.

Petuntse—A feldspar found in China. Early Chinese potters mixed it with kaolin to make porcelain.

Pink oxide—*See* Maroon base.

Plaster of Paris—Calcium sulfate ($CaSO_4 \cdot \frac{1}{2}H_2O$). Made by calcining gypsum, used for making molds and casts.

Plastilene—Clay ground with oil so that it becomes nondrying. Used to model forms from which casts are made.

Potash—Potassium carbonate (K_2CO_3). Also called pearl ash, a flux, extremely soluble, rarely used except in fritted form.

Potassium dichromate—($K_2Cr_2O_3$). A source of color in glazes; produces yellow, red.

Pumicite—An ash formed by volcanic action, a kind of natural frit that can be used as a glaze ingredient.

Red lead—*See* Minium. *Poisonous*.

Rutile—An ore containing titanium oxide (TiO_2) and iron; produces light shades of yellow and tan in glazes; also produces broken color and mottled effects; with copper or cobalt, produces beautifully textured colors.

Salt, common—Sodium chloride (NaCl); produces a hard glaze on stoneware when thrown into the kiln at its highest temperature.

Salts, soluble—Metallic salts such as copper sulfate, silver nitrate, gold chloride, bismuth subnitrate, and others, used to produce lusters; also used to brush light washes of color over glazes.

Sand—Silica.

Selenium—A source of red in glazes and glaze stains.

Silica—(Si). Flint, most abundant substance in the earth's rocky crust, a major component of clays and glazes. Flint is used in glazes to change the coefficient of expansion and control crazing and shivering.

Silicon carbide—(SiC). Used very finely ground, as a reducing agent in glazes; coarse ground it produces lava-type glazes. Also used as an abrasive (carborundum) and an electric kiln element (Globar).

Size (potter's soap)—A neutral soap manufactured especially for ceramic work, used as a separator in mold making.

Soapstone—Talc.

Soda—Sodium oxide (Na_2O), an active flux, useful in glazes from the lowest to the highest temperature. Has some disadvantages—high coefficient of expansion; glazes are soft, easily scratched. Many feldspars contain soda. Glazes with high soda content have beautiful colors, especially the turquoise blue produced by copper.

Soda ash—Sodium bicarbonate (Na_2CO_3), a source of soda in glazes; soluble, hence usually fritted. Also used as an electrolyte.

Sodium chloride—(NaCl). Common salt.

Spodumene—($Li_2O \cdot Al_2O_3 \cdot 4SiO_2$). A flux used in high-fire glazes.

Strontium oxide—(SrO). Acts in a glaze in a manner similar to calcium; rarely used—too expensive.

Talc—($3MgO \cdot 4SiO_2 \cdot H_2O$). Pulverized steatite, a flux used in glazes; its most important use is as a flux in low-fire bodies.

Tin oxide—(SnO_2). The most effective opacifier; 10% added to a clear colorless glaze will make it opaque white.

Titanium dioxide—(TiO_2). *See* Rutile.

Umber—A natural source of red iron oxide (Fe_2O_3), used as a colorant in clay bodies to produce shades of brown.

Uranium—Formerly used as a source of color in glazes; produces shades of yellow, orange, and red; used as uranium oxide (U_2O_3).

Vanadium—(V). Used to produce vanadium stain, a yellow colorant for glazes.

Vermiculite—Bloated mica, used as an insulater in kiln construction.

Volcanic ash—*See* Pumicite.

Wallastonite—A material resembling feldspar with a lower melting point. Used to lower the maturing temperature of clay bodies. Promotes resistance to thermal shock and to crazing.

Water glass—Sodium silicate.

Wax emulsion—A liquid wax used in making wax resist designs.

White lead—Lead carbonate ($2PbCo_3 \cdot Pb(OH)_2$). The usual source of lead in glazes. *Poisonous*.

Whiting—Calcium carbonate ($CaCO_3$), the usual source of calcium in glazes, used also as a flux in clay bodies.

Yellow base—Vanadium stain.

Zinc oxide—(ZnO). Used as a glaze flux in middle and high temperature ranges (above cone 1); added to low-fire glazes produces a mat surface; distinguishing ingredient of Bristol glazes; affects the colors of other oxides—makes iron dull, makes copper turquoise green; promotes crystallization in glazes. Zinc oxide should be calcined before use, otherwise it tends to make glazes crawl.

Zirconium—An opacifier similar to tin but not as strong; 20% added to a clear colorless glaze makes it opaque white. Zirconium oxide (ZrO) is too refractory for most glaze use; Zircopax or Opax, commercial silicates of zirconium, are used instead.

Zircopax—*See* Zirconium.

Index

320

About the Author

JOHN B. KENNY is known to ceramists the world over through his two previous books, *The Complete Book of Pottery Making* and *Ceramic Sculpture,* both of which have been widely praised both here and abroad.

The enormous success of these two books, their adoption by a large number of schools, colleges and universities, as well as by artists and craftsmen, is due to the author's wide background as a skilled potter and experienced teacher. For over twenty years Mr. Kenny has been principal of the High School of Art and Design, New York City's specialized high school for preparing young people for professional careers as artists and designers.

Examples of Mr. Kenny's work are included in private collections in this country and in Europe. His wife Carla, with whom he recently visited ceramic manufacturing plants, studios, and colleges in both the United States and Europe, has helped in the preparation of *Ceramic Design* with her drawings. She is an illustrator and a member of the Society of Illustrators.

Mr. Kenny holds the degree of Master of Fine Arts in ceramics from Alfred University and is also a member of the Society of Illustrators.